The Special Educator's Survival Guide

Second Edition

Roger Pierangelo, Ph.D.

JOSSEY-BASS
A Wiley Imprint
www.josseybass.com

Published by Jossey-Bass
A Wiley Imprint
989 Market Street, San Francisco, CA 94103-1741 www.josseybass.com

Jossey-Bass books and products are available through most bookstores. To contact Jossey-Bass directly call our Customer Care Department within the U.S. at 800-956-7739, outside the U.S. at 317-572-3986, or fax 317-572-4002.

Jossey-Bass also publishes its books in a variety of electronic formats. Some content that appears in print may not be available in electronic books.

Readers should be aware that Internet Web sites listed in this work may have changed or disappeared between when this work was written and when it is read.

Library of Congress Cataloging-in-Publication Data

Pierangelo, Roger.
The special educator's survival guide / Roger Pierangelo.— 2nd ed.
p. cm.
Rev. ed. of: A survival kit for the special education teacher. c1994.
Includes bibliographical references (p. 307).
ISBN 0-7879-7096-4 (alk. paper)
1. Children with disabilities—Education—Handbooks, manuals, etc. 2. Special education—Handbooks, manuals, etc. I. Pierangelo, Roger. Survival kit for the special education teacher. II. Title.
LC4015.P52 2004
371.91—dc22

2003028273

Printed in the United States of America
SECOND EDITION
PB Printing 10 9 8 7 6 5 4 3 2

I dedicate this book to my loving family: to my wife, Jackie, who has supported me in all my endeavors, and my very special children, Jacqueline and Scott; to my parents, who always believed in me and always made me feel special; to my sister, Carol, whose humor and genuine caring have always been an inspiration; and to my brother-in-law, George, for his guidance, insight, support, and dependability.

ABOUT THE AUTHOR

R*oger Pierangelo* has over thirty years' experience as a regular classroom teacher, school psychologist in the Herrick's Public School system in New Hyde Park, New York, administrator of special education programs, associate professor in the Department of Special Education and Literacy at Long Island University, licensed clinical psychologist, member of committees on special education, evaluator for the New York State Education Department, director of a private clinic, diplomate fellow in forensic psychology, and consultant to numerous private and public schools and PTA and SEPTA groups.

Pierangelo earned his B.S. from St. John's University, M.S. from Queens College, professional diploma from Queens College, Ph.D. from Yeshiva University, and diplomate fellow in forensic psychology from the International College of Professional Psychology.

He is a member of the American Psychological Association, New York State Psychological Association, Nassau County Psychological Association, New York State Union of Teachers, and Phi Delta Kappa.

Pierangelo is the author of *Survival Kit for the Special Education Teacher* and *The Special Education Teacher's Book of Lists*, and coauthor of the *Parent's Complete Guide to Special Education*, *The Special Educator's Complete Guide to Transition Services*, and *The Special Educator's Guide to 109 Diagnostic Tests*, all published by Prentice Hall. He is coauthor of *The Special Education Yellow Pages*, published by Merrill Publishing, *Assessment in Special Education—A Practical Approach* and *Transitional Services in Special Education—A Practical Approach*, published by Allyn & Bacon, *The Special Educator's Book of Lists*, published by Jossey-Bass, coauthor of *Why Your Students Do What They Do—and What to Do When They Do It—Grades K–5*, *Why Your Students Do What They Do—and What to Do When They Do It—Grades 6–12*, *Creating Confident Children in the Classroom—The Use of Positive Restructuring*, and *What Every Teacher Should Know About Students with Special Needs*, all published by Research Press, and *301 Ways to Be a Loving Parent*, published by Shapolsky Publishers.

ACKNOWLEDGMENTS

I wish to thank Ollie Simmons, a very special person, who could put a smile on anyone's face with her humor, kindness, and loving personality. I also wish to thank Helen Firestone, a truly instrumental individual in my life and a remarkably bright and energetic woman who has touched so many. Bill Smyth, an extraordinary ordinary man and a truly great person and mentor, helped form my skills. I also thank Dr. Steve Thompson of Jossey-Bass, who was very supportive and available during the writing of this book. And finally, I wish to thank my colleagues and the staff of the Graduate School of Special Education at C. W. Post College, Long Island University.

PURPOSE OF THE BOOK

This unique guide has been developed to help all teachers survive the pressures and derive greater rewards when working with exceptional children. Many texts are filled with theories, but few offer practical advice. From my twenty-eight years of teaching special educators, thirty years in psychology and education, twenty years in private practice, and seventeen years participating in committees on special education, I have come to realize the need that all teachers have for a wide variety of important and pertinent information that can be obtained at a moment's notice. This book is organized to give teachers that wealth of practical advice.

Many special education teachers do not have a perspective on the entire special education process or the specific knowledge and tools required at each stage. Awareness of this global concept of special education allows teachers to fulfill the requirements in any role they may encounter.

Filled with practical tools and suggestions, the book takes special education teachers through the various stages in understanding the processes of referral, parent intakes, evaluation, interpretation, diagnosis, remediation, prescription, placement, recommendations, parent conferences, committee on special education referrals, Individualized Education Program (IEP), classroom management, curriculum, materials, and special education law.

It is the responsibility of all special education teachers to keep themselves abreast of the latest techniques, laws, tools, and evaluative measures that exist. Having one book that reviews all this necessary information can only facilitate the process of teaching exceptional children.

Who Can Use This Guide?

This book will be very useful not only for special education teachers but for regular classroom teachers, administrators, college students, and parents of exceptional children. The information it provides will answer the questions that many of these individuals have about their students, children, and educational techniques.

Helpful and Unique Features

This book contains the most up-to-date information possible. It is a unique survival guide for special education teachers because of several features:

- The book's developmental, step-by-step approach takes readers through a variety of topics and procedures necessary for a realistic, complete awareness of exceptional children.

- Written in an easy-to-read format, the book contains a wealth of tried-and-true suggestions based on the author's extensive experience.
- The material is presented in such a way that readers will be able to make an easy transition to classroom applications.
- The focus is on the more practical and common issues, avoiding more obscure subjects.
- Numerous examples reinforce the concepts presented in the book.
- A wealth of practical tips gives teachers the opportunity to share with parents on a variety of topics.

In conclusion, I wish you all the best in your journey as a special education teacher and hope that this book acts like a beacon to help you work more positively with children with disabilities.

Roger Pierangelo

CONTENTS

Part Three: The Special Educator's Role in the Special Education Process

Part Four: Working as a Special Education Teacher

Part Five: What Special Educators Need to Know and Do About . . .

Part Six: Dealing with Parents of Children with Disabilities

Part Seven: A Law Primer for Special Educators

Part Eight: Appendixes

PART ONE

INTRODUCTION: ROLES AND RESPONSIBILITIES

Chapter 1

What Do Special Education Teachers Do?

Each day in the United States millions of children go off to school, all with different strengths and weaknesses, abilities and disabilities. Over five million of these children have been identified as having a specific disability, including autism, mental retardation, or cerebral palsy; emotional, physical, visual, or hearing disabilities; or learning disabilities that necessitate some type of special instruction. These children are referred to as children with disabilities or children with special needs. To address these children's special needs, schools rely on people who have been trained to help them: special education teachers. Special education teachers play a critical role in the proper education of exceptional students, in their daily lives, and in their long-term achievements in learning. As you will soon realize, this is a role that can change the course of a child's life, placing that child on a road to positive self-worth, a sense of accomplishment, and assimilation into society.

Special educators work in many settings and play many roles. Whatever the setting or role, they are sure to encounter a variety of situations that require making practical decisions and relevant suggestions. No matter what role you will play in special education, you will need to understand fully symptoms, causality, evaluation, diagnosis, prescription, and remediation. You will have to communicate vital information to professionals, parents, and students. You will encounter a whole new language, with lots of terminology and abbreviations, and you will need to know it and recognize it. There is no doubt that you will need to learn a great deal, have a good base of knowledge in legal and educational areas, and be ready for an exciting, rewarding, but demanding profession.

This survival guide is designed to give you the basic knowledge you will need.

Chapter 2

Disability Classifications

As a special educator you will come into contact with and be responsible for the educational needs of children with a wide range of disabilities. These children will require a variety of different services, as well as modifications and accommodations in their educational experiences. If you plan to be involved in or are already working in the field of special education, it is crucial for you to have knowledge of each type of disability and the specific needs of children with that disability. The various categories of disabilities are clearly defined in the Individuals with Disabilities Education Act (IDEA) of 1997.

Autism

This disorder is characterized by difficulty in responding to people, events, and objects. Responses to sensations of light, sound, and feeling may be exaggerated, and delayed speech and language skills may be associated features. The onset of this condition is usually observed before two and a half years of age.

Autistic children do well in a classroom environment that is structured so that the program is consistent and predictable. Children with autism or Pervasive Developmental Disorder (PDD) learn better and are less confused when information is presented visually as well as verbally. Interaction with nondisabled peers is also important, for these students provide models of appropriate language, social, and behavior skills. To overcome frequent problems in generalizing skills learned at school, it is very important for teachers to develop programs with parents. Learning activities, experiences, and approaches can then be carried over into the home and community.

Visual Impairments

The visually impaired category is divided into two subcategories: blind and partially sighted. Children who are classified as blind require special Braille equipment and reading materials. The condition is severe; they do not have what is considered functional sight. Children classified as partially sighted have some functional sight, usually 20/70 or better with best correction. These students may be able to learn to read regular print with glasses or special books that are printed with large type.

Students with visual impairments may need help with special equipment and modifications in the regular curriculum to emphasize listening skills, communication, orientation and mobility, vocation-career options, and daily living skills. Students with low vision or those who are legally blind may need help in using their residual vision more efficiently and in working with special aids and materials. Students who have visual impairments combined with other types of disabilities need an interdisciplinary approach and may require greater emphasis on self-care and daily living skills.

Hearing Impairments

The hearing impaired category is divided into two subcategories: deaf and hard of hearing. Individuals classified as deaf have a loss of hearing so severe—usually above an eighty-decibel loss—that it hinders effective use of the sense of hearing. Children with this disability usually need specialized services or equipment in order to communicate. Students who are hard of hearing have a hearing loss that may or may not be permanent, and have some sense of hearing with or without an aid. However, such students still require specialized instruction and special education assistance.

Children who are hard of hearing will find it much more difficult than children with normal hearing to learn vocabulary, grammar, word order, idiomatic expressions, and other aspects of verbal communication. Among children who are deaf or have severe hearing loss, early, consistent, and conscious use of visible communication modes (such as sign language), amplification, and aural-oral training can help reduce the language delay. By age four or five, most children who are deaf are enrolled in school on a full-day basis and do special work on communication and language development. It is important for teachers and audiologists to work together to teach these children to use their residual hearing as much as possible, even if the preferred means of communication is manual. Because the great majority of deaf children (over 90 percent) are born to hearing parents, programs should provide instruction for parents on implications of deafness in the family.

Emotional Disturbance

Students classified as emotionally disturbed have behavior disorders over a long period of time and to such a degree that they are unable to do well in school. These disturbances may interfere with their developing meaningful relationships, result in physical symptoms or irrational fears, and limit their overall production. Educational programs for children with an emotional disturbance need to provide emotional and behavioral support as well as help them to master academics, develop social skills, and increase self-awareness, self-control, and self-esteem. A large body of research exists on methods for providing students with positive behavioral support (PBS) in the school environment so that problem behaviors are minimized and more positive, appropriate behaviors are fostered.

Learning Disabilities

These students have difficulty receiving, organizing, or expressing information. They are of average intelligence but find it hard to listen, think, speak, read, write, or do arithmetic, which results in a significant discrepancy between ability and achievement. This is not due to emotional, mental, physical, environmental, or cultural factors. The specific instruction these students receive will vary depending on their needs and capabilities. Some need related services as well: a notetaker (for a student with a fine motor disability), a word processor, a laptop computer, books on tape, or extra time when taking tests. The Individuals with Disabilities Education Act (IDEA) requires schools to provide these special education and related services at no cost to families.

Mental Disabilities

These students have a developmental delay that causes them to learn at a slower pace than other children. They also exhibit significantly lower intelligence and marked impairment in social skills. The mentally disabled category includes educable mentally disabled, with an IQ usually between fifty-five and approximately eighty, and trainable mentally disabled, with an IQ below fifty-five. Many children with mental retardation need help with adaptive skills—skills needed to live, work, and play in the community. Teachers and parents can help such children work on these skills both at school and at home. These skills include the following:

- Communication with others
- Personal needs (dressing, bathing, going to the bathroom)
- Health and safety
- Home living (helping to set the table, cleaning the house, or cooking dinner)
- Social skills (manners, rules of conversation, how to get along in a group, playing games)
- Reading, writing, and basic math
- Among older children, skills that will be helpful in the workplace

Multiple Disabilities

Children who are multiply disabled have disabilities in more than one category, such as deafness and blindness. Frequently, classroom arrangements must take into consideration students' needs for medications, special diets, or special equipment. Adaptive aids and equipment enable these children to increase their functional range. For example, in recent years computers have become effective communication devices. Other aids include wheelchairs, typewriters, headsticks (headgear), clamps, modified handles on cups and silverware, and communication boards. Computerized communication equipment and specially built vocational equipment also play important roles in adapting working environments for people with serious movement limitations.

Orthopedic Impairments

These students are physically disabled, and their educational performance is directly affected by this condition. Such conditions as cerebral palsy and amputation are included in this category. In addition to therapy services and special equipment, children with orthopedic impairments may need what is known as *assistive technology*, including communication devices and computer technology. Communication devices can range from the simple to the sophisticated. Communication boards, for example, have pictures, symbols, letters, or words attached. The child communicates by pointing to or gazing at the pictures or symbols. Augmentative communication devices are more sophisticated and include voice synthesizers that enable the child to "talk" with others. Computer technology can range from electronic toys with special switches to sophisticated computer programs operated by simple switch pads or keyboard adaptations.

Other Health Impairments

Students who are classified in this category have limited strength, vitality, or alertness because of chronic or acute health problems. Conditions that fall into this category include heart conditions, asthma, Tourette's syndrome, attention deficit hyperactive disorder (ADHD), diabetes, and so on. It is important for teachers to learn as much as possible about the child's medical condition in order to provide the proper services to prevent frustration and increase the chances for success.

Speech Impairments

Children with speech impairments have a communication disorder. They are unable to produce speech sounds correctly, have difficulty understanding or using words or sentences, or exhibit stuttering or some other vocal impairment. The speech language pathologist may assist vocational teachers and counselors in establishing communication goals and suggest effective strategies for the important transition from school life to employment and adult life. Technology can help children whose physical conditions make communication difficult. Electronic communication systems allow nonspeaking people and people with severe physical disabilities to engage in the give-and-take of shared thought.

Traumatic Brain Injury

Traumatic brain injury (TBI) is defined as an acquired injury to the brain caused by an external physical force, resulting in total or partial functional disability, psychosocial impairment, or both, adversely affecting a child's educational performance. The term applies to open or closed head injuries resulting in impairments in one or more areas, such as cognition; language; memory; attention; reasoning; abstract thinking; judgment; problem solving; sensory, perceptual, and motor abilities; psychosocial behavior; physical functions; information processing; and speech. The term does not apply to brain injuries that are congenital or degenerative, or to brain injuries induced by birth trauma. When children with TBI return to school, their educational and emotional needs are often very different from before the injury. Their disability has happened suddenly and traumatically. They may well remember how they were before the brain injury. This can bring on many emotional and social changes. The child's family, friends, and teachers also recall what the child was like before the injury. These other people in the child's life may have trouble changing or adjusting their expectations of the child.

Chapter 3

The Special Educator's Responsibilities

Now that we have reviewed the different types of children you may encounter as a special educator, you can see that it would be difficult to give a simple picture of a special educator's daily life, because the children's disabilities are so varied. In addition, special educators may have many roles and responsibilities in any given school setting. Their everyday activities will be determined by the types of children they are teaching, the kinds and severity of their disabilities, their ages, and the school setting. For example, the activities and responsibilities are very different for a high school special education teacher who is coteaching a class with a general education teacher, a special education teacher working in a self-contained middle school classroom with children who have emotional and behavior disorders, an elementary special education teacher in a resource room who has children coming in and out of the classroom all day, and an educational diagnostician. But no matter what setting they are working in or whom they are teaching, special education teachers usually have three main responsibilities: direct teaching (and preparing for it), preparing appropriate reports and doing other paperwork, and collaborating with other professionals and parents. Juggling the many demands on their time is a challenging and sometimes frustrating endeavor.

Direct Teaching

One of the primary responsibilities of the special education teacher is to provide instruction and adapt, modify, and develop materials to match the learning styles, strengths, and special needs of each of their students. The majority of special education teachers spend most of their classroom time actually teaching their students (Allinder, 1994). The methods they use and the learning goals they develop are determined by their students' abilities and age, the setting, and many other variables. In addition, they spend time after the regular school day preparing lesson plans, grading papers, meeting with other professionals, calling and meeting with parents, attending child study team meetings (more on these teams follows), meeting with related service providers, and attending meetings of special education committees (also called eligibility committees). More on these committees follows later in the book.

It has been said that in general education the school system dictates the curriculum, whereas in special education the child's individual needs dictate the curriculum (Lieberman, 1985). For example, dressing, eating, and toileting might be a regular part of the curriculum for students with severe disabilities but are not normally taught in general education classrooms. Similarly, a child who has a hearing impairment may receive special training in sign language, and a child who is blind may need specific instruction in Braille. These students may be using assistive technology to help them meet the goals of their educational plan. These devices would obviously not be a part of the typical general education curriculum and are areas that every special educator needs to know about.

The challenge for special education teachers is to identify the children's strengths and weaknesses, assess how each child learns best, and then determine the best way to design or modify instruction so that each can achieve the expected educational outcome. This can be especially challenging for a teacher who has several students with different disabilities of varying severity in the same classroom, which may be the case in a resource room, a self-contained classroom, or an inclusion setting. The special education teacher must meet the needs of all of these students. For example, a special education teacher in elementary school could have a class of ten children, two with hearing impairments, one with autism, and seven with varying developmental delays. This teacher has quite a challenge to develop learning activities and strategies that will be effective for all of these students.

Paperwork

Special education teachers have a great deal of paperwork and forms to complete. They have the same kinds of paperwork demands that general education teachers do—filling out attendance reports and discipline reports, and grading homework and tests, just to mention a few. But they are also required to prepare other forms and reports; for example, special education teachers usually play a lead role in preparing each student's Individualized Education Program (IEP). They also maintain the records that document students' progress in meeting the goals and objectives specified in their IEPs.

The IEP is a list of goals, needs, and objectives for every disabled student. IEPs include strategies to address the children's behavior, including positive behavioral interventions and supports. IEPs may outline psychological or counseling services; these are important related services that are available by law and are provided by a social worker, psychologist, guidance counselor, or other qualified personnel. In addition, career education (both vocational and academic) is a significant part of secondary education and should be included in every adolescent's IEP transition plan. The development of the IEP occurs at the Eligibility Committee meeting with the parent present.

Special education teachers also have to become familiar with federal, state, and local school district regulations and policies that require complete reports on student placement and progress. It is usually the special education teacher who has to write up these reports. These regulations and policies may change from year to year (some say, from day to day). Every change may mean a change in the documentation. Indeed, special education teachers who choose to leave the field often cite the abundance of paperwork as a primary contributor to their high level of stress and decision to change jobs (Billingsley, 1993). The increase in the number of lawsuits filed against school districts over the placement and education of children with disabilities has made it even more critical for teachers to maintain accurate and complete records.

Collaboration and Consultation

Special education teachers never work completely on their own. Even those who work in self-contained classrooms work in some way as part of a team. Some schools have established teams to help plan appropriate adaptations and educational interventions for students who are having difficulty in general education classes. These teams, which we will discuss later, are sometimes referred to as child study teams (CSTs) or pupil personnel teams (PPTs).

Depending on the disability and the school setting, special education teachers need to work with speech language pathologists, school psychologists, occupational therapists, physical therapists, school social workers, general education teachers, and community workers to plan and implement the best education strategy for each child. Special education teachers who work in inclusive settings or who coteach or team-teach with general education teachers must spend adequate time planning, developing, and implementing an educational environment that is challenging and appropriate for all the students in the class, including those with disabilities and those without.

Special education teachers usually serve as a resource on special education issues to other staff in the school—teachers, administrators, speech language pathologists, parents, and others. Furthermore, they provide crucial assistance to parents who may be struggling at home; the overall well-being of the child depends on their knowing what to recommend.

Special education teachers not only teach their students when they are in the classroom, but usually also keep tabs on them throughout the day, wherever they may be. To do all of this effectively, special education teachers need to maintain positive relationships with the principal, parents, other teachers, and other personnel.

Special educators act as liaisons between community agencies or organizations and their school. At no time is this more important than when a child begins the transition from school to adult life. Assisting in this process, which begins when the child is around age thirteen or fourteen, is a major responsibility of the special education teacher. For example, a teacher may need to work with the local vocational training agency with regard to a student. This might mean being the contact in the school for the agency, job coach, and employer. The teacher can also advise the agency of any meetings with the student and coordinate any necessary activities. In another example, a teacher may work with the local independent living agency and the vocational rehabilitation agency to set up a transition plan for a student getting ready to graduate from school.

All of this collaboration and consultation requires time—something that many special educators do not have. It is probably true that educators never have enough time to do all they want to do. But it is certainly true that to work effectively, and to be as effective as possible for children with disabilities, special education teachers need the time to work and plan with parents and other professionals. Many special education teachers are not given enough free time in the regular school day to make appointments with other staff members or parents and consequently have to meet outside of regular school hours or during lunch or other breaks. A second reason given by many special education teachers for deciding to leave the field is lack of time to meet all of their responsibilities (Billingsley, 1993).

Chapter 4

Roles in Special Education

As we have already seen, special education teachers are unique in that they can play many different roles in the educational environment. However, each of these roles is distinct and each involves particular responsibilities and functions. If you understand these responsibilities, it can only help you better understand the role and increase your chances for success on the job.

As we have already mentioned, special education teachers work in a variety of different educational settings. The following figure summarizes these settings, which are discussed in depth in the rest of this chapter.

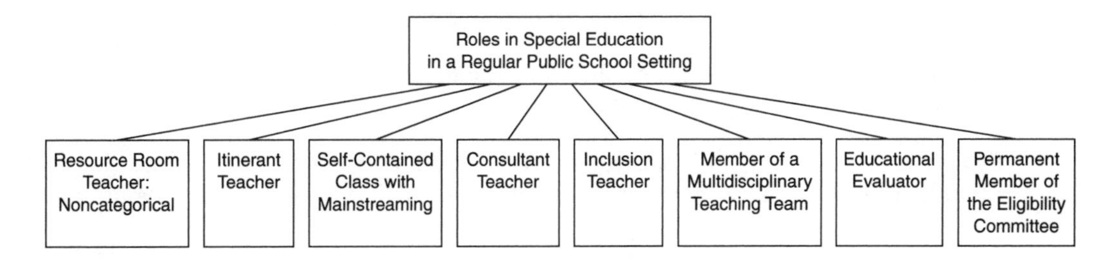

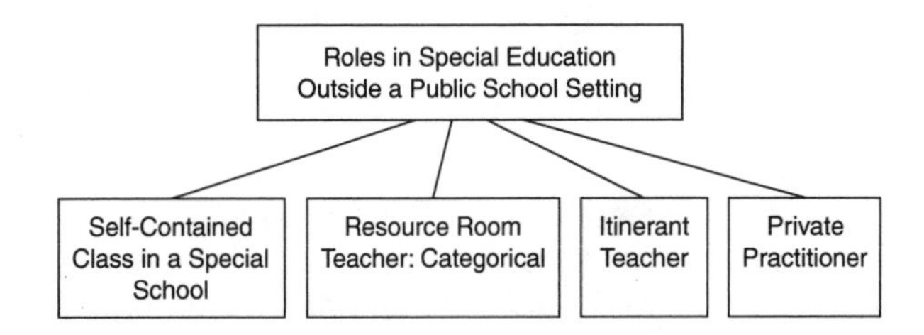

Teacher in a Self-Contained Special Education Classroom in a Regular School

In this role, special education teachers must work with a number of disabled students in a special education setting. The teacher in a self-contained classroom usually works with a teaching assistant.

This setting allows for *mainstreaming*, which means that the disabled children may be involved in a regular classroom for part of the school day when they are ready to make this transition.

In the self-contained special education classroom, the educator is likely to face a variety of responsibilities, including curriculum development, parent conferences, and pre- and posttesting using group standardized tests. They are also involved in the annual review—an annual meeting held by the eligibility committee to discuss the progress of each child with a disability and plan the next year's Individualized Education Program (IEP). The teachers are also involved in the triennial evaluation process, which, as the name implies, takes place every three years to determine if the conditions for the original classification are still present or need to be modified. The requirement here would be limited to progress reports and recommendations for the following year. Finally, special education teachers monitor the IEP, making modifications and accommodations.

A DAY IN THE LIFE OF A SPECIAL EDUCATOR IN A SELF-CONTAINED CLASSROOM IN A REGULAR SCHOOL

Name: Sharon Mierow

Where: Dallas, Texas

Education: Bachelor's in music; certification as a special educator

Teaching: Has taught LIFE (living and functional environment) skills class for the past five years

Students: First- through fourth-graders with moderate to severe disabilities (for example, autism, cerebral palsy, mental retardation, and Fragile X and other rare syndromes)

Class type: Self-contained special education class in a regular school; students participate in art, library, physical education, music, and lunch with the other students in the school

We have a very structured routine. Each day we start with class breakfast, which is followed by personal hygiene activities: using the bathroom, brushing teeth, and washing hands. After this, we have reading time. Each student's reading time activity is tailored to his or her ability level. After reading, we have fifteen minutes of free time. During this time, I change the diapers of those students who need it.

Next, we have what we call "Larger Group." This is a combination of the two LIFE skills classes and consists of fourteen students ages six to twelve. During Larger Group we work on the unit of the week–nutrition, going to the zoo, space, health. We do many activities, including sign language, music therapy, and large motor activities.

Then, we return to our regular class size and do seat work. We do different activities with each student: fine motor skills, cutting, pasting, tracing, and range of motion. During this part of the day, the occupational therapist and speech pathologist come in to work with the students.

Each afternoon we have our "working" part of the day. We do a different adaptive social skill each day of the week. Monday, we wash our classroom windows. Tuesday, we clean our tables. Wednesday, we sweep the floor. And so on throughout the week. It's basically vocational education on a very small scale. The last hour of each day is devoted to music, physical education, library, or art class.

What do I like best about teaching? The kids. It's very rewarding to see their improvements.

Source: "Who's Teaching Our Children with Disabilities?" *NICHCY News Digest,* 1997, *27,* 14.

Resource Teacher in a Categorical or Noncategorical Resource Room

A categorical resource room is a resource room in a special school that deals with only one type of disability. A noncategorical resource room is usually found in a regular, mainstream school, where children with varied disabilities are educated at one time. Special education teachers in the latter settings must work closely with each child's homeroom teacher and help transfer practical techniques and make suggestions to facilitate the child's success in the regular setting.

Special educators in resource rooms have a variety of responsibilities, including the following:

- *Modifying the child's curriculum.* The resource teacher assists the classroom teacher in modifying the curriculum to meet the learning style and needs of the child with a disability.
- *Participating in parent conferences.*
- *Doing pre- and posttesting.* The teacher gives the children group standardized tests.
- *Acting as educational evaluator.* Often the resource room teacher is asked to complete the educational evaluations for initial evaluations, screening, and triennial evaluations.
- *Getting involved in the annual review.* The teacher works with the eligibility committee to discuss each child's progress and plan the following year's IEP.
- *Getting involved in the triennial evaluation process.* The teacher participates in this evaluation to help determine if the conditions for the original classification are still present or need to be modified. Involvement here would be limited to either discussing test results or updating the student's progress report and making recommendations for the following year.
- *Monitoring the IEP.* The teacher must make modifications and accommodations to the IEP throughout the year.

Educational Evaluator on the Child Study Team (CST)

The child study team (CST) is a school-based support team that discusses and makes recommendations for high-risk students. (See Part Two for more on the CST.) The educational evaluator on this team must have a complete and professional understanding of testing and evaluation procedures, as well as diagnosing and interpreting test results.

As educational evaluator on the CST, special educators face a variety of responsibilities. They may act as educational evaluator during initial evaluations (evaluations performed on students being classified for the first time); be involved in the triennial evaluation process, which, as noted previously, takes place every three years to determine if the conditions for the original classification are still present or need to be modified; or interpret diagnostic results from outside evaluations.

Member of the Eligibility Committee

Depending on the state, the eligibility committee may also be referred to as the committee on special education (CSE) or the IEP committee. Whatever name it goes by, this committee is a district-based committee mandated by federal law. Responsibilities include the classification, placement, and evaluation of all disabled children in the district. This involves interpreting educational test results, making recommendations, and diagnosing strengths and weaknesses for the IEP.

In this setting, the special educator may face a variety of responsibilities, including interpreting educational test results; making recommendations for the eligibility committee, the IEP, classification, or placement; and diagnosing strengths and weaknesses for the IEP.

Member of a Multidisciplinary Teaching Team for Secondary Students in a Departmentalized Program

These programs are fairly new to secondary schools. Students with disabilities follow departmentalized programs, like other students, but all their classes are taught by special education teachers.

In this type of setting, special educators may be involved with curriculum development, parent conferences, the annual review, the triennial evaluation process, and monitoring the IEP.

Consultant Teacher

Sometimes, the eligibility committee decides that it is in the best interests of a child to receive services in his or her own classroom rather than leave to go to a so-called pull-out program, such as a resource room. This may be the best decision when a child has problems with fragmentation—that is, when the schedule has him or her leave the class to go to the resource room in the middle of one lesson and return in the middle of another. Fragmentation can create severe confusion for some children. In such cases, a consultant teacher is assigned to work with the child right in the mainstreamed class.

In this type of setting, the special educator may be involved with parent conferences, pre- and posttesting using group standardized tests, the annual review, the triennial evaluation process, and monitoring the IEP. Consultant teachers also help the regular classroom teacher modify the curriculum to meet the learning style and needs of the child with a disability.

Itinerant Teacher

This is a special education teacher employed by an agency to visit various schools in several districts and work with children with disabilities. As a result, each child is provided with the required auxiliary services and the district can meet requirements without having a program of its own.

In this setting, special educators may be involved in parent conferences, pre- and posttesting using group standardized tests, the annual review, the triennial evaluation process, monitoring the IEP, and making modifications and accommodations to it. In addition, itinerant teachers are involved in curriculum modification—assisting the regular classroom teacher in modifying the curriculum to meet the learning style and needs of the child with a disability. They may also be asked to make educational evaluations; the district usually pays the agency a fee for this service.

A DAY IN THE LIFE OF AN ITINERANT SPECIAL EDUCATOR

Name: Ellie White

Where: Chicago

Education: Bachelor's in animal science, minor in education; master's in special education

Teaching: First year as an elementary-level itinerant special educator in a suburban school district; teaches in two schools

Students: Nine students from various general education classes; students' disabilities include autism, Down's syndrome, and learning disabilities

Class type: Pullout and in-class support

I spend two hours each day with my student with Down's syndrome–three mornings and two afternoons each week, so I'm able to get the full spectrum of his day. Since he does well with loud, interactive activities that aren't adaptable to his regular classroom, most of the time I work with him in a pullout situation. Then I drive to the other school I work in.

I spend one to one and a half hours each day with my student with autism. I work with him both in his regular classroom and out. Since getting him involved in lots of social interaction is a very high priority, we've developed a volunteer "peer buddy" helping system for him.

My seven students with learning disabilities all come to work with me in my classroom. I teach them both math and reading, working with them both in groups and one-on-one. Many of them are a grade level behind in reading. Since self-esteem is an issue with my students with learning disabilities, I make sure I work on something they are good at as well as something they have difficulty with.

We have weekly team meetings for both my student with Down's syndrome and my student with autism. All of the people involved with each student attend (general educator, speech therapist, occupational therapist, paraprofessional, physical therapist), and we discuss techniques that will enable the student to participate with the rest of the class. I also make sure that I'm available to the regular classroom teachers to answer questions, and I check in with them during the week to see how things are going.

I love working with the kids. It demands a lot of creativity and a lot of time. It's wonderful to see the students learning, to see their faces when they finally understand something.

Source: "Who's Teaching Our Children with Disabilities?" *NICHCY News Digest,* 1997, *27,* 14.

Inclusion Teacher in a Partial Inclusion or Full Inclusion Program

An inclusion class is a mainstream class with a population of children with and without disabilities. A regular education teacher and a special education teacher work together as a team. (For an explanation of the different types of inclusion settings, see Chapter Sixteen.)

In this type of setting, special educators may be involved in parent conferences, pre- and posttesting using group standardized tests, the annual review, the triennial evaluation process, and making modifications and accommodations to the IEP. In addition, inclusion teachers are involved in curriculum development and modification. Here, special education teachers assist the classroom teacher in developing and modifying the curriculum to meet the learning style and needs of the children with disabilities. They also assist the students themselves. They may circulate among these children during a lesson to ensure that they understand the concepts being taught, give help with note-taking, and answer questions.

A DAY IN THE LIFE OF COTEACHERS IN AN INCLUSION CLASS

Names: Debbie Boyce, general educator; Chris Ohm, special educator

Where: Frederick, Maryland

Education: Debbie: Bachelor's in math and science education, master's in counseling; Chris: Bachelor's in public relations and psychology, master's in special education

Teaching: Debbie: seven years general education, one year coteaching; Chris: two years, both coteaching

Students: Twenty-two students, half have special education classification, half are not in special education but need extra support in math

Class type: Coteach (team teaching) seventh-grade mathematics

CHRIS: The key to making coteaching work is joint planning. As a special education coteacher, you can't just walk into the classroom and expect to be able to work together as equals. You must take the time to plan how to handle each lesson. You must both know all the curriculum so that you can switch back and forth with your coteacher and support each other's efforts, and teach the class yourself if your coteacher is absent. You have to have the attitude that you are a teacher first and a special educator second. If you don't know the curriculum, you are not a coteacher; you are just an assistant.

DEBBIE: At first, it takes a while to get used to having another adult in the classroom with you. Teachers are used to having their classroom be their own domain. It takes a little while to get used to sharing, to become accustomed to the other person's methods of doing things, perspective, and pace.

DEBBIE: I would recommend to any general educator who has the opportunity to coteach to absolutely do it! It's a unique inclusive technique, and without it some students would not get out of their self-contained classroom. Before coteaching I was interested in students with special needs, but I felt incompetent to teach them because I didn't know much about how to meet their needs. Working with Chris has influenced how I will teach for the rest of my life and has made me a better teacher in all my classes.

CHRIS: I love coteaching. It has a lot of benefits. You get to bounce ideas off each other, and help each other if one of you is having difficulty getting the students to understand part of the lesson. It's also great for the kids because you are modeling good interactive behavior. I would suggest to any interested special educator to take a class in coteaching. It's important to learn how to coteach the right way—equally.

Source: "Who's Teaching Our Children with Disabilities?" *NICHCY News Digest,* 1997, *27,* 11.

Teacher in a Self-Contained Special Education Classroom in a Special School

These teachers work with more seriously disabled students in a special education setting. Teachers in self-contained special education classrooms in special schools usually have the help of both a teaching assistant and aides because of the seriousness of the disabilities of this population of students.

In this setting, special educators may be faced with a variety of responsibilities, including curriculum development, parent conferences, pre- and posttesting using group standardized tests, involvement at the annual review, involvement in the triennial evaluation process, and making modifications and adjustments to the IEP. These teachers also work very closely with related service providers, especially vocational and transition specialists at the secondary level.

A DAY IN THE LIFE OF A SPECIAL EDUCATOR IN A SELF-CONTAINED SPECIAL SCHOOL

Name: Laura Zappia

Where: Suffolk County, New York

Education: Bachelor's and master's in special education

Teaching: Fifteen years

Students: Middle-school–aged children who have severe emotional disturbances and behavioral disorders (ED/BD)

Class type: Self-contained class in a self-contained public school that serves twelve school districts; class size of six students

I work on subjects and tasks that may be harder and more frustrating for my students, such as vocabulary, spelling, and reading, early in the day when everyone is fresher. In the afternoon I do review work and go over basic skills.

Besides academics, the focus of what I do is work on each student's behavior problems. During the day the classroom aide monitors each student's behavior and keeps behavior minutes or "point sheets." Each student's behavior is assessed every fifteen to thirty minutes. If the students are lower functioning, behavior is assessed more often. The point sheets help you monitor the students' behavior, but also how your own behavior as a teacher is either working or not working.

One of the keys to teaching students with ED/BD is to find out what is valuable to them. If a student likes to go to extra gym time, you reward him with that when he participates more in class or does something positive.

Since many of these students have great problems with self-control, our main goal is to try to decrease their worst behavior. For instance, if a student is cursing twenty times a day, then you work on getting it down to ten times a day. Then you cut it down to five. We work on achieving our ultimate goal in small steps.

My students also need help in thinking about the consequences of their actions. If a student throws his book across the room saying he won't read anymore, I coach him along. "You've already read ten pages, and you only have two paragraphs left. You're having a good day. You can either read the rest of the page, or lose the reward you've earned." More likely than not the student will finish the reading. When their worst behavior is under control, you focus on the next most apparent one. By the end of the year you are working on more typical problems, such as getting them to turn in their homework.

I keep notes every day on every child. This way I can assess both the students' behavior and my own. The children I work with change gradually. You have to try a technique for at least thirty days to see if it is making any difference. Many times a behavior will get worse before it gets better. We start each day with a clean slate.

Source: "Who's Teaching Our Children with Disabilities?" *NICHCY News Digest,* 1997, *27,* 11.

Private Practitioner

Private practitioners work in the evaluation and remediation of children as an auxiliary service after school. In other words, these special education teachers provide evaluation and remediation services for children with disabilities in addition to those provided by the district.

These special educators are likely to be involved in the annual review and the triennial evaluation process. In addition, they usually make suggestions to the classroom teacher for modifying the curriculum to meet the learning style and needs of the child with a disability.

Whatever the role you play in special education, you will always encounter a variety of situations that require practical decisions and relevant suggestions. There will always be the need to fully understand symptoms, causality, evaluation, diagnosis, prescription, and remediation, as well as to communicate vital information to professionals, parents, and students. You will also encounter a whole new language filled with terminology and abbreviations that you will need to know and recognize. As part of this survival guide, you will find a vast glossary in Appendices C through G as well as a thorough list of abbreviations used in special education in Appendix B.

There is no doubt that you will need to learn a great deal, have a good base of knowledge in legal and educational areas, and be ready for an exciting, rewarding, but demanding profession.

PART TWO

THE SPECIAL EDUCATION PROCESS

Chapter 5

Overview of the Special Education Process

When a student has difficulties in school, the professional staff makes many attempts to resolve the problem. When these interventions do not work, a more extensive look at the student is required. The process by which children are identified as having a disability is called the *special education process.* It involves a number of steps that follow federal, state, and district guidelines. The guidelines have been created to protect the rights of students, parents, and school districts.

Special education teachers must be knowledgeable enough about this complicated process to help parents and students get through it. Working together under these guidelines ensures comprehensive assessment of students and proper special education services and modifications.

The chapters in this part of the book provide the information you will need to guarantee that any child you work with is given the most comprehensive opportunity to define clearly his or her symptoms, problems, needs, learning styles, strengths and weaknesses, classroom placements, modifications, and so on. Several different steps are involved in the process. As a future special education teacher, you should review each in terms of your responsibilities, the legal procedures, parental rights and responsibilities, and the implications for the student. Although the specific steps of the process may vary from state to state, district to district, and even school to school, those described here will give you a good idea of those required in any system.

A Two-Stage Process

The special education process actually has two stages. During the first stage, the staff looks at potential high-risk children and determines the most suitable direction for them. There is a wide range of options to choose from, from change of program to consolidation of program, disciplinary actions, parent counseling, and so on. However, when the child study team—the local school committee assigned to monitor children with potential problems—determines that the child fits the criteria for a suspected disability, the second stage begins.

Chapter 6

Identification of a Suspected Disability

Every staff member in a school should be trained to identify certain behaviors in children that may indicate a serious problem. When such behaviors begin to interfere with the child's ability to function in school, the child is described as *high risk.* As a special educator, you are likely to focus on children who have already been classified as having a disability. However, your skills and your knowledge of high-risk children should always be used to assist in the identification of other children with suspected disabilities who have not yet been classified. Whether you are sitting in the teacher cafeteria and overhear two regular education teachers talking about a student, are a member of a child study team (discussed at length later in this chapter), or are listening to a teacher speak about a parent interview, you will undoubtedly at some time hear high-risk symptoms being mentioned. In this case, an investigation into the child should be initiated immediately.

Sources of Referral

Potential high-risk students are referred by a variety of people, including the classroom teacher, a special education teacher who identifies a potential problem, the child's special teachers (art teacher, music teacher, and so on), the child's parents, the school support staff (psychologist, speech and language therapist, occupational therapist), outside professionals (the child's therapist, medical doctor), the child herself, clergy, and legal personnel such as the police.

When one of these individuals feels a child needs to be reviewed, a referral form is filled out and forwarded to a local school committee. This local committee, or team, may be called the child study team, the school-based support team, or the pupil personnel team, or have another, similar name, depending on the school district. For the purposes of this chapter, we will refer to it as the child study team, or CST.

This local school-based team should not be confused with either the multidisciplinary team (MDT) or the eligibility committee, which become involved later in the process. The MDT and eligibility committee are only utilized if the CST determines that a suspected disability exists; otherwise, the CST alone resolves the issue. The MDT includes participants from the school and the community, and the eligibility committee is a district-based team. The CST does not have a parent member and is not required to have one; in contrast, both the MDT and eligibility committee are required to do so. (MDTs are described later in this part of the book; eligibility committees are discussed in more detail in Part Three.)

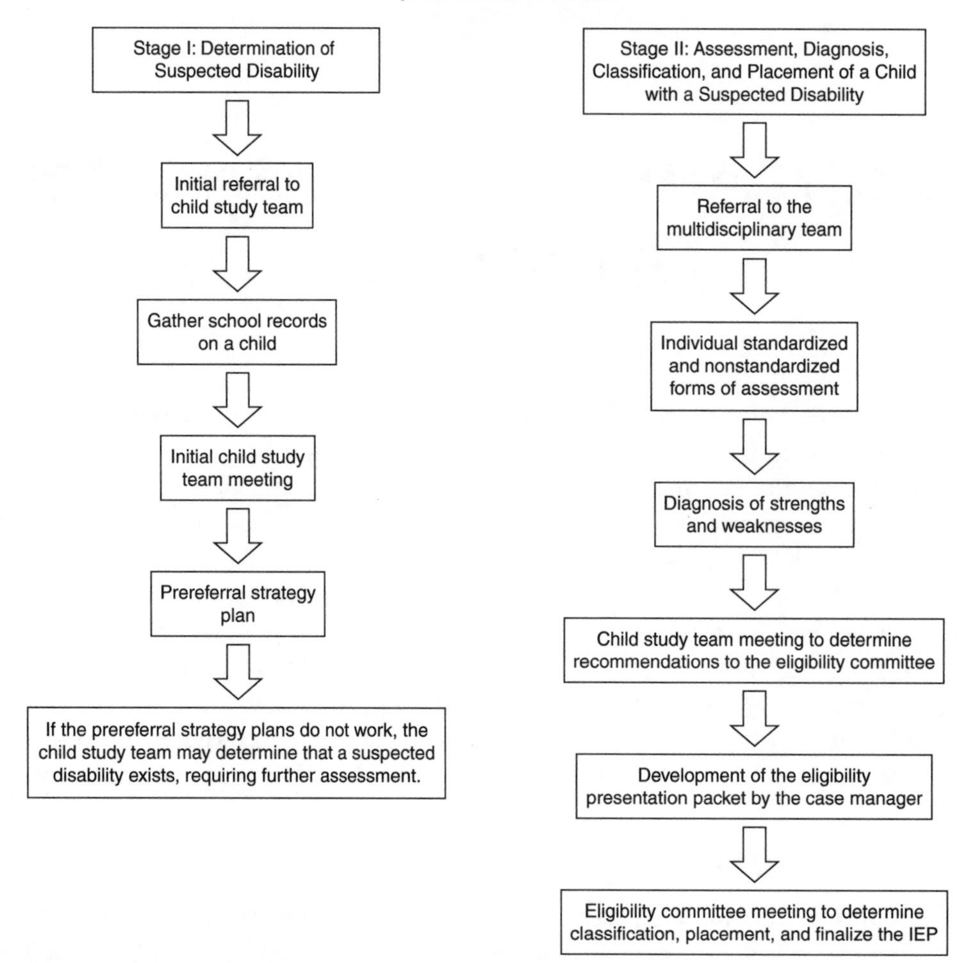

The Child Study Team (CST)

The members of the CST work as a unit to determine the possible cause (etiology), contributing factors, educational status, outcome (prognosis), and recommendations for the referred student. Bringing together many disciplines to work on a case is the primary concept behind the CST. In this way, many experts cover many fields and disciplines, which is more effective than having a single individual try to determine all of the factors. The CST usually includes the following individuals: school administrator (usually the principal or assistant principal), school psychologist, school nurse, classroom teacher, school social worker, guidance counselor (at the secondary level), reading teacher, speech and language teacher, and special education teacher.

The team members usually meet on a regular basis—once or twice a week, depending on the caseload.

Schools usually have a wealth of information about all their children, but it is distributed among a number of people and in a number of records. Gathered together, this information provides a very thorough picture of the child and his or her abilities and patterns. This information is usually gathered once a referral has been made, but prior to the initial CST meeting. Each member of the CST will bring certain information to the first meeting.

School Administrator

The administrator may have prior knowledge of the student, such as information gained through contact with the family or student, prior disciplinary or suspension information, or legal information communicated to the school by outside professionals. The administrator is also likely to bring information obtained through prior conferences between previous teachers and parents or between previous administrators and parents. This may be important in understanding the child's patterns and history.

School Psychologist

The school psychologist can provide past psychological reports, information gained from observation, reports from therapists or outside mental health facilities, clinical interviews, and screening information. The school psychologist may also bring prior teachers' reports. The various comments written on report cards or in permanent record folders may provide a different view of the child under a different style of teaching. Successful years with positive comments may be a clue to the child's learning style and provide information about the conditions under which the child responds best. If these reports or comments are not available, then someone on the CST should interview prior teachers to determine patterns of strengths and weaknesses. Although certain pieces of information may be brought by several different team members, the school psychologist is most likely to bring group intelligence test information. This information is usually found in the permanent record folder. It should be noted that in some districts and on some tests the term School Abilities Index (SAI) has replaced the term Intelligence Quotient, or IQ.

School Nurse

The school nurse may bring past and present medical information, medical reports, medication information, screening results on eyesight and hearing, observation information, and other medical screening information. This information will need to be reviewed for indications of visual or hearing difficulties, prescribed medications (for example, antihistamines) that may be affecting the child's behavior, and medical conditions in need of attention or that may be contributing to the child's behavior.

Classroom Teacher

The classroom teacher will bring examples of class work, informal testing results, anecdotal records, observations of social interactions, information on academic level, and parent intake information. (The parent intake is described later in this part of the book.) This individual will also bring comments or reports of his or her prior interviews with parents. The classroom teacher will usually bring attendance records, which need to be reviewed for patterns of lateness or absence. If such patterns exist, the reasons should be investigated to rule out medical causes (hospital stays, illnesses), psychological causes (dysfunctional family patterns, school phobia, and so on), or social causes (peer rejection or isolation). Two children both absent ten days a year can be absent for very different reasons. One may have been out twice for five days each due to illness, whereas the other may have been out ten Mondays in a row, possibly indicating a problem.

At times, teachers assess students in their classroom using a variety of nonstandardized assessment measures such as portfolios or informal reading inventories. If it is available, the teacher should bring this kind of nonstandardized assessment information to the initial meeting of the CST.

School Social Worker

If a school has a social worker on staff, this individual may bring family history or information, history of outside agency involvement, observation, or experiences with the student in group interaction.

Guidance Counselor

At the secondary level, it is important to include a guidance counselor on the CST because these individuals stand in for all the child's teachers in communicating classroom progress, strengths, and weaknesses. Because it is not realistic for all seven or eight of a child's teachers to attend the CST meeting, the guidance counselor reviews the child's situation and progress with all of them prior to the meeting and then reports the results to the team. This individual may also bring past report cards, standardized group test results, the permanent record folder, parent consultation information, aptitude testing results, observations, and past teacher comments.

Reading Teacher

The reading teacher may bring observation information and past and present reading diagnostic and screening or standardized test results.

Speech and Language Teacher

This individual may bring any past test results, outside test reports, observation if required, and screening results.

Special Education Teacher

A special education teacher is always a sitting member of the CST. It is up to the school administrator to choose which special education teacher in the school will fill this position. If you are chosen, you will need to be prepared for that role. This section of the book will help prepare you.

The special education teacher may provide past academic testing results, perceptual testing results, observations, prior special education services, outside educational test results and reports, any screening results, and copies of IEPs on students who have already been involved in special education. (As already noted in Part One, the IEP is a list of goals, needs, and objectives that is drawn up for every student with a disability.) The special education teacher may also be asked to bring standardized test score information on the child being discussed. These scores should be analyzed for patterns of strengths and deficiencies across the same skill area. Also, inconsistencies across the same skill areas over time may offer some clues about the child's real issues.

These standardized scores are usually in the permanent record folder found in the main office; the secretary will likely know where they are stored. And in fact, it is a good idea to bring the entire permanent record folder on the child to the meeting. Furthermore, it is important not to assume that someone else (other than you, the special education teacher) will bring it. Besides the previously mentioned information, this folder may contain teacher comments dating back to kindergarten, records from previous schools, individual reading test results, family information, and, most importantly, a history of the child's report card grades. All of this will be very helpful to the committee as it looks for patterns of strengths and weaknesses in academic, social, and behavioral areas over the years as well as number and types of schools attended. Sometimes children are enrolled in several schools in several years. The reasons for the many moves should be investigated because they may add to the child's adjustment difficulties.

Observation

The law usually requires that any child who is referred for special education be given a classroom observation. This observation is required at some time during the process, and it is helpful to do it before the initial CST meeting. One member of the team—usually the psychologist, social worker, guidance counselor, or special education teacher—observes the child in a variety of situations. Based on their expertise, special education teachers are often asked to do the observation. Observing children in different settings is a necessary part of the referral process; it offers another perception of the child. While only a classroom observation is required, it is strongly suggested that a child who has been referred should be observed in a variety of environments, including the playground, gym, and lunchroom in order to draw a conclusion.

Basic behaviors to observe include attention, focus, aggressiveness, compliance, flexibility, rigidity, oppositional behavior, shyness, controlling behavior, distractibility, impulsivity, social interaction, and so on.

Many types of prepared observation forms are available. This section of the chapter provides examples of several forms available for use.

Unstructured Observation Checklist

The unstructured observation checklist allows you to fill in any information that you feel is important about a series of behaviors. An example follows.

UNSTRUCTURED OBSERVATION CHECKLIST

Name of student observed:

Observer:

Date of observation:

Place of observation:

Classroom **Playground** **Lunchroom** **Gym**

Behaviors to observe:

1. Impulsivity
2. Attention to task

3. Attention span
4. Conformity to rules
5. Social interaction with peers
6. Aggressiveness
7. Level of teacher assistance required
8. Frustration levels
9. Reaction to authority
10. Verbal interaction
11. Procrastinating behaviors
12. Organizational skills
13. Developmental motor skills

As this example shows, any of a number of general areas can and should be observed. This is an informal working scale for the user's own information. The spaces provided allow for comments and notes that may shed some light on the child's overall pattern and severity of symptoms.

Structured Observation Checklist

The structured observation checklist defines the specific target behaviors that need to be observed. An example of this form follows.

STRUCTURED CLASSROOM OBSERVATION CHECKLIST

Student's name/ID # ______________________________

Date of birth ______________ **Dominant language** ______________

Date of observation ______________ **Length of observation** ______________

Observer ______________ **Position** ______________

Classroom observed ______________ **Location** ______________

Teacher's name ______________________________

Subject area being taught ______________________________

Task-Individual

A. When assigned task, the student:

1. Initiates task without need for teacher's verbal encouragement.
2. Requests help in order to start task.
3. Complains before getting started on task.

4. Demands help in order to start on task.
5. Actively refuses to do task despite teacher's encouragement.
6. Passively retreats from task despite teacher's encouragement.

B. While working on task, the student:

7. Works independently.
8. Performs assigned task without complaints.
9. Needs teacher's verbal encouragement to keep working.
10. Needs teacher in close proximity to keep working.
11. Needs physical contact from teacher to keep working.
12. Seeks constant reassurance to keep working.
13. Is reluctant to have work inspected.
14. Belittles own work.

C. At the end of assigned time, the student:

15. Completes task.
16. Takes pride in completed task.
17. Goes on to next task.
18. Refuses to complete task.

Social Interaction

The student:

19. Establishes a relationship with one or two peers.
20. Shares materials with peers.
21. Respects property of peers.
22. Gives help to peers when needed.
23. Accepts help from peers when needed.
24. Establishes a relationship with most peers.
25. Teases or ridicules peers.
26. Expresses prejudiced attitudes toward peers.
27. Physically provokes peers.
28. Physically hurts peers.
29. Seeks to be attacked by peers.
30. Participates appropriately in group activities.
31. Postpones own needs for group objectives.
32. Withdraws from group.
33. Is overly assertive in group.
34. Disrupts group activities (calling out, provocative language, and so on).
35. Exhibits aggressive behavior in group not amenable to teacher intervention.

Relationship to Teacher

The student:

36. Tries to meet teacher's expectations.
37. Functions adequately without constant teacher encouragement.
38. Interacts with teacher in nondemanding manner.
39. Responds to teacher without haggling.
40. Tests limits, tries to see how much teacher will allow.
41. Seeks special treatment from teacher.
42. Responds to teacher's criticism without fear.
43. Responds to teacher's criticism without verbal anger.
44. Responds to teacher's criticism without physical outbursts (for example, temper tantrums).
45. Defies teacher's requirement.
46. Scorns or ridicules teacher's support.
47. Responds with anger when demands are thwarted by teacher.
48. Blames and accuses teacher ("not helping," "not liking me").
49. Abuses teacher verbally (no apparent cause).
50. Abuses teacher physically (no apparent cause).
51. Requires close and constant supervision because behavioral controls are so limited.

Comments

Questions to Ask

If you are chosen to sit on the CST, be sure to review the available records in the school, as suggested in the previous section, and be ready to ask the necessary questions about this information. For example, when the CST discusses the observation information, they should look at the following issues.

Is There a Difference Between the Child's Behavior in Structured Settings and Unstructured Settings?

The answer may determine if the child needs a more structured learning environment. Children who do not have well-developed internal control systems need a highly structured environment to maintain focus and appropriate behavior. Some children cannot shift between structured and unstructured environments and then back again (for example, classroom, playground, classroom). They may not possess the internal monitor that regulates conformity and logical attendance to rules. For example, these children may be more successful in a structured play setting set up by teachers during the lunch hour.

Does the Child Seem to Respond to External Boundaries?

This is important, because it is a monitor of potential learning style. If a child who lacks internal controls does conform to external boundaries, such as time-outs or teacher proximity during work time, then this needs to be taken into consideration when prescribing classroom management techniques. When the child conforms to such boundaries, this behavior sends a message about what works for him.

What Is the Child's Attention Span During Academic Tasks?

Attention span at different ages is normally measured in minutes or hours. As a special education teacher, you should be aware of the normal attention span for children of all ages. If you are the one to do the observation, compare the particular child over several activities and days to see if a pattern of inattention is present. If the attention span is very short for a child of that age, then modifications to the workload—shorter but more frequent assignments, for example—may be needed.

Does the Child Require Constant Teacher Supervision or Assistance?

A child who requires constant teacher supervision or assistance may be exhibiting a wide variety of symptomatic behaviors that may result from attention deficit disorder, processing problems, emotional difficulties involving need for attention, need for control, high anxiety, internal stress, limited intellectual capacity, hearing problems, and so on. All of these areas need to be checked out, and a good evaluation should determine the roots of such behavior. The key is always the frequency, intensity, and duration of the symptoms.

Does the Child Interact Appropriately with Peers?

Observing children at play can tell us a great deal about their self-esteem, tension levels, social maturity, physical development, and many other factors. Social interaction is more common in children over age six or seven, while parallel play is common in younger children. Appropriate social interaction gives us insight into a child's internal boundaries and organization. A child who always needs to control may be masking high levels of tension. The more controlling a child is, the more out of control she is likely feeling. A child who can conform appropriately to group rules, delay his or her needs for the good of the team, and conform to rules and various changes or inconsistencies in rules, may be very self-assured and have low anxiety levels. The opposite is usually typical of at-risk children. However, developmental stages should always be taken into consideration, because certain behaviors, such as seeking to control, are more typical at early ages.

Is the Child a High- or Low-Status Child?

Observing a child in different settings offers the opportunity to see the social status of the child and its impact on his behavior. Low-status children, as children with learning disabilities often are, are more apt to feel insignificant and therefore fail to receive the positive social cues that help reinforce feelings of self-esteem.

Referral Forms

As noted earlier, before a child can be reviewed by the CST, the team must receive a referral. The referral form itself varies from school to school, district to district, and state to state. Its main purpose is to alert school professionals to a student who is exhibiting difficulties and may require further attention. Referral forms usually appear in two formats: open-ended and structured. An example of an open-ended referral form follows.

OPEN-ENDED REFERRAL FORM

Name: Matthew Jones

Date of referral: November 3, 2003

Grade: 4

Date of birth: December 5, 1993

Teacher: Mrs. Brown

Why are you referring this child?

Matthew is experiencing severe academic difficulties in the classroom. He procrastinates, is easily distracted, refuses to hand in work, has a short attention span, and has poor social skills. The other children tolerate him but are losing patience. I have contacted the mother and she has mentioned that these problems have been around for some time.

I have estimated his ability to be at least average, but his academic performance is well below grade level in all areas.

He further exhibits low frustration tolerance, an unwillingness to attempt new concepts, self-criticism, and intolerance for those around him.

I am very concerned about Matthew's deterioration this year and would like some advice on how to handle the situation.

Has parent been notified of this referral? Yes __X__ **No** ____

Administrator's signature ____________________ **Date** ____________________

This type of referral form allows the individual filling it out to include what he or she considers to be the child's most important issues. However, the information may not be the type the team needs to get an overall indication of severity, history, and nature of the symptoms presented. Therefore, some schools use a structured referral form. This form takes the individual filling it out through a series of questions that provide the information desired by the team. An example of this type of form follows.

STRUCTURED REFERRAL FORM

Student name: Mary Williams

Grade level: 3

Teacher: Mrs. Lacy

Parents' names: Mary/John

Date of referral: December 1, 2003

Date of birth: September 21, 1995

Chronological age: 8 years, 2 months

Phone: 455-8976

Please answer the following questions using behavioral terms:

1. **What symptoms is the child exhibiting that are of concern at this time?**
   Mary is having a great deal of trouble in my class. She exhibits numerous problems. She rarely hands in work; fails many tests, especially spelling and math; procrastinates; makes excuses; and has great difficulty handing in homework assignments.

2. **What have you tried that has worked?**
   The only thing that seems to work is contacting her parents, but that is short-lived and any noticeable changes only last for a day or two and Mary is right back to her patterns.

3. **What have you tried that does not seem to work toward alleviating these symptoms?**
   I have attempted several things including peer tutoring, limiting assignments, change of seat, parent conferences, small group interventions, all to see if she could accomplish anything but nothing has worked.

4. **What are the child's present academic levels of functioning?**
   From informal testing I consider Mary to be low average in all academic skills and ability.

5. **Any observable behavioral or physical limitations?**
   Mary does not seem to have any physical limitations.

6. **What is the child's social behavior like?**
   Mary does not seem to avoid any social contact with the other children. She spends a great deal of her time with her friends.

7. **Current performance estimates (below, on, or above grade level)**
   Reading: average. Math: below average. Spelling: below average.

8. **Have the parents been contacted? Yes** __X__ **No** ____ **If no, why not?**

9. **Further comments?**
   Parents are concerned. Not sure what to do next.

As this example shows, the individual filling out the form is guided through a series of questions that define the specific areas determined to be important by the child study team. Room is also given at the end for any further comments that the individual feels are necessary to the understanding of the child.

Initial CST Meeting

Once the referral is made and the available information has been gathered by the team members, the initial child study team meeting can be held. The team will try to review everything available on the child and make some recommendations for the next step to take on this case. The team should consider certain issues to help them make the best decisions. As the special education teacher on the team, you should try to make sure that they consider the following issues.

Has This Child Previously Been Referred to the CST?

Prior referral may indicate a historical disturbance or long-term problem and therefore a serious situation, especially if the same pattern still exists. Situational disturbances, with no prior problems, usually have a better prognosis.

Are There Any Prior Psychological, Educational, Language, or Other Evaluations?

This information is very important and can avoid putting the child through unnecessary testing. These reports also offer the team another perspective on the problem.

What Are the Comments from Past Teachers?

Never assume that the child is always the problem. Comments from past teachers may give a different picture and also help pinpoint the changes that have led to the referral. A child who had positive teacher feedback for the past four years and all of a sudden begins to deteriorate may have experienced something over the summer, experienced changes in the home, or be having a personality conflict with the teacher.

Is Anyone Familiar with Other Family Members?

Family patterns of behavior may help define contributing factors to the child's problem. Knowledge of this behavior may also provide the team with some ideas for the best approach to take with this family.

What Is Going On at Home?

Many symptoms in school are the result of tension or problems in the home. If confused as school-related problems, the true issue will be overlooked; you will be treating symptoms, not problems. Home issues affect every child, and some more than others. A short conversation between a staff member and the parents may determine situational disturbances (brief but intense patterns of tension, such as loss of a job, death of a relative, separation, and so on) that may be causing the child to have difficulty focusing or performing in school.

What Does the Developmental History Look Like?

A child's developmental history can be like a fingerprint in indicating possible causes or influences that are contributing to the present problem. A thorough parent intake that covers all areas of a child's history is a crucial factor in the proper diagnosis of a child's problems. A look at developmental milestones, traumatic experiences, hospitalizations, prior testing, and so on offers a closer look at the total child. (The following section discusses the parent intake in detail.)

Are There Any Medical Issues That Might Affect This Case?

Medical issues are crucial. The existence of medical problems should always be determined. Difficulties with hearing or eyesight, taking medication, severe allergies, and so on may be significant contributors to poor performance, while the child may be improperly described as "unmotivated," "lazy," "stubborn," and so on.

When Were Vision and Hearing Last Checked?

Vision and hearing problems should be ruled out immediately as having any influence on the presenting problem. If the child has not been evaluated in either area in at least one year, or if symptoms indicate possible visual or auditory involvement (squinting, eye fatigue, failure to hear directions, and so on), then a retest is indicated.

Has Anyone Observed This Child?

The observation should always be a piece of the contributing information presented to the CST. As explained earlier, one member of the team—usually the psychologist, social worker, guidance counselor, or special education teacher—should observe the child in a variety of situations prior to the first CST meeting. It is very important for the team to know how the child functions in both structured and unstructured settings.

Are There Samples of the Child's Class Work?

Samples of class work over a period of time offer a clearer view of the child's abilities and attitude toward class work. They also give several team members an opportunity to observe possible academic symptoms that may first appear in written work.

Have the Parents Been Notified of the Teacher's Concerns?

It is not up to the team to notify parents of a potential problem. It is the responsibility of the classroom teacher to alert them about his concerns, and that he would like the CST to take a closer look. Parents do not have a legal right to refuse such a request because it is considered normal school procedure. The teacher should also explain that someone from the team will be in touch with them to gather more information and review any findings.

Obtaining Further Information

Discussion of a specific child may take one or several meetings, depending on the complications and needs of the case. Sometimes the CST may need further information not available during the initial meeting. For example, the CST may request the following.

Educational Screening

The CST will likely make this recommendation when a child's academic skill levels (reading, math, writing, and spelling) are unknown or inconsistent. A screening is not a formal evaluation but a series of short, brief measures that offer some basic academic information on which the team can make other decisions. An example of an educational screening test is the Wechsler Individual Achievement Test-II Screener (WIAT-II Screener). It is likely that the special educator on the team will be the one to carry out this type of evaluation.

Language Screening

The recommendation for language screening usually occurs when the child is experiencing significant delays in speech or language development, problems in articulation, or problems in receptive or expressive language. Some symptoms that might warrant such a screening are difficulty pronouncing words through third grade, immature or delayed speech patterns, difficulty labeling thoughts or objects, and difficulty putting thoughts into words.

Intellectual Screening

The CST will make this recommendation when the child's intellectual ability is unknown. An example of a brief intelligence screening is the Kaufman Brief Intelligence Test (KBIT) or the screening form of the Wechsler scales. The school psychologist will administer these tests.

The Parent Intake

In addition to the educational screening, language screening, and intelligence screening, the CST may recommend a parent intake. We break out this item in greater depth because it contains several steps.

The recommendation for a parent intake is usually made when family background information is missing or needs to be updated. The CST may feel that this information will shed some light on the present situation. This intake may be assigned to any member of the team.

Points to Keep in Mind

If you are chosen to do the parent intake, it is important to keep some points in mind.

Sensitivity and Diplomacy

A parent intake should be done with sensitivity and diplomacy. Although the questions may not be of concern to most parents, they may be perceived as intrusive by others. The questions should be specific enough to help diagnose the problem, but not so specific as to place the parent in a vulnerable and defensive position. Four main areas are usually covered in a parent intake: identifying data and family information, developmental history, academic history, and social history.

Identifying Data and Family Information

Get confirmation of names, addresses, phone numbers, and dates of birth; siblings' names, ages, and dates of birth; parents' occupations; other adults residing in the home; marital status of parents; and so on.

Developmental History

Find out about length of delivery, type of delivery, complications if any, approximate ages of critical stages (that is, walking and talking), hospital stays, illnesses other than normal ones, sleeping habits, eating habits, high fevers, date of last eye exam, date of last hearing exam, falls or injuries, traumatic experiences, medications, and any prior developmental testing.

Academic History

Learn the number of schools attended, types of schools attended, adjustment to kindergarten, best school year, worst school year, best subject, worst subject, prior teacher reports, prior teacher comments, and homework behavior.

Social History

Ask about the child's groups or organizations, social behavior in group situations, hobbies, areas of interest, circle of friends, and sports activities.

Arranging for the Parent Intake

As you can see, the parent intake provides a complete social history, which can be regarded as a description of the family life situation. In some cases it may not be possible to obtain this information because of a number of variables such as parents' work restrictions, inability to obtain coverage for younger siblings, resistance, or apathy. However, if you are able to arrange for a parent intake, there are several things to consider before the meeting.

- Always make the parents feel comfortable and at ease by setting up a receptive environment. If possible, hold the meeting in a pleasant setting, use a round table—or any table instead of a desk—and offer some type of refreshment to ease possible tension of the situation.
- Never view the parents as adversaries, even if they are angry or hostile. Keep in mind that their anger or hostility is a defense because they may not be aware of what you will be asking or have had negative school meetings over the years. Because this may be an opportunity for parents to "vent," listen to their concerns, do not get defensive, and be understanding without taking sides.
- Inform them of the purpose of the meeting and the steps involved in the referral process. Reassure them that no recommendation will be made without their input and permission.
- Be solution-oriented and offer realistic hope even if past experiences have resulted in frustration. Remind the parents that children can be more motivated, resilient, and successful at different developmental stages.
- You may want to offer them a pad and pen so that they can write down information, terms, or notes. Let them know that they should feel free to call you with any questions or concerns they may have.

- Reassure the parents about the confidentiality of the information gathered. Explain which individuals on the CST will be seeing the information and the purpose for their review.
- Explain the next step and who will be getting back to them with the results of the CST meetings.

The Parent Intake Form

An example of a parent intake form completed by the special education teacher is shown here. This intake was done with the mother of the child, Mrs. Jane Jones.

PARENT INTAKE FORM

Identifying Data

Name of client: Matthew Jones

Address: 12 Court Street

Phone: 675-7863

Date of birth: March 4, 1993

Age: 9

Brothers (names and ages): Brian, 15

Sisters (names and ages): Karen, 4

Mother's name: Jane

Father's name: Ben

Mother's occupation: Medical technician

Father's occupation: Accountant

Referred by: Teacher

Grade: 4

School: Holland Avenue

Developmental History

Length of pregnancy: Full term, 22-hour labor

Type of delivery: Forceps

Complications: Apgar score 7, jaundice at birth

Long hospital stays: None

Falls or injuries: None

Allergies: Early food allergies, none recently

Medication: None at present

Early milestones (walking, talking, toilet training): According to parent Matthew was late in walking and talking in comparison to brother. He was toilet-trained at age three. Parent added that he seemed to be slower than usual in learning things.

Traumatic experiences: None

Previous psychological evaluations or treatment (please explain reasons and dates): None. However, parent indicated that it was suggested by first-grade teacher but teacher never followed through.

Any previous psychiatric hospitalizations? No

Sleep disturbances: Trouble falling asleep, somnambulism at age 5 but only lasted a few weeks. Talks a great deal in his sleep lately.

Eating disturbances: Picky eater, likes sweets

Last vision and hearing exams and results: Last eye test in school indicated 20/30. Last hearing test in school was inconclusive. Parent has not followed through on nurse's request for an outside evaluation.

Excessively high fevers: No

Childhood illnesses: Normal ones

Academic History

Nursery school experience: Matthew had difficulty adjusting to nursery school. The teacher considered him very immature and his skills were well below those of his peers. He struggled through the year.

Kindergarten experience (adjustment, comments, etc.): Matthew's difficulties increased. According to the parent he had reading problems and social difficulties. His gross and fine motor skills were immature.

First grade through sixth grade (teachers' comments, traumatic experiences, strength areas, etc.): According to past teachers Matthew struggled through the years. He was a nice boy and polite and at times tried hard. But in the later grades (second and third), his behavior and academics began to falter. Teachers always considered referral but felt he might grow out of it.

Subjects that presented the most difficulty: Reading, math, spelling

Subjects that were the least difficult: Science

Most recent report card grades (if applicable): Matthew has received mostly "Needs to improve" on his report card.

Social History

Groups or organizations: Tried Boy Scouts but dropped out. Started Little League but became frustrated.

Social involvement as perceived by parent: Inconsistent. He does not seem to reach out to kids and lately he spends a great deal of time alone.

Hobbies or interests: Baseball cards, science

Prereferral Strategies

After analyzing all the information presented at the meeting, the CST has to make a decision: What do they recommend at this point? If this is the first time a student is being reviewed by the team, then prereferral strategies will likely be recommended to the classroom teacher. These are techniques and suggestions to attempt to resolve the child's issues without more comprehensive assessment. The team, along with the teacher, will choose strategies from those listed here and develop a prereferral strategy plan. This plan, as outlined in the Individuals with Disabilities Education Act (IDEA), is an attempt to try every possible alternative prior to making a formal referral for assessment. The special education teacher plays a critical role in the development of this plan, which contains classroom suggestions for management, modifications, assessment, and accommodations.

Once the plan is developed, the classroom teacher will collaborate with the support personnel assigned to assist her. There may be meetings and conferences between staff and classroom teacher, or sometimes there will be direct participation and assistance by support personnel in the classroom. The special education teacher may be called upon to provide the classroom teacher indirect collaboration (nonparticipation suggestions) or direct assistance involvement (working with the teacher in the classroom).

In sum, prereferral interventions include the following:

- Team meetings with the classroom teacher
- Parent interviews
- Help classes
- Remedial reading or math services
- In-school counseling
- Daily or weekly progress reports
- Disciplinary action
- Medical exam
- Change of program
- Consolidation of program
- Referral to Child Protective Services
- Teacher-made tests
- Further observation
- Screening tests

Two additional strategies, classroom management techniques and hearing and vision tests, are discussed in more detail here.

Classroom Management Techniques

There are times when the real issue may not be the child, but rather the teaching style of the classroom teacher. Perhaps the teacher has unrealistic expectations, is critical, or is overly demanding. In this case, help for the teacher can come in the form of classroom management techniques. These include the following:

- Display daily class schedule with times so the student has a structured idea of the day ahead.
- Change seating.
- Seat student with good role models.
- Use peer tutors when appropriate.
- Limit number of directions.
- Simplify complex directions.
- Give verbal as well as written directions.
- Provide extra work time.
- Shorten assignments.
- Modify curriculum.
- Identify and address preferred learning styles.
- Provide manipulative materials.
- Provide examples of what is expected.
- Color-code materials to foster organizational skills.
- Develop a homework plan with parental support.
- Develop a behavior modification plan.
- Use lots of positive reinforcement.
- Use technology as an aid.

Hearing Tests

Some symptoms that suggest this option include the following:

- Child asks speaker to repeat frequently.
- Child consistently misinterprets what he or she hears.
- Child does not respond to auditory stimuli.
- Child slurs speech, speaks in a monotone voice, or articulates poorly.

Vision Tests

Symptoms that may require this option include the following:

- Child turns head when looking at board or objects.
- Child squints excessively.
- Child rubs eyes frequently.
- Child holds books and materials close to the face or at unusual angles.
- Child suffers frequent headaches.

- Child avoids close work of any type.
- Child covers an eye when reading.
- Child consistently loses place when reading.

Moving to the Next Stage

If, after some time, the teacher reports to the CST that the problems still exist despite all the prereferral strategies, then the team must consider if the child has a more serious educational disability. The team will usually look at the following criteria:

- The level of the discrepancy between the child's ability and his or her performance.
- Historical patterns of this discrepancy.
- Behavioral manifestations of a suspected disability. For instance, such behaviors as distractibility, problems in attention, problems in memory, social difficulties, gross motor coordination issues, and fine motor concerns may indicate a learning disability.

If these factors are present and the prereferral strategies were unsuccessful, then it is the responsibility of the CST to refer the child for a more formal assessment. With the referral for a more formal assessment, the second stage of the special education process begins.

Chapter 7

Assessment, Diagnosis, Classification, and Placement of a Child with a Suspected Disability

As explained earlier, the child study team is a local school committee whose responsibilities include the monitoring and disposition of cases involving high-risk students. Once the CST has tried everything possible and the issues still exist, a referral is made to another team, a team that will be responsible for the formal assessment. This team is called the *multidisciplinary team* (MDT).

Sources of Referral

A referral for this formal individualized evaluation and possible special education services is usually initiated by written request from the CST. However, just as with the earlier referral to the CST in the first place, other people have the right under due process to initiate this formal referral. (Due process is discussed at length later in the book. See in particular Part Seven.) Those other people include:

- The child's parent and advocate or person in parental relationship
- A classroom teacher
- Any professional staff member of the public or private school district
- A judicial officer (a representative of the court)
- The student on his or her own behalf if he or she is eighteen years or older, or an emancipated minor—that is, a person under the age of eighteen who has been given certain adult rights by the court
- The chief school officer of the state or designee responsible for the welfare, education, or health of children

The Multidisciplinary Team (MDT)

Although specific state regulations differ on the membership of the MDT, the members are usually drawn from the school and the community. A special education teacher will be assigned as the team member responsible for the educational and perhaps perceptual evaluations of the child. The law mandates that an individual who is an expert in the field of the suspected disability be a member of the MDT. For instance, if there is a suspected learning disability, the special education teacher will be considered the expert on the team in this area. As a special education teacher, it will be important for you to be familiar with the other professionals who are likely to be on this team. Many are similar to those who were on the CST. The MDT differs from the CST in that it may include other outside members such as parents, students, psychiatrists, pediatricians, agency officials, and so forth.

School Psychologist

The school psychologist on the MDT administers individual intelligence tests, projective tests, and personality inventories, and observes the student in a variety of settings.

School Nurse

The school nurse reviews all medical records, screens for vision and hearing, consults with outside physicians, and may refer to outside physicians if necessary.

Classroom Teacher

The classroom teacher works with the local school-based child study team to implement prereferral strategies, and plans and implements, along with the special education team, classroom strategies that create an appropriate working environment for the student.

School Social Worker

The social worker's role on the MDT is to gather and provide information on the family system. This may be accomplished through interviews, observations, conferences, and so on.

Special Education Teacher

The special education teacher consults with parents and classroom teachers about prereferral recommendations; administers educational and perceptual tests; may be called on to observe the student in a variety of settings; may be involved in the screening of students with suspected disabilities; writes IEPs, including goals and objectives; and recommends intervention strategies to teachers and parents.

Educational Diagnostician

The educational diagnostician, who is usually trained in special education, administers a series of evaluations, including norm-referenced and criterion-referenced tests, observes the student in a variety of settings, and makes educational recommendations that get applied to the IEP as goals and objectives.

Physical Therapist

The physical therapist evaluates a child who is experiencing problems in gross motor functioning, living and self-help skills, and vocational skills necessary for functioning in certain settings. This professional may screen, evaluate, provide direct services, or consult with the teacher, parent, or school.

Behavioral Consultant

This individual works closely with the MDT in providing direct services or consultation on behavioral and classroom management techniques and programs.

Speech-Language Clinician

This professional screens for speech and language developmental problems, provides a full evaluation on a suspected language disability, provides direct services, and consults with staff and parents.

Audiologist

This professional will evaluate a student's hearing for possible impairment, and as a result of the findings, may refer the student for medical consultation or treatment. The audiologist may also help students and parents obtain equipment, such as hearing aids, that may improve the child's ability to function in school.

Occupational Therapist

The occupational therapist evaluates a child who may be experiencing problems in fine motor skills and in living and self-help skills, for example. This professional may screen; evaluate; provide direct services; consult with the teacher, parent, or school; and assist in obtaining appropriate assistive technology or equipment.

Guidance Counselor

This individual may provide aptitude test information; provide counseling services; work with the team on consolidating, changing, or developing a student's class schedule; and assist the child study team in developing prereferral strategies.

Parents

Unlike in the CST, parents play an extremely important role on the MDT: providing input for the IEP; working closely with members of the team; and carrying out, assisting with, or initiating academic or management programs in the home.

The Written Referral

Regardless of who makes the referral, a referral form is always required. A referral should include a great deal of information to assist the MDT in its assessment. Documentation as to why a possible disability exists, descriptions of attempts to remediate the child's behaviors (prereferral strategies), and performance prior to the referral should all be included. As explained earlier, if the referral is not from the parent, the district must inform the parent in writing immediately that the child has been referred for assessment because of a suspected disability. The referral states that the child may have a disability that adversely affects educational performance. An important point to remember is that a referral to the MDT does *not* necessarily mean that the child has a disability. It simply signals that the child is having learning difficulties and that there is a concern that the problem *may* be due to a disability.

If the CST is making the referral, it is likely that the special education teacher or the school psychologist, or both together, will be asked to fill out this form. Therefore, it is important for you to become familiar with what will be asked.

INITIAL REFERRAL TO THE MDT FROM THE SCHOOL STAFF

To: Chairperson of the MDT

From: Sara Block **Name-title:** Chairperson of the Child Study Team

School: Baily High **Date:** April 15, 2002

The following student is being referred to the eligibility committee for suspicion of a disability:

Student name: Ben Aziza **Sex:** M **Grade:** 4 **Ethnicity:** Hispanic

Parent/guardian name: Maria/Calo

Address: 10 Spring Street

City: Morris **State:** NJ **Zip:** 11786

Telephone: (201) 786-0987 **Date of birth:** March 2, 1993

Current program placement: Regular mainstream

Teacher (elementary): Mrs. Stowe **Guidance counselor (secondary):** ___________

Reasons for referral: Describe the specific reason and/or needs that indicate the suspicion of a disability. Specify reason why referral is considered appropriate and necessary.

Ben is being referred for a formal assessment as the result of suspected learning disability. The school has attempted a variety of prereferral strategies but has been unable to change Ben's level of impaired performance. While he is a bright boy, and articulates appropriately, his written expression is well below average and continues to impair his performance. Ben also needs a great deal of encouragement and monitoring in the classroom. His performance still falls far below those of his classmates.

Describe recent attempts to remediate the pupil's performance prior to referral, including regular education interventions such as remedial reading and math, teaching modifications, behavior modifications, speech improvement, parent conferences, and so on, and the results of those interventions.

The referral is considered necessary at this time because Ben continues to do poorly in school despite numerous interventions such as classroom modifications, parent training and conferences, portfolio assessment, observation, remedial reading and math intervention, and changes in teaching strategies and management. The results of these intervention strategies have been unsuccessful and have even added to Ben's sense of frustration and lack of confidence.

Do you have a signed parent assessment plan? Yes __X__ No ____ (If yes, attach copy.)

Is there an attendance problem? Yes __X__ No ____

Did student repeat a grade? Yes ____ No __X__ (If yes, when?)

Is an interpreter needed? Yes ____ No __X__ (Deaf?)

Is a bilingual assessment needed? Yes ____ No __X__ (If yes, what language?)

Language spoken at home: English

Is student eligible to receive ESL (English as a Second Language) services? Yes ____ No __X__

If yes, how many years receiving ESL services? __NA__ If yes, determine how student's educational, cultural, and experiential background were considered to determine if these factors are contributing to the student's learning or behavior problems.

Test Scores Within Last Year

(Standardized Achievement, Regents Competency, etc.)

Area Test Name	*Percentile Measured*	*Score*	*Comment*
1. Wechsler Individual Achievement Test	Basic reading	42	Screening
2. Wechsler Individual Achievement Test	Reading comprehension	10	Screening
3. Wechsler Individual Achievement Test	Numerical operations	22	Screening
4. Wechsler Individual Achievement Test	Oral expression	67	Screening
5. Wechsler Individual Achievement Test	Written expression	5	Screening
6. Kaufman Brief Intelligence Test	Intelligence	57	

Has school staff informed parent/guardian of referral to eligibility committee? Yes __X__ No ____

By whom? School psychologist

What was the reaction of the parent/guardian to the referral? Positive

To Be Completed by School Nurse: Medical Report Summary

Any medication? Yes ___ No _X_ If yes, specify:

Health problems? Yes ___ No _X_ If yes, specify:

Scoliosis screening: Positive ___ Negative _X_

Date of last physical: August 1999 **Vision results:** Normal **Hearing results:** Normal

Relevant medical information: None

School Nurse signature:

Principal's signature:

To Be Completed by the Appropriate Administrator

Date received: **Signature:**

Chairperson:

Date notice and consent sent to parent/guardian:

Parent consent for initial evaluation received:

Date agreement to withdraw referral received:

Projected eligibility meeting date:

If eligible, projected date of implementation of services:

Projected eligibility board of education meeting date:

This initial referral to the MDT from the school staff alerts the chairperson of the MDT that the local school CST has made every attempt to resolve the student's difficulties before making the formal referral. It also informs the chairperson that guidelines for dealing with parental rights have been followed. As noted earlier, a student's parent or guardian may initiate a referral to the MDT if they suspect a disability (allowed under special education laws or Section 504 of the Rehabilitation Act). A referral form for parents is provided later in this chapter. The parent sends this form to the appropriate special education administrator. Usually on the receipt of a parent referral, the chairperson of the MDT will send the parent an assessment plan and a due process rights statement.

If a release for testing (the assessment plan) is not secured at a separate meeting—usually the initial parent intake—the chairperson of the MDT will mail one to the parent along with the letter indicating that a referral has been made. No formal evaluations may begin until the district has received this signed permission from the parent or guardian.

Obtaining Consent for Evaluation

As previously stated, the release for testing form can be obtained in several ways. Most of the time it is attached to a letter to the parents from the district's office of special services indicating that their child has been referred for a formal evaluation. According to the law it should:

- Be written in a language easily understood by the general public.
- Be provided in the primary language of the parent or other mode of communication used by the parent, unless doing so is clearly unfeasible.
- Explain the types of assessments to be conducted.
- State that no Individualized Education Program (IEP) will result from the assessment without the consent of the parent.
- Explain that no assessment shall be conducted unless the written consent of the parent is obtained. The parent shall have at least fifteen days (this may vary from state to state) from the receipt of the proposed assessment plan to arrive at a decision. Assessment may begin immediately on receipt of the consent.
- Include a copy of the notice of parent rights, which include the right to electronically record the proceedings of the eligibility committee meetings that will eventually take place.
- Explain that the assessment will be conducted by persons competent to perform the assessment, as determined by the school district, county office, or special education local plan area.
- Explain that any psychological assessment must be conducted by a qualified school psychologist.
- Explain that any health assessment of pupils will be conducted only by a credentialed school nurse or physician who is trained and prepared to assess cultural and ethnic factors appropriate to the pupil being assessed.

The Assessment

Once the parents have been informed of their rights, a release is obtained, and the assessment plan is signed, the assessment can begin. The MDT has several evaluation options to choose from, depending on the specializations of the MDT members. Keep in mind that the special educator on the team will do the academic and perceptual evaluations because the special educator's role on the MDT is that of educational diagnostician. The big difference between the MDT and CDT evaluations is the extent, depth, and types of testing and assessment done. The MDT most often considers assessing children with a suspected disability in the following areas.

Academic Evaluation

In most cases when there is a suspected disability, the academic evaluation is a part of the formal evaluation. The academic evaluation is usually recommended when a child's academic skill levels (reading, math, writing, and spelling) are unknown or inconsistent and when his or her learning process shows gaps (for example, memory and expression). Some symptoms that might suggest the need for an academic evaluation are consistently low test scores on group achievement tests, indications of delayed processing when faced with academic skills, labored handwriting after grade three, poor word recall, poor decoding (word attack) skills, discrepancy between achievement and ability, and consistently low achievement despite remediation.

The academic evaluation will determine if a discrepancy between intellectual potential and academic achievement required for the classification exists, and it will determine strengths and weaknesses in the child's academic and processing areas. The objectives of an academic evaluation are as follows:

- To help determine the child's stronger and weaker academic skill areas. This information is useful when making practical recommendations to teachers about academic expectations, areas in need of remediation, and how best to input information to assist the child's ability to learn.
- To help the teacher gear materials to the learning capacity of the individual child. A child reading two years below grade level may require modified textbooks or greater explanations prior to a lesson.
- To develop a learning profile. This can help the classroom teacher understand the best way to present information to the child and therefore increase his or her chances of success.
- Along with other information and test results, to help determine if the child's academic skills are suitable for a regular class. If the disabilities are severe, the child may require a more restrictive educational setting—that is, an educational setting or situation other than a full-time regular class placement, such as a resource room, a self-contained class, a special school, and so on.

Whatever the achievement battery (that is, group of tests) chosen, it should be one that covers enough skill areas to make an adequate diagnosis of academic strengths and weaknesses.

For a detailed explanation of all tests mentioned here, as well as many others not included due to space limitations, refer to *The Special Educator's Guide to 109 Diagnostic Tests* (Pierangelo and Giuliani, 2000) or *The Special Educator's Book of Lists* (Pierangelo, 2003).

Some tests used to measure academic levels are the following:

- *Reading assessment measures* are normally administered by the special education teacher, psychologist, or classroom teacher. Some examples are the Decoding Skills Test (DST); Durrell Analysis of Reading Difficulty (DARD); Gates-MacGinitie Silent Reading Test-Third Edition; Gates-McKillop-Horowitz Reading Diagnostic Tests; Gilmore Oral Reading Test; Gray Oral Reading Test-3 (GORT-3); Nelson-Denny Reading Test (NDRT); Slosson Oral Reading Test-Revised (SORT-R); Spache Diagnostic Reading Scales (DRS); Test of Reading Comprehension-Third Edition (TORC-3); Woodcock Reading Mastery Test-Revised (WRMT-R).
- *Arithmetic assessment measures* are normally administered by the special education teacher, psychologist, or classroom teacher. Some examples are the Key Math Diagnostic Arithmetic Test-Revised (Key Math-R); the Steenburgen Diagnostic-Prescriptive Math Program and Quick Math Screening Test (Steenburgen); Test of Early Mathematics Ability-2 (TEMA-2); Test of Mathematical Abilities-2 (TOMA-2).
- *Spelling assessment measures* are normally administered by the special education teacher, psychologist, or classroom teacher. They include the Diagnostic Word Patterns and the Test of Written Spelling-3 (TWS-3).

- *Handwriting assessment measures* are normally administered by the special education teacher, psychologist, speech and language therapist, classroom teacher, or occupational therapist. They include the Denver Handwriting Analysis (DHA); the Picture Story Language Test (PSLT); Test of Early Written Language-2 (TEWL-2); Test of Written Language-3 (TOWL-3); Written Language Assessment (WLA).
- *Comprehensive achievement measures* are normally administered by the special education teacher, psychologist, or classroom teacher. They include the Brigance Diagnostic Inventory of Basic Skills; Kaufman Test of Educational Achievement (KTEA); Norris Educational Achievement Test (NEAT); Peabody Individual Achievement Test-Revised (PIAT-R); Test of Academic Achievement Skills-Reading, Arithmetic, Spelling, and Listening Comprehension (TAAS-RASLC); Wechsler Individual Achievement Test-II (WIAT-II); Wide Range Achievement Test-3 (WRAT-3).

Language Evaluation

This recommendation usually occurs when the child is experiencing significant delays in speech or language development, problems in articulation, or problems in receptive or expressive language. Some symptoms that might warrant such an evaluation are:

- Difficulty pronouncing words through grade three
- Immature or delayed speech patterns
- Difficulty labeling thoughts or objects
- Difficulty putting thoughts into words

Expressive and receptive language measures are normally administered by the speech and language therapist. They include the Boehm Test of Basic Concepts-Revised (BTBC-R); Comprehensive Receptive and Expressive Vocabulary Test (CREVT); Goldman-Fristoe Test of Articulation; Goldman-Fristoe-Woodcock Test of Auditory Discrimination (G-F-WTAD); Kaufman Survey of Early Academic and Language Skills (K-SEALS); Peabody Picture Vocabulary Test-III (PPVT-III); Test for Auditory Comprehension of Language-Revised (TACL-R); Test of Adolescent and Adult Language-Third Edition (TOAL-3); Test of Early Language Development-Second Edition (TELD-2); Test of Language Development-Intermediate-2 (TOLD-I:2); Test of Language Development-Primary-2 (TOLD-P:2).

Psychological Evaluation

As with the academic assessment, the psychological evaluation is a normal part of every referral for a suspected disability. This recommendation is appropriate when the child's intellectual ability is unknown or when there is a question about inability to learn. It is useful when the MDT suspects potential learning, emotional, or intellectual problems. The psychological evaluation can rule out or rule in emotionality as a primary cause of a child's problem; ruling this factor out is necessary before the learning disability diagnosis can be made. Some symptoms that might signal the need for such an evaluation are:

- High levels of tension and anxiety exhibited in behavior
- Aggressive behavior
- Lack of motivation or indications of low energy levels

- Patterns of denial
- Oppositional behavior
- Despondency
- Inconsistent academic performance, ranging from very low to very high
- History of inappropriate judgment
- Lack of impulse control
- Extreme and consistent attention-seeking behavior
- Pattern of provocative behavior

Objectives of the psychological assessment include these:

- Determine the child's present overall levels of intellectual ability.
- Determine the child's present verbal intellectual ability.
- Determine the child's nonlanguage intellectual ability.
- Explore indications of greater potential.
- Find possible patterns involving learning style—for example, verbal comprehension, concentration.
- Ascertain possible influences of tension and anxiety on testing results.
- Determine the child's intellectual ability to deal with present grade-level academic demands.
- Explore the influence of intellectual ability as a contributing factor in a child's past and present school difficulties (for example, limited intellectual ability found in retardation).

Assessment measures used in this area include the following:

- *Measures of intellectual ability* are normally administered by the psychologist: Columbia Mental Maturity Scale (CMMS); Comprehensive Test of Nonverbal Intelligence (CTONI); Kaufman Assessment Battery for Children (K-ABC); Mental Processing Scales; Kaufman Brief Intelligence Test (K-BIT); McCarthy Scales of Children's Abilities (MSCA); Otis-Lennon School Ability Test (OLSAT); Slosson Intelligence Test-Revised (SIT-R); Stanford Binet Intelligence Test; Test of Nonverbal Intelligence-Third Edition (TONI-3); Wechsler Scales of Intelligence.
- *Psychological measures* are normally administered by the psychologist: Attention Deficit Disorders Evaluation Scale-Revised (ADDES); Children's Apperception Test (CAT); Conners' Parent and Teacher Rating Scales (CRS); Draw-A-Person: Screening Procedure for Emotional Disturbance (DAP:SPED); Goodenough-Harris Drawing Test (GHDT); Kinetic-House-Tree-Person Drawings (K-H-T-P); the Polite Sentence Completion Test (PSCT); Rorschach Psychodiagnostic Test; Thematic Apperception Test for Children and Adults (TAT).
- *Social maturity and adaptive behavior scales* are normally administered by the psychologist: AAMR Adaptive Behavior Scale-School-2 (ABS-S:2); AAMR Adaptive Behavior Scales-Residential and Community-2 (ABS-RC-2); Developmental Assessment for the Severely Handicapped (DASH); Light's Retention Scale (LRS); Adaptive Behavior Evaluation Scale-Revised (ABES-R); Vineland Adaptive Behavior Scale (VABS).

Perceptual Evaluation

A perceptual evaluation is suggested when the team suspects discrepancies in the child's ability to receive and process information. This assessment may focus on a number of perceptual areas, including:

- *Auditory modality:* delivery of information through sound
- *Visual modality:* delivery of information through sight
- *Tactile modality:* delivery of information through touching
- *Kinesthetic modality:* delivery of information through movement
- *Reception:* initial receiving of information
- *Perception:* initial organization of information
- *Association or organization:* relating new information to other information and giving meaning to the information received
- *Memory:* storage or retrieval process, which facilitates the associational process to give meaning to information or help in relating new concepts to other information that might have already been learned
- *Expression:* output of information through vocal, motoric, or written responses

The objectives of the perceptual assessment are as follows:

- To help determine the child's stronger and weaker modalities for learning. Some children are visual learners, some are auditory, and some learn well through any form of input. However, if a child is a strong visual learner in a class where the teacher relies on an auditory form, such as lectures, then his or her ability to process information may be hampered. This information is very useful when making practical recommendations to teachers about how best to provide information to assist the child's ability to learn.
- To help determine a child's stronger and weaker process areas. A child having problems in memory and expression will quickly fall behind the rest of the class. The longer these processing difficulties continue, the greater the chance that secondary emotional problems (emotional problems resulting from continued frustration with the ability to learn) will develop.
- To develop a learning profile that can help the classroom teacher understand the best way to present information to the child and therefore increase his or her chance of success.
- Along with other information and test results, to help determine if the child's learning process deficits are suitable for a regular class or are severe enough for a more restrictive educational setting, such as a resource room, self-contained class, special school, and so on.

Tests used to measure this area include these:

- *Tests that specifically measure areas of visual perception* are normally administered by the special education teacher or psychologist: Developmental Test of Visual Motor Integration-Fourth Edition; Bender Visual Motor Gestalt Test

(BVMGT); Marianne Frostig Developmental Test of Visual Perception (DTVP); Motor-Free Visual Perceptual Test-Revised (MVPT-R).

- *Tests that specifically measure areas of auditory perception* are normally administered by the special education teacher, psychologist, classroom teacher, or speech language therapist: Goldman-Fristoe-Woodcock Test of Auditory Discrimination (GFW); Lindamood Auditory Conceptualization Test (LACT); Tests of Auditory Perceptual Skills-Revised (TAPS-R); Wepman Test of Auditory Discrimination-2 (ADT-2).
- *Comprehensive measures of perceptual abilities* are normally administered by the special education teacher, psychologist, classroom teacher, speech language therapist, or occupational therapist: Bruininks-Oseretsky Test of Motor Proficiency; Detroit Tests of Learning Aptitudes-Third Edition (DTLA-4); Illinois Test of Psycholinguistic Abilities (ITPA); Slingerland Screening Tests for Identifying Children with Specific Language Disability; Test of Gross Motor Development (TGMD); Woodcock-Johnson Psycheducational Battery-Revised (WJ-R).

Occupational Therapy Evaluation

The team may consider this evaluation when the child is exhibiting problems involving fine motor or upper body functions, such as abnormal movement patterns, sensory problems (sensitive to sound, visual changes, and so on), hardship with daily living activities, organizational problems, attention span difficulties, equipment analysis, and interpersonal problems. Typical measures used to evaluate this area include these:

- Milani-Comparetti Motor Development Test
- Miller Assessment for Preschoolers (MAP)
- Quick Neurological Screening Test (QNST)
- Sensory Integration and Praxis Test (SIPT)
- Purdue Perceptual Motor Survey (PPM)

Nonstandardized Forms of Assessment

When a child is referred to the MDT, the team is required by law to do a comprehensive assessment. This involves standardized and nonstandardized forms of assessment. Nonstandardized forms of assessment include the following.

Ecological Assessment

Ecological assessment basically involves directly observing and assessing the child in the many environments in which he or she routinely operates. The purpose of conducting these observations is to probe how the different environments influence the student and his or her school performance. Where does the student manifest difficulties? Are there places where he or she appears to function appropriately? What is expected of the student academically and behaviorally in each type of environment? What differences exist in the environments where the student manifests the greatest and the least difficulty? What implications do these differences have for instructional planning?

Direct Assessment

Direct assessment of academic skills is one alternative that has recently gained popularity. Although a number of direct assessment models exist (Shapiro, 1989b), they are similar in that they all suggest that assessment needs to be directly tied to instructional curriculum.

Curriculum-based assessment (CBA) is one type of direct assessment. "Tests" of performance in this case come directly from the curriculum. For example, a child may be asked to read from his or her reading book for one minute. Information about the accuracy and the speed of reading can then be obtained and compared with other students in the class, building, or district. CBA is quick and offers specific information about how a student may differ from peers.

Because the assessment is tied to curriculum content, it allows the teacher to make curriculum adaptations or modifications. Unlike many other types of educational assessment, such as intelligence tests, CBA provides information that is immediately relevant to instructional programming (Berdine and Meyer, 1987). CBA also offers information about the accuracy and efficiency (speed) of performance. The latter is often overlooked when assessing a child's performance but is an important piece of information when designing intervention strategies. CBA is also useful in evaluating short-term academic progress.

Dynamic Assessment

Dynamic assessment refers to several different but similar approaches to evaluating student learning. The goal of this type of assessment "is to explore the nature of learning, with the objective of collecting information to bring about cognitive change and to enhance instruction" (Sewell, 1987, p. 436).

One of the chief characteristics of dynamic assessment is a dialogue or interaction between the examiner and the student. Depending on the specific dynamic assessment approach used, this interaction may include modeling the task for the student, giving the student prompts or cues as he or she tries to solve a given problem, asking what the student is thinking about while working on the problem, sharing on the part of the examiner to establish the task's relevance to experience and concepts beyond the test situation, and giving praise or encouragement (Hoy and Gregg, 1994). The interaction allows the examiner to draw conclusions about the student's thinking processes (for example, why he or she answers a question in a particular way) and his or her response to a learning situation (that is, whether with prompting, feedback, or modeling, the child can produce a correct response, and what specific means of instruction produce and maintain positive change in the child's cognitive functioning).

Usually, dynamic assessment involves a test-train-retest approach. The examiner begins by testing the student's ability to perform a task or solve a problem without help. Then a similar task or problem is given to the student, and the examiner models how the task or problem is solved or gives the student cues to assist his or her performance. In Feuerstein's (1979) model of dynamic assessment, the examiner is encouraged to interact constantly with the student—an interaction that is called *mediation*—which is felt to maximize the probability that the student will solve the problem. Other approaches to dynamic assessment use what is called *graduated prompting* (Campione and Brown, 1987), in which "a series of behavioral hints are used to teach the rules needed for task completion" (Hoy and Gregg, 1994, p. 151). These hints do not evolve from the student's responses, as in Feuerstein's model, but rather are scripted and preset, a standardization that allows for comparison across students. The prompts are given only if the student needs help in solving the problem. In both these approaches, the "teaching" phase is followed by a retesting of the student with a similar task but with no assistance from the examiner. The results indicate the student's "gains" or responsiveness to instruction—whether he or she learned and could apply the earlier instructions of the examiner and the prior experience of solving the problem.

Portfolio Assessment

Perhaps the most important type of assessment for the classroom teacher is the portfolio assessment. According to Paulson, Paulson, and Meyer (1991, p. 60), a portfolio is "a purposeful collection of student works that exhibits the student's efforts, progress, and achievement in one or more areas. The collection must include student participation in selecting contents, the criteria for selection, the criteria for judging merit, and evidence of student self-reflection." A portfolio collection contains work samples, permanent products, and test results from a variety of instruments and measures. For example, a portfolio of reading might include a student's test scores on teacher-made tests, including curriculum-based assessments, work samples from daily work and homework assignments, error analyses on work and test samples, and the results of an informal reading inventory with miscues noted and analyzed (Overton, 2000).

Authentic Assessment

Another technique that teachers can use to assess classroom performance is authentic assessment. This is a performance-based technique that involves the application of knowledge to real-life activities, real-world settings, or a simulation of such a setting using real-life, real-world activities (Taylor, 1997). For example, when students are assessed in artistic ability, they present artwork and are evaluated according to various criteria set up by the teacher; it is not simply the person's knowledge of art, the materials, artists, or the history of art that is measured as would be the case on an achievement test.

Outcome-Based Assessment

Outcome-based assessment has been developed, at least in part, in response to concerns that, to be meaningful, education must be directly related to what educators and parents want the child to gain in the end. Outcome-based assessment involves considering, teaching, and evaluating the skills that are important in real-life situations. Learning such skills will result in the student becoming an effectively functioning adult. From this point of view, assessment starts by identifying what outcomes are desired for the student (for example, being able to use public transportation). In steps similar to those in task analysis (see next section), the team then determines what competencies are necessary for those outcomes to take place (that is, the steps or subskills the student needs to master in order to achieve the outcome desired) and identifies which ones the student has mastered and which he or she still needs to learn. The needed instruction can then be pinpointed and undertaken.

Task Analysis

Task analysis is very detailed; it involves breaking down a particular task into the basic sequential steps, component parts, or skills necessary to accomplish it. The degree to which a task is broken down into steps depends on the student in question. "It is only necessary to break the task down finely enough so that the student can succeed at each step" (Wallace, Larsen, and Elksnin, 1992, p. 14).

This assessment approach has several advantages for the teacher. For one, the process identifies what is necessary for accomplishing a particular task. It also tells the teacher whether or not the student can do the task, which part or skill causes him to falter, and the order in which skills must be taught to help him learn to perform the task. According to Bigge (1990), task analysis can be used to guide decisions made about

- What to teach next
- Where students encounter problems when they attempt but are unable to complete a task
- The steps necessary to complete an entire task
- What adaptations can be made to help the students accomplish a task
- Options for those students for whom learning a task is not a possible goal

Learning Styles Assessment

Learning styles theory suggests that students learn and problem-solve in different ways and that some ways are more natural for them than others. When they are taught or asked to perform in ways that deviate from their natural style, they are thought to learn or to perform less well. A learning style assessment, then, would attempt to determine those elements that affect a child's learning and "ought to be an integral part of the individualized prescriptive process all special education teachers use for instructing pupils" (Berdine and Meyer, 1987, p. 27).

Some of the common elements included here are the way in which material is usually presented (visual, auditory, tactile) in the classroom, the environmental conditions of the classroom (hot, cold, noisy, light, dark), the child's personality characteristics, expectations for success held by the child and others, the response the child receives while engaging in the learning process (for example, praise or criticism), and the type of thinking the child generally employs in solving problems (for example, trial and error, analysis). Identifying the factors that positively affect the child's learning may be very valuable in developing effective intervention strategies.

Other Areas of Assessment

Sometimes the MDT requires other professionals to evaluate a child. Although these evaluations are used less frequently, they still play an important role in the assessment process. Examples of instruments used in these categories follow:

- *Early childhood assessment measures:* The Battelle Developmental Inventory (BDI); Bayley Scales of Infant Development-Second Edition (BSID-II); Boehm Test of Basic Concepts-Preschool Version; Bracken Basic Concept Scale (BBCS); Child Behavior Checklist (CBCL); Degangi-Berk Test of Sensory Integration (TSI); Denver Developmental Screening Test-Revised (Denver II); Developmental Profile II (DP-II); Kindergarten Readiness Test (KRT); Metropolitan Readiness Tests-Sixth Edition (MRT-6); Preschool Language Scale-3 (PLS-3); the Preschool Evaluation Scales (PES).

- *Hearing impaired assessment measures:* Auditory Perception Test for the Hearing Impaired (APT/HI); Carolina Picture Vocabulary Test for Deaf and Hearing Impaired (CPVT); Hiskey-Nebraska Test of Learning Aptitude; Leiter-R International Performance Scale; Rhode Island Test of Language Structure (RITLS); Screening Instrument for Targeting Educational Risk (SIFTER); Test of Early Reading Ability-2-Deaf or Hard of Hearing (TERA-2-D/HH).
- *Bilingual assessment measures:* ESL Literacy Scale (ESL); Language Proficiency Test (LPT); Matrix Analogies Test—Expanded Form (MAT-Expanded Form); Test of Spanish Grammar; System of Multicultural Pluralistic Assessment (SOMPA).

Understanding a Child's Behavior During Assessment

As we have seen, critical observation takes place during the assessment period. When the special education teacher administers these tests, it gives him or her a firsthand opportunity to view the child under these conditions. The way a child approaches different types of evaluations may be very similar to his or her style in the classroom. Therefore, many behaviors should be observed when administering tests. If you record these observations, it will greatly facilitate your report writing (see the next major section for more on this).

Adjustment to the Testing Situation

Some behaviors to observe during assessment include what the child's initial reaction was, how the child reacted to the examiner, and if there were any initial signs of overt tension.

Several factors need to be considered when the child first encounters the testing situation.

- Children's initial adjustment to the testing situation can vary greatly. Children are usually initially nervous but relax as time goes on with the reassurance of the examiner. However, children who maintain a high level of discomfort throughout the sessions may be having more serious problems that need to be explored.
- Examiner variables—that is, examiner style, gender, tension, expectations, and so on—may need to be considered, especially if test results vary greatly from examiner to examiner.
- Overt signs of tension—that is, observable behaviors indicative of underlying tension—may affect the test results. Some overt signs of behavior often manifested by children include constant leg motion, little or no eye contact with the examiner, consistent finger or pencil tapping, oppositional behaviors (behaviors that test the limits and guidelines of the examiner), singing or making noises while being tested, keeping a jacket on or almost covering the face with a hat, and so on. If this type of tension is extreme, the results of the test may be minimal indications of actual ability.

Reaction Time

Were responses delayed, blocked, irregular? Was there any indication of negativism? Were responses impulsive or well thought out?

The speed with which a child answers questions on a test can indicate several things.

- The child who impulsively answers incorrectly, without thinking, may have high levels of anxiety that interfere with his ability to delay and concentrate.
- The child who is negative or self-defeating—making such comments as "I'm so stupid, I'll never get any of these right"—may be exhibiting very low self-confidence or hiding a learning problem.
- The child who blocks or delays may be afraid of reaction or criticism and uses these techniques to ward off what she perceives as an ego-deflating situation.

Nature of Responses

Are some responses nonsensical, immature, childlike? Are they inconsistent? Does the child ask to have responses repeated? Is the child critical of his or her responses?

The types of response a child gives during an evaluation may indicate the following:

- A child who continuously asks to have questions repeated may have hearing difficulties. As noted several times earlier, this should always be ruled out first, along with vision problems, prior to testing.
- The child who asks to have questions repeated may be having problems processing information and may need more time to understand questions.

Verbalizations

Is the child verbose? Is the child spontaneous in responding? Does he or she have peculiarities of speech?

The verbal interaction with the examiner during an evaluation can be very telling.

- Some children with high levels of anxiety may vent through constant verbalizations. When these verbalizations begin to interfere and the child has to be constantly reminded to focus on the task at hand, it may indicate high levels of anxiety.
- Verbal hesitations may be due to immature speech patterns, expressive language problems, poor self-esteem, or lack of understanding of the question because of limited intellectual capacity.

Organizational Approach Used During Testing

Does the child plan and work systematically? Does the child make false starts? Does he or she use trial and error?

The manner in which a child handles individual tasks and organizes his or her approach may indicate several things.

- A child who sizes up a situation and systematically approaches a task using trial and error may have excellent internal organization, the ability to delay, and low levels of tension and anxiety. However, some children with emotional problems may also perform well on short-term tasks because they see them as a challenge and can organize themselves to perform over a relatively short period of time. Their particular problems in organization and consistency may come when they are asked to perform over an extended period.

- Children with chaotic internal organization may seem to know what they are doing, but the overall outcome of a task indicates a great deal of energy input with very low production. It is almost like "spinning wheels"; the energy output is a cover for not knowing what to do.
- Some children may become less organized under the stress of a time constraint. The factor of style under time restrictions is one aspect in determining the child's overall learning style.
- Children with ADHD may also exhibit a confused sense of organization. However, other factors as well as problems in attention go into the diagnosis of this disorder. (See Part Five for a discussion of common disabilities, including ADHD.)

Adaptability During Testing

Does the child shift from one test to the next? Is interest sustained in all types of test items?

The ability of a child (or adult, for that matter) to adapt or shift from one task to another without difficulty is a very important factor in determining learning style and may be one predictor for successful outcome of a task.

- Adaptability in life is crucial to adjustment. When a person can shift from task to task without spending a great deal of energy, the person has more available resources for the next task. A child who is rigid or does not adapt well is using up much of his or her available energy, thus reducing the chances of success on the subsequent task.
- Sustaining interest may also be a direct result of available energy. A child who loses interest quickly may be immature, overwhelmed, or preoccupied. Some of these reactions may be normal at the early ages. However, as the child gets older such reactions may be symptomatic of other factors, such as learning problems, emotional issues, or limited intellectual capacity.

Effort During Testing

Is the child cooperative? Does he or she give evidence of trying hard? Does the child become frustrated easily?

The effort that a child puts into a testing situation may be similar to the effort exhibited in the classroom and may indicate the following.

- A child who is oppositional or uncooperative may need to control. Always keep in mind that the more controlling children are, the more out of control they likely feel. Control on the part of children is aimed at securing predictability so that they can deal with a situation even though their energy levels may be lowered by conflict and tension. If they can control a situation or person, they know what to expect. Because of their level of tension, they do not adapt well and are easily thrown by new situations or people.

- A child who tries hard to succeed may do so for several reasons. He or she may enjoy success and find the tasks normally challenging. This type of child is usually not thrown by a mistake and can move to the next task without difficulty.

In conclusion, always keep in mind that *all behavior sends a message.* The way a child interacts with the examiner offers clues to learning style or problem areas. If you can "hear" a child's behavior by being aware of significant signs, you may come to a better understanding of the child's needs.

Once the members of the MDT complete their evaluations, they must diagnose strengths and weaknesses and determine if the discrepancy is significant enough to substantiate the suspected disability.

The Educational Report

As we have seen, many different professionals provide input in the assessment of a child with a suspected disability. A comprehensive report based on the findings must then be written. This report may be called the psychoeducational or the academic report. It may be presented to the parents, sent to an outside doctor or agency, or presented to the eligibility committee. Its purpose is to communicate results in such a way that readers will understand the rationale behind the recommendations and be able to use the recommendations as practical guidelines for intervention. The report needs to be as professional, comprehensive, and as practical as possible.

Report writing is a real skill. No matter how wonderful the data collection, it is useless if it is not interpreted and explained in a clear and concise manner. For example, being too general or poorly explaining results creates many problems and confusion for readers. If numerous general recommendations are made, it will not be helpful for the school, teacher, or parents. A report that contains loads of jargon that few readers will understand is also useless. Similarly, an extremely lengthy report that attempts to be too comprehensive will only lose the reader.

Guidelines for Report Writing

Here are some practical guidelines. As you review each section here you may wish to refer to Appendix A at the back of this book. Appendix A provides examples of two reports, one for an elementary school student and one for a secondary school student.

Write in the Third Person

Use phrases such as "According to the examiner . . . . " "It was felt that . . . . " "There seems to be . . . . " "It is the professional opinion of this evaluator that . . . . "

Never write "I think" or "If it were up to me." This is not a term paper; it is a legal document. The professional approach is to remain in the third person.

Single-Space to Reduce Length

A report of three to five pages is not overwhelming. You will learn several tips later in this chapter for breaking up the report so that the format is easy on the reader.

Separate the Recommendation Section into Three Parts

One part is for the school, one for the teacher, and one for the parents. This approach will make it easy to follow the recommendations and allow the interested parties to see their responsibilities.

Write the Report in the Past Tense When Possible

Since the data was already collected and you have already done the assessment, using the past tense is most appropriate. For example:

> On the reading subtest, Billy scored in the ninety-fifth percentile.
>
> During testing, Sally exhibited shyness.
>
> Throughout the interview, Tommy showed no signs of hyperactivity.
>
> Karen appeared to lack confidence when doing tasks that required hand-eye coordination.

Separate Sections

For example, separate "Reason for Referral" and "Background History" by skipping two lines. This is done simply for purposes of clarity.

Underline Paragraph Headings So They Are Easy to Locate

Any time you create a new section in your report, underline it so that readers know this starts a different area of the report.

Use Complete Sentences

A report should never read like a telegram. Be sure that all sentences are complete and clear. Check spelling and grammar to make sure there are no errors. Nothing looks more unprofessional than a sloppy report that contains many mistakes.

Outline of the Report

Educational reports can take many forms and it is usually up to the personal choice of the examiner. However, it is important that certain information not be overlooked. These reports usually contain the following sections:

- Identifying data
- Reason for referral
- Background history
- Behavioral observations
- Tests administered
- Test results (test-by-test analysis, content-area-by-content-area analysis)
- Conclusions
- Recommendations

Identifying Data

The first section, "Identifying Data," contains all the necessary basic information about the child:

Name:	**Parents' names:**
Address:	**Teacher:**
Phone:	**Referred by:**
Date of birth:	**Dates of testing:**
Grade:	**Date of report:**
School:	**Examiner:**

Chronological age (CA) at time of testing:

Although most of this information can usually be found in the school records, having it all in one place saves a great deal of time. Make sure that the dates of testing and the date of the report are always included for comparison. Some evaluations are finished several months before the report is typed, and the scores can be misleading if the reader assumes they represent the child's present levels on the date of the report when in fact they may reflect ability levels in prior months. It is always more acceptable when the two dates are within a month of each other.

Reason for Referral

The second section, "Reason for Referral," explains the specific reasons why an evaluation has taken place. This section should not be more than two to three sentences, but should be comprehensive enough to clarify the purpose. Following are some examples of information to include in this section:

John was referred by his teacher for evaluation as a result of inconsistent academic performance and poor social skills.

Mary was referred by her parents for evaluation in order to determine if a learning disability was interfering in her ability to learn.

Benjamin was being tested as part of the triennial evaluation.

This section should not contain a great deal of parent or teacher information. That goes into another section that offers a more detailed explanation of the child.

Background History

The third section, "Background History," contains a thorough description of the child's family history, developmental history, academic history, and social history. (See the earlier section on the parent intake for details on these histories.)

Behavioral Observations

The fourth section, "Behavioral Observations," includes a description of the child's behavior during the testing sessions. (See the earlier section, beginning on page 60, on what to look for in behavior during testing for more information on what to include here.) This is a very important section because it may reinforce what is seen in the class or be very different, in which case the structure of the testing environment should be explored for clues to learning style.

Tests Administered

The fifth section, "Tests Administered," provides a simple list of the individual tests included in the test battery and any procedures used to enhance the report, such as classroom observation, review of records, parent intake.

Test Results

The sixth section, "Test Results," is crucial because it analyzes the results of each test and looks at the child's individual performance on each measure. There are several approaches to this section, but the two most widely used are the test-by-test analysis and the content-area-by-content-area analysis. The approach chosen is a personal choice and preference of the diagnostician.

A test-by-test approach analyzes the child's performance on each test separately. It analyzes the results of the different subtests and provides indications of strengths and weaknesses, manner of approach, and indications of whether the scores on the specific test should be considered valid.

A content-area-by-content-area approach takes all the reading subtests, math subtests, spelling subtests, and writing subtests from each evaluation measure and analyzes the results separately by content area.

Conclusions

The next section is probably the essence of the report. In the "Conclusions" section the diagnostician indicates in very simple terms the trends in the child's testing results that may indicate academic strengths and weaknesses, modality strengths and weaknesses, process strengths and weaknesses, and overall diagnosis and level of severity of the problem areas indicated.

Recommendations

The last section of the report is probably the most valuable for readers. Ideally, the "Recommendations" section makes practical recommendations that will bring some hope and direction for the identified problem areas. As noted earlier, it may be broken up as follows:

- *Recommendations to the school:* This section might contain suggestions for further testing from other professionals on staff, vision or hearing tests by the school nurse, a review by the eligibility committee, remedial reading assistance, or an ESL evaluation.
- *Recommendations to the teacher:* This section should contain useful information for the teacher, including an indication of the conditions under which the child learns best. The teacher is probably mainly interested in "What do I do?" to help the child learn. Keep in mind that even before the evaluation process is begun, the teacher should have been asked what he or she has already tried in an attempt to alleviate the problems. In this way, the recommendations in this

report will not include suggestions already attempted by the teacher and will not be viewed as "nothing I haven't already tried before."

- *Recommendations to the parents:* This part should be very practical, direct, and also diplomatic. The suggestions should be inclusive enough to explain "why" and "how" so that parents do not have to interpret them.

Finally, it is helpful to number each recommendation separately for purposes of clarity.

Second Child Study Team Meeting: Development of the Eligibility Presentation Packet

Once the MDT has considered all the information and completed its evaluations, the team will meet with the CST to report back and review the findings. The CST may feel that a referral to the eligibility committee is warranted for several reasons:

- An initial review on a new student who may have a suspected disability
- An annual review meeting where a child's present disability and placement are reviewed
- A triennial evaluation
- A request for a special eligibility committee meeting to change an existing IEP

When the CST makes the referral to the eligibility committee, one individual will be designated as case manager. The case manager is usually the psychologist, the special education teacher, or an administrator. The case manager's job is to develop the presentation packet for the eligibility committee.

This information packet will be viewed by the members of the eligibility committee, the parents, and other individuals so designated, such as advocate or lawyer. This packet is a crucial part of the special education process because most of the eligibility committee members will not be familiar with the child. The information gathered and forwarded will be used to determine the child's educational future. Therefore, it is imperative that it contain the most thorough and practical information.

All districts have their own specific forms and guidelines for presentation to the committee. However, in most cases the information presented is similar. The rest of this chapter details a typical list of materials included in the eligibility packet.

What You Need to Know If Asked to Be the Case Manager for a Presentation at the Eligibility Committee (EC)

Prior to an eligibility committee meeting, someone at the school, usually on the CST, will be asked to develop what is called the eligibility committee presentation packet. The chances, again, are that either the special education teacher on the team or the school psychologist will be asked to perform this task. This person will be designated as the case manager for that particular case. The presentation packet contains all materials that will be sent to the eligibility committee chairperson and eventually presented at the eligibility committee meeting. If you are the case manager, you will be required to gather materials for the eligibility committee for several reasons:

1. An initial review on a new student who may have a suspected disability
2. An annual review meeting in which the child's present disability and placement are reviewed
3. A triennial evaluation
4. A request for a special eligibility committee meeting, that is, a change in an existing IEP

While state requirements may differ, a complete and well-organized packet should be sufficient for any situation. In order to accomplish this task, the case manager's responsibility is to ensure that all required materials are placed in the packet. In order to survive this task if you are chosen, become familiar with the following requirements. Remember that each district will have its own requirements for this packet, but many of these materials would most likely be part of most district packets. A well-organized presentation packet could include the following information.

Eligibility Committee Packet Checklist

The case manager will want to be sure that you have included everything necessary. Therefore, use this checklist to ensure that you have included all the necessary materials for the presentation packet. An example of this form follows.

ELIGIBILITY COMMITTEE PACKET CHECKLIST

Name of student ______________________ School ____________________ Grade ____

Type of meeting:

Initial ______________ Special ______________ Annual review ______________

Required Forms

Initial meeting:

_____ Presentation packet information form
_____ Initial referral to MDT from school staff or
_____ Initial referral to MDT from parent/guardian
_____ Parent consent for evaluation

Special meeting:

Name of current/contact teacher ____________
____

_____ Special meeting referral form
_____ Current teacher's report
_____ Recommended goals and objectives
_____ New evaluations if completed

Other documents, specify:

Evaluation:

_____ Social history
_____ Medical report
_____ Classroom observation
_____ Psychological
_____ Educational
_____ Speech/language
_____ Vocational (secondary level only)
_____ Other (for example, occupational therapist, physical therapist)

Goals/objectives, specify: _______________

Annual review:

_____ Prep sheet
_____ Current IEP
_____ Evaluations completed, specify:
_____ Other documents, specify:

Guidance materials:

_____ Child's schedule
_____ Transcript of past grades
_____ Latest report card
_____ Teachers' reports

Recommended eligibility committee participants:

Triennial evaluation documents:

_____ Copy of the parent notice of triennial evaluation form
_____ Psychological
_____ Educational
_____ Speech/language

Other:

_____ Discipline information
_____ CST-related documents (minutes)
_____ SAT scores
_____ Report cards
_____ Needs (Levels of development: social, physical, academic, management)
_____ Recommended goals and objectives (draft)
_____ Attendance records
_____ Other, specify:

Case manager: Date:

Required Forms

Several forms may be required in the packet. These forms are used for initial reviews, special meetings, and triennial evaluations.

Presentation Packet Initial Information Form

This form provides the eligibility committee with all the necessary identifying data on a child with a potential disability. It can also serve as a worksheet for the chairperson during the meeting. The following is an example of such a form.

PRESENTATION PACKET INITIAL INFORMATION FORM

Goals submitted and attached to packet: _______ Yes ______ No Student ID no.: ____________

Goals changed (re-review): _______ Yes ______ No Student date of birth: _______

Eligibility Committee Date: ______________________________ (For eligibility committee use only)

Committee: ____

____

Also present (For eligibility committee use only) ________________________________

____

Case presented by ____

Student name ____

Parents' names ____

Parents' status: Married ________ Single _______ Divorced ______ Widowed _______

Address ____

____

All correspondence and information should be sent to:

Mother _____ Father _____ Both _____ Legal guardian _____

Current school ____

Current teacher (Elementary level only)____

Current grade __________

Current contact teacher if previously classified (Middle school-high school only) __________________

Guidance counselor ____

Dominant language, student ____

Dominant language, home ____

Ethnicity ____

Reason for the meeting:

(Check one) Initial review _____ Review of present classification _____ Declassification _____

Review of placement _____ Pendency _____ Annual review _____ Triennial review _____

Date entered program (For review cases only) ______________________________

Diploma type ______________________________

Other ______________________________

Evaluation information (Test names and score type: G.E., %)

IQ test information

Test ________________ VIQ ____________ % Rank __________ PIQ ____________ % Rank ____________ FSIQ ____________ % Rank ________

Psychoeducational Test Information

Area measured (for example, reading)

Test name ________________ Percentile ________________ Test date ____________

Test name ________________ Percentile ________________ Test date ____________

Test name ________________ Percentile ________________ Test date ____________

Examiner:

Psychological ____________ Educational ____________ Speech/language ____________

Student Name ______________________ Eligibility Committee Date ____________

Student ID ______________ Student DOB ____________ School ______________

A Copy of the Initial Referral to the Multidisciplinary Team (MDT) from School Staff

As previously mentioned, this form is used to alert the eligibility committee that a case of a child with a suspected disability may be coming up for a review depending on the outcome of evaluations. This occurs when the school suspects a possible disability. This form is forwarded with or without signed parent consent for evaluation. If it is sent without the signed evaluation, the eligibility committee chairperson will send one to the parent, requesting it be signed and returned. Again, local policy may differ and many schools try to have the parent sign this consent when they meet with parents to discuss the initial reasons for the referral.

Initial Referral to the Multidisciplinary Team from the Parent or Guardian

This form is the one used if a parent, rather than the CST, makes a referral to the MDT for a formal evaluation. If this is the case, then include this specific form, which may look like the following.

INITIAL REFERRAL TO THE MULTIDISCIPLINARY TEAM FROM PARENT OR GUARDIAN

Date: ____________________

To: ____

Principal or Eligibility Committee Chairperson

I am writing to refer my child ______________________, age __________, to the eligibility committee. I am asking you to conduct an individual evaluation to determine whether a handicapping condition exists that would make my child eligible for Special Education Services. I am concerned about my child's educational difficulties in the following areas:

Please contact me as soon as possible to discuss my referral.

Sincerely,

Parent/guardian ___________________________ Phone ______________

Address ____

State ____________ Zip__________

Child's birth date _______________ School ____________________________ Grade ____________

Date received by eligibility committee ____________________

Parent Consent for Evaluation

A signed and dated copy of this release by a parent or guardian, obtained by the CST or by the chairperson of special education when the parents are initially informed about a referral for a formal evaluation, should be included in the eligibility packet. Even though you will not make up this form—because it is likely to be a district form—as special education teacher you should be familiar with its contents. You may be the one to attempt to secure the signature of the parent to perform the formal evaluation. Such a form may look as follows.

PARENT CONSENT FOR EVALUATION

To the parent/guardian of: _________________ Birth date __________

School _________________________________ Grade _____________

We would like to inform you that your child ____________________ has been referred for individual testing because of the suspicion of a disability. Testing results will help us in determining your child's educational needs and in planning the most appropriate program. The evaluation procedures and/or tests may include the following:

Intelligence
Communication/language/speech
Physical
Behavior/emotional
Academic
Vocational
Other

Before we can begin testing, it is necessary that the school's multidisciplinary team have your written permission to evaluate your child. You have had the opportunity to discuss the need for this testing and the possibilities for special educational services with the school principal/designee. The multidisciplinary team that will share the results of said evaluation with you at a building-level meeting will conduct the evaluation(s). Both this meeting and an eligibility committee meeting will be held within thirty school days of receipt of this notice.

I grant permission for the evaluation(s) mentioned above ______

I do not grant permission for the evaluation(s) mentioned above ______

Date ____________ Parent's signature______________________________

Date ____________ Administrator/designee___________________________

Evaluations

Evaluations will be discussed in the packet as follows.

Psychological Evaluation

A full psychological evaluation, including all identifying data, reason for referral, background and developmental history, prior testing results, observations, tests administered, test results (including a breakdown of scaled scores), conclusions, and recommendations, is required. This evaluation must be conducted within one year of the eligibility committee meeting. It may also be helpful to include any prior evaluations done over the years. This report may be obtained from the individual or agency that completed the testing—that is, the school psychologist, outside agency, or outside professional. Keep in mind that this evaluation should be within a year. If you are the person completing this packet, then be sure to check with your district to see the time requirements for a recent evaluation; they may vary from state to state.

Educational Evaluation

The educational evaluation is the report of the special education teacher or the special education diagnostician who completed the evaluation. (See the earlier section on assessment for more details on this report.)

Speech and Language Evaluation

If the child is being referred for suspected speech or language impairment, then this report should be obtained from the speech pathologist who performed this evaluation. The report should contain a description of the type and severity of the impairment, and if possible, the prognosis.

Vocational Evaluation Aptitude Test Results

If the child is in high school, then it is a good idea to include a copy of the Differential Aptitude Test results or other measures of vocational aptitude if applicable. The child's guidance counselor will know if such a test has been administered.

Other (Occupational Therapist, Physical Therapist, ESL, Reading)

From time to time, parents or the school will have a variety of reports from outside agencies: medical, neurological, psychiatric, occupational therapy screening, physical therapy screening, psychological, audiological, visual training, and so on. These reports should be included only when they are relevant to the possible disability. If outside reports are to be used instead of the district's own evaluations, they should be fairly recent (done within the past six months to a year).

Nonstandardized Assessment Results

If nonstandardized assessment results were used in the overall evaluation—as they should be—then these write-ups should be included in the packet. Such assessments include portfolio assessments and curriculum-based assessments.

Academic Data

Academic data to include are as follows.

SAT Data from All Grades

This information should reflect standardized test score results including percentiles as far back as possible. This allows committee members to see patterns, strengths, and weaknesses in the child's scores. This can be found in the child's permanent folder. Make copies of these scores and include them in the packet.

Report Card Grades from All Grades

Copies of all report cards, including teacher comments, should be included for grades K–6. Beginning with grade seven, copies should reflect quarter grades, final grades, absences, and so on.

Present Classroom Teachers' Reports

This report should include a behavioral description of the child's academic, social, intellectual, behavioral, and physical status from the child's present teachers. Observations should be worded in behavioral terms, and any informal testing results should be included.

On the secondary level, it is important to have copies of checklists, reports, summaries, and so on from every one of the child's teachers. Every secondary school uses a different system to gain information on a child from the large number of teachers involved.

Past Classroom Teachers' Reports

The packet should include written reports, comments, anecdotal records, and so on from past teachers. These reports will be invaluable in determining patterns of strengths and weaknesses in a child's academic profile. As many of these as possible should be gathered by searching through records or interviews.

Attendance and Disciplinary Reports

A listing of all disciplinary reports from elementary through secondary level, with reason for referral and disposition, should be included. An accurate attendance record should also be included.

Student Class Schedule

A copy of the child's present class schedule that clearly outlines the level of classes enrolled (modified, regents, and so on) should be included, with teachers' names.

Classroom Observation Report

This form must be included in the eligibility committee packet for an initial referral. Examples of this type of form can be found in Chapter Six.

Developmental Data

Developmental data must be included as well.

Social and Developmental History Form

The information gained during the parent intake provides the information for this form. It is important that it include answers to all the information requested so that the committee members have a thorough understanding of the child's history. (See the example of a completed form in Chapter Six.)

Eligibility Committee Medical Report Form from Nurse

This district form was filled out by the nurse and should be included in the eligibility committee packet. It should contain the entire child's pertinent medical history and should include results from a medical examination within the past year. The nurse will be very familiar with this form.

Other Required Information and Procedures

Other information is as follows.

Statement of Least Restrictive Educational Environment

If the CST is recommending additional services under a classifying condition, the case manager, along with other members of the CST, will have to state the reasons why additional services or a less restrictive environment would be necessary. This statement is also very important if the CST feels that the child's needs may be better served in an out-of-district placement. Although the final decision for placement will be made by the eligibility committee, the school still needs to substantiate its recommendation.

Parents Given State Rights Booklet Prior to Eligibility Committee Meeting

As noted earlier, it is very important to give parents a copy of the state booklet on parental rights prior to the eligibility committee meeting. This gives them the opportunity to become familiar with the procedure and allows them time to develop any questions that they might have. This booklet can be obtained from the district office or from the state education department. As a special educator, you should keep several of these on hand.

Agreement to Withdraw Eligibility Committee Referral (Optional)

Sometimes the parents and the school will agree that the evaluation and findings do not seem to substantiate the suspected disability. When this occurs, members of the CST and the parents must meet to discuss other methods to remediate the student's problems. At the time of the meeting an "Agreement to Withdraw the Eligibility Committee Referral" form must be filled out and forwarded to the principal, and then to the eligibility committee chairperson. This will officially withdraw the original referral and stop the eligibility committee process.

There are usually time requirements and constraints after which this option is not acceptable; district and state policies should be checked. As the special educator, you may be the one to fill out this form. An example follows.

AGREEMENT TO WITHDRAW ELIGIBILITY COMMITTEE REFERRAL

Initial Conference

Student name ____________________

Date of birth ____________________

Date of agreement ____________________

Date of referral ____________________

Current program ____________________

Name of referring party ____________________

Position of referring party ____________________

Persons present at conference ____________________

The following method(s) will be used to attempt to resolve ________________ identified learning difficulties: (attach additional sheets, as needed)

If necessary, a follow-up conference to review the student's progress will be held on ____________

____.

We agree to the above conditions. The referral is hereby withdrawn.

Referring party signature ______________________________ Date ______________

Parent/guardian signature ______________________________ Date ______________

cc: Student's Cumulative Educational Record, Parent/Guardian, Referring Party

SPAMS (Social, Physical, Academic, Management Needs)

A list of these needs will provide the committee with an idea of the environmental, educational, social, and physical requirements under which the child may learn best.

Draft IEP, Including Goals and Objectives

In some states and some school districts, a working copy of the IEP is prepared before the eligibility committee meeting. This is a basic draft of the IEP, not the final draft, and is used as a working model during meeting discussions. In other districts, the IEP is developed only at the time of the eligibility committee meeting, with the parent present. The case manager is responsible for filling out this draft document. More about IEPs can be found in Chapter Ten.

Recommended Testing Modifications Worksheet

This worksheet outlines the suggested test and classroom modifications being suggested and the supporting data for such recommendations. The special education teacher will probably help fill this out with other members of the CST.

Extended School Year Worksheet

This worksheet provides the eligibility committee with the information and criteria necessary to make a recommendation for extended school services in July and August. At annual review meetings, parents of students with disabilities may ask for special education services during the summer (that is, the extended school year). This service may be recommended for the child at the formal meeting of the eligibility committee, and the input of the special education teacher may be requested. Be aware of the child's skills and ability to maintain a break from formal education without losing skills. If you feel that the child's issues will result in problems if he does not receive continuity of services over the summer, then make the recommendation at the time of the meeting.

In conclusion, the forms and information shown in this chapter will present a clear picture of the child with a suspected disability, including strengths, weaknesses, recommendations, and any other information that will assist the eligibility committee in making the most educationally sound decisions.

Eligibility Committee Meeting

Once the eligibility committee presentation packet is received by the chairperson of that committee, a date will be set up for the initial meeting. After the eligibility committee reviews the case, the committee will determine classification and proper service placement. The eligibility committee meeting and review and the role of the special educator in that process are described in the next part of this book.

PART THREE

THE SPECIAL EDUCATOR'S ROLE IN THE SPECIAL EDUCATION PROCESS

Chapter 8

Reporting Formal Assessment Results to Parents

Before the official eligibility committee meeting, it is very important to meet with the parents to go over the results of all the tests that have been carried out. This meeting will have several objectives:

- To share the results of testing, scores, and recommendations.
- To inform the parents of their due process rights and again provide them with a copy of those rights (this information is usually available from the district office).
- To inform the parents of the process that will be used during the eligibility committee meeting and notify them of the participants at that meeting.
- To answer any questions that the parents may have about the process. However, it is important not to discuss the classification or placement, because that will be up to the eligibility committee to decide.

Often parents leave a conference having been "bombarded" with jargon and statistics and understanding nothing. An important skill for special education teachers is the ability to report test results to other professionals and to parents in such a way that these people can understand the causes, specific areas of strength and weakness, and practical recommendations to alleviate the situation. In order to report results in an understandable way, it is helpful to do the following.

First, when you call parents to set up the appointment, never begin the explanation of the results over the phone, even if they insist on a "quick" idea of how the child performed. If they do request this, gently explain that the type of information you have is better explained and understood in person. If you sense anxiety, try to reassure them that you will meet as soon as possible. It is important to see the parents in front of you so that you can explain things they seem confused about or uncomfortable with. Face-to-face contact also provides a more human touch. It is like hearing results from a doctor over the phone—it may be more difficult than hearing results in person.

As with an intake, it is important to make the parents feel at ease by setting up a receptive environment. If possible, hold the meeting in a pleasant setting, use a round table (or any table instead of a desk), and offer some type of refreshment to ease possible tension in the situation.

It may be helpful to refresh the parents' memory about the reasons for the evaluation and the symptoms that brought the child to the team's attention. Explain the tests in your test battery, why they were used, and what specific types of information you hoped to arrive at by using these measures.

Go over strengths first, no matter how few these may be. You can also report positive classroom comments, and any other information that may help set the tone for acceptance of problem areas.

Provide a typed outline of the tests and scores for parents to take with them if the report is not ready. However, always try to have the report typed and ready to hand them. It looks more professional and may help alleviate problems that may occur when a report is sent home and read without a professional present.

Explain in simple terms any statistical terms you may use, such as percentiles, stanines, mental ages, and so on. In fact it may be a good idea to define these on the same sheet with the scores so the parents will have a key when they go back and review the scores. (For an explanation of many terms used in assessment, see Appendix D at the back of this book.)

Also as with the intake, offer a pad and pen so parents can write down information or terms or take notes on the meeting. Let them know they should feel free to call you with any questions or concerns they may have.

Put aside a sufficient amount of time for difficult conferences. This is not the type of situation where you want to run out of time. The parents should leave in a natural manner, not feeling rushed.

Take time to explain the differences between symptoms and problems. This explanation can go a long way in alleviating a parent's frustration.

It is helpful for parents to hear how the problems or deficiencies you found contributed to the symptomatic behavior in the classroom and at home. It is reassuring for parents to know that what they have been seeing are only symptoms, even though they may be quite intense, and that the problems have been identified and recommendations are available. Offer them as much realistic hope as possible.

Be as practical and specific as possible when offering suggestions on how parents can help at home. Give them printed sheets with step-by-step procedures for any recommendation that you make. Parents are not teachers (most aren't, anyway!) and should never be given general recommendations that require their interpretation. This may aggravate an already tense situation at home. Offer them supportive materials that they can use with their child. Although it can be a positive experience for a parent to work with a child, in some cases—such as when parental frustration levels are low—you may want to discourage this type of interaction.

If the case is going to be reviewed by the eligibility committee, take some time to alleviate the parents' fears by explaining the process and what they can expect. Indicate that your report is part of the packet that will be presented and that they are entitled to a copy of all materials. Some school districts may charge a fee for these copies; inform parents if this is the case.

Finally, reassure the parents about the confidentiality of the information gathered. Explain which individuals will be seeing the information and the purpose for their review of the facts. Also explain that in order to send out this information, you need parental permission in the form of a signed release.

Chapter 9

Participating in the Eligibility Committee

The responsibilities of the special education teacher on the eligibility committee depend on the committee's role in the district. Your responsibilities when making a presentation will vary, but proper preparation is crucial.

As Educational Evaluator

If you have been selected to sit on the committee based on your educational and perceptual evaluation of the child, then you need to keep the following in mind:

- Before the meeting, meet with the parents and go over your results. Follow the procedures outlined in Chapter Eight.
- Make sure you have your report complete and typed at least a week to ten days before the eligibility committee meeting. In some districts, the committee requires that the entire packet be forwarded a week in advance.
- Before the meeting, outline the important points that you wish to make. Do not go through the report while you are at the meeting, looking for the issues you want to discuss. Preparation will make you look more professional.
- Make sure you report strengths as well as weaknesses.
- Even though all the committee members should have a copy of your report in front of them, the length of the report may make it impossible for them to filter out the crucial sections in the time allotted for the meeting. Therefore, it is a good idea to develop a one-page summary sheet that clearly outlines what you will be presenting. You may hand this out as you begin your presentation.
- Remember that this is not a parent conference where you review the entire report. Several other individuals may need to report results or speak, and the eligibility committee may have several meetings that day. Keep your presentation brief and highlight the important issues.
- If you feel that the case may require more time than that normally set aside for a review, call the chairperson and make a request for a longer meeting time. It is very uncomfortable when crucial meetings have to be ended because of time constraints.
- Be prepared to be questioned about your findings or some aspect of the report by either a parent, a committee member, a lawyer (sometimes brought by the parent), or others. Even though this may not happen, you should be ready to answer without being defensive or anxious. It is best to look over your report carefully and be well prepared.

As Child's Classroom Teacher

Sometimes the child's classroom teacher is asked to attend an eligibility committee meeting either for a review of classification, placement, annual review, change in IEP, or a special meeting requested by the parent. If you are in this role, keep the following in mind.

The first thing you need to do when you receive a request to attend an eligibility committee meeting is to find out the reason for the meeting. The material required may vary, but your preparation prior to the meeting is crucial. If the parents called the meeting, you may want to have them in for a conference to discuss their concerns.

Once you know why the meeting will be held, organize yourself so that you will have information in front of you in the following areas:

- The child's present academic levels in reading, math, spelling, and writing. These may be available as a result of recent individual or group achievement tests, informal evaluations that you may have administered, observations, class tests, and so on. Determine grade levels if possible, and where the child falls compared with others in the class.
- The child's present pattern of classroom behavior. Write this up in behavioral terms (factual, observable, descriptive notes of behavior that do not include analysis or judgment).
- The child's present levels of social interaction and social skills.
- The child's interest areas and areas of strength.
- The child's present schedule.
- Samples of the child's work.
- Outline of parent conferences, phone conversations or meetings, and the purpose and outcome of each. These notes should be kept on an ongoing basis.
- Your opinion about whether the child is benefiting from his present placement.
- Any physical limitations noted and their implication for the learning process.
- Your opinion of the child's feelings of self-esteem.
- Any pertinent comments made by the child that may have an impact on his present situation.

You should be well prepared to answer any questions if you have this information at hand. When it is your turn to present, do it in an organized manner. Here too you may want to provide the participants with an outline of what you will be covering.

Try not to be defensive even if the reason for the meeting is the parents' concern over the child's placement in your class, the workload, and so on. Try to listen carefully to what the parent is really asking for. It may not be so big a problem as you think. Try to be solution-oriented, even if the parent is blame-oriented.

As Member of the Eligibility Committee

Sometimes as a special education teacher you are asked to sit on an eligibility committee to review a case even if you do not have the child in your class or know the child and have not evaluated him. Your participation in this situation is based on your expertise in reviewing the academic and perceptual material that will be presented. This material may come from other evaluators in the district or from an outside agency or professional. If you find yourself in this position, then keep the following in mind.

First, get a copy of the reports before the meeting. In some districts this is the standard procedure. If not, request the reports so you can review the findings and make notes.

Your role here is to review and analyze the test results and offer concrete and practical suggestions to the committee in the following ways:

- Explain what you see as indications of areas of strength and weakness.
- Explain what you believe to be the level of severity of the problem—mild, moderate, or severe.
- Explain the educational implications in determining least restrictive placement. (See Chapter Thirty for a discussion of least restrictive placement.)
- Explain whether the recommendations coincide with the test results. For example, in some cases outside agencies or professionals will recommend a resource room even though the child's scores do not reflect a disability.
- See whether the new findings support or disagree with past scores. Do some research into the child's historical academic patterns, reviewing any prior reports, achievement test scores, report card grades, and so on.
- Explain if you think the findings require modifications and which ones they should be—revised test format, flexible scheduling, and so on.

Finally, be prepared. Do not wait until the last minute. It will look more professional if you come with notes, questions, and suggestions.

Chapter 10

Individualized Education Programs (IEPs)

The Individualized Education Program (IEP) is a legally binding contract of services provided by a school district to a child classified as having a disability. Only children who are classified by the eligibility committee receive an IEP. Although certain information is required by each state to be included in this document, there is no specific form for school districts to follow. As a result, there are as many different-looking IEPs as there are school districts.

Nevertheless, all IEPs have seven basic sections:

- General identifying data
- Current placement data
- Recommendations by the eligibility committee
- Goals and objectives
- Mastery levels
- Evaluation measures
- Alternate testing modifications

This chapter deals with each section of the IEP individually, but all are tied together to form one plan.

General Identifying Data

In this section of the plan, the school district provides information on the child's background. The information comes from the background history form. This section is likely to include name, address, phone, date of birth, parents' names, dominant language of child, and dominant language spoken at home. The date the child entered the program is provided if the child has been previously classified. It basically informs the reader about when the child first started receiving special education services.

Current Placement Data

This section contains all necessary information on the child's current educational placement. This information is usually gleaned from evaluation reports, prior IEPs (if the child has already been classified), school records, and so on. Included in this section are the following: classification (if the child is presently classified), present grade, current placement (regular class if this is an initial review by the eligibility committee, present special education setting if child has already been classified), class size ratio (for previously classified students, length of program (ten or twelve months), present school, name of child's present teacher or guidance counselor if a secondary level student, and diploma (either a local diploma or an IEP diploma, which can be given to classified students who do not meet the school requirements for graduation but have accomplished all the objectives on their IEP). Information on transportation is provided if the child is presently receiving special transportation arrangements. Also provided is information on physical education (present class type, whether regular or adaptive), annual review date (usually April, May, or June of the school year), triennial review date (usually three years from the date of the last full evaluation), intelligence test results (must be within one year of review by eligibility committee and indicate verbal, performance, or full-scale IQ).

Recommendations by the Eligibility Committee

In this section, the eligibility committee meeting recommendations are recorded, indicating the proposed plan of placement and services until the next annual review or an eligibility committee meeting is called to reevaluate the IEP. This may be done if the school or parent requests a change or addition to the IEP. This document cannot usually be modified without a full meeting of the eligibility committee.

This is a very important section of the IEP because it describes the plan for special educational services for the coming year. This section is likely to contain the following information:

Classification: The child must fit the criteria for one of the state-defined classification categories, and the disability must significantly impede his or her ability to learn.

Grade: Projected grade for the coming year.

Placement: Based on the child's least restrictive educational setting.

Class size ratio: This indicates the maximum student population allowed, the number of teachers required, and the number of assistant teachers or aides required.

Length of program: Some special education programs maintain a ten-month calendar. Programs for more seriously disabled students may be twelve months.

School: Projected school for the coming year.

Teacher: The child's contact teacher for the coming year. When a child has several special education teachers, as in a departmentalized special education high school program, one teacher is assigned as the contact teacher. At the elementary and secondary levels, this can also be the resource room teacher, if the child is assigned there, or the child's self-contained special education teacher if this more restrictive program is used.

Program initiation date: When the special education services will begin.

Transportation: Whether the child has special transportation needs. For example, a severely physically handicapped child may require door-to-door service with a special bus to allow easy access and departure.

Physical education: Explains if the child is being recommended for regular physical education or adaptive physical education—that is, a specially designed program of developmental activities, games, sports, and rhythms suited to the interests, capacities, and limitations of students with disabilities who may not safely or successfully participate in the regular physical education program.

Related services: Other services the child will be receiving to support the academic special education process. Also noted in this section would be the number of sessions per week, minutes per session, maximum group size, start date, and end date. Related services may include in-school individual counseling, in-school group counseling, resource room, speech or language therapy, occupational therapy, physical therapy, art therapy, and adaptive physical education.

Mainstreamed courses: The IEP must specify if the child's disability allows for participation in any mainstreamed classes.

Special classes: The types of special education classes the child will have in the coming year, such as math, social studies, and health.

Testing information: In this section, the academic test results are reviewed, including the tests administered, date administered, and percentile and or age or grade equivalents.

Comments: This section is reserved for any questions, reminders, reviews, parents' concerns, identified areas of strength and weakness, and progress to date.

Goals and Objectives

There are usually two separate parts to this section. The first deals with general social, physical, academic, and management goals (SPAM goals) that relate to the environment and specific conditions under which the child will be learning or learns best. For example:

Social development: The degree and quality of the child's relationships with peers and adults, feelings about self, and social adjustment to school and community environments.

Physical development: The degree or quality of the child's motor and sensory development, health, vitality, and physical skills or limitations that affect the learning process.

Academic characteristics: The level of knowledge and development in subject areas and skills, including activities of daily living, level of intellectual functioning, adaptive behavior, expected rate of progress in acquiring skills, and information and learning style.

Management needs: The nature and degree to which environmental modifications and human material resources are required to enable the child to benefit from instruction.

The second part of the goals and objectives section deals with the specific academic goals and objectives. The basis for these goals is the evaluation and the diagnosis of strengths and weaknesses. This section may include specific content area goals, such as in science, social studies, math, and English if the child is in a special education setting for these subjects.

Mastery Levels

A *mastery level* is a predetermined level of competence indicating a clear understanding of a particular skill. This is the teacher's way of validating a child's movement to the next objective.

Setting the mastery levels too low will increase the possibilities of luck or chance influencing success, but setting them too high may cause frustration and failure. Mastery levels may be set as follows:

- *Ratio-based:* John will be able to do ... eight out of every ten times he attempts to do so.
- *Percent-based:* Mary will be able to do ... 75 percent of the time.
- *Time-based:* Ben will be able to ... and provide twelve responses in a ten-minute period.

Sometimes one general mastery level standard may apply to all objectives—for example, all objectives will be completed with 80 percent accuracy.

Evaluative Measures

Some IEPs specify measures or techniques to use to evaluate success levels for each objective. These measures are used to qualify the mastery levels applied to each objective and indicate whether the child has accomplished it and is competent enough to move on to the next one. Many such measures are available: student assignments and projects, informal conferences between student and teacher, student self-evaluation, textbook tests and quizzes, standardized tests, review of quarterly report cards, discussions with classroom teachers, parent-teacher conferences, record of attendance, Stanford Diagnostic Test, teacher-made tests, teacher evaluations, homework assignments, and criterion-referenced tests.

Alternate Testing Modifications

The final section, testing modifications, will be discussed in the next chapter.

Chapter 11

Alternate Testing Modifications

As a special educator, you will frequently be asked about the need for students to have modifications on their IEP. Alternate testing techniques take into account the individual needs of a child with a disability. As a result, you modify testing procedures or formats. These modifications are designed to give these students an equal opportunity to participate in the testing situation.

These techniques must be described on the student's IEP. They must provide the child the opportunity to demonstrate mastery of skills without being unfairly restricted by his disability.

Children classified as disabled are entitled to alternate testing and classroom modifications as long as the testing or background of the child provides evidence of such a need. There are no limits on the number of modifications that may be made, but they should only be included in the IEP if they will enable the child to be more successful in school. Here is a list of some testing modifications: requires flexible scheduling in testing, requires testing in a flexible setting, requires a revised test format, requires extended time for testing, requires revised test direction, requires the opportunity to record answers in any manner, requires the use of a calculator for testing, requires the use of a tape recorder for testing, requires the use of a typewriter or word processor, needs a Braille writer, requires questions to be read aloud (test may be read aloud), should not be penalized for spelling errors on tests, has to use a computer or word processor for written work to compensate for handwriting or spelling deficits, requires enlarged print, or requires enlarged answer sheets.

A sample of an IEP can be found in Appendix K at the back of this book.

Student Eligibility for Alternate Testing Techniques

Only students who have been identified as having a disability by the eligibility committee are normally allowed to use alternate testing techniques. However, there are three other possible reasons for providing alternate testing techniques.

First, the law usually gives the school principal the authority to approve testing modifications that do not alter the intended purpose of the test for students who may have a disability but one that is not severe enough to warrant identification by the eligibility committee. For example, a student with attention deficit disorder (ADD) may have some mild problems that do not cause severe disruption in functioning.

Second, with certain tests, such as SAT exams, two pieces of documentation from outside professionals (who are not working in the same agency) that indicate the need for alternate testing techniques (such as untimed tests) may allow a student these privileges even though she has not been classified by the eligibility committee.

Finally, services will continue to be provided to students having been declassified by the eligibility committee. Further, they may use their modifications throughout their school career even though they have been declassified; however, this may vary from state to state.

Criteria for Allowing Use of Alternate Testing Techniques

The eligibility committee determines if a student would benefit from alternate testing techniques. The committee takes into account several variables when making this determination:

- The individual needs of the child as determined by evaluation, observation, background history, and other pertinent information presented at the eligibility committee meeting
- The necessity for modification in light of the student's past academic and test performance without modifications
- The student's potential benefit from the modification

Of course, all students could benefit from alternate testing techniques. As a result, a recommendation based only on potential to enhance performance may be inappropriate. The need for modifications must be substantiated in the evaluation results.

Techniques That Modify Presentation

Alternate testing techniques that modify manner of presentation are the most common to appear on a student's IEP. These are separated into several categories, and each contains several options.

- *Flexible scheduling.* This modification is usually made for students who have problems with the rate at which they process information. They may have physical disabilities such as motor or visual impairments. Examples of modifications that fall in this category include untimed tests, administration of a test over several sessions in the course of the day, or administration of a test in several sessions over several days.
- *Flexible setting.* This modification allows disabled students to take a test in a setting other than a regular classroom. This may be necessary in cases if a child is unable to leave home or the hospital, or if a child's disability interferes with his ability to remain on task or if he is easily distracted. In some cases, a disabled student requires special lighting or acoustics or a specifically equipped room. Examples of such modifications are individual administration of a test in a

separate location, small group administration of a test in a separate location, special lighting, special acoustics, adaptive or special furniture, or administration of the test in a location with minimal distractions.

- *Revised test format.* This modification is made for students whose disability interferes with their ability to take a test in the standard test format—for example, students with visual or perceptual disabilities who cannot read regular-sized print. Examples include use of a large print edition, increased spacing between items, reduced number of items per page, use of a Braille edition, larger-sized answer bubbles on test answer forms, or rearrangement of multiple-choice items with answer bubble right next to each choice.
- *Revised test directions.* This allows students with certain disabilities a better chance of understanding directions and thereby successfully completing a test. For example, they may be allowed to have directions read to them, reread the directions for each page of questions, be given directions in simplified language, or be given additional examples.
- *Use of aids.* Some disabled students, such as hearing-impaired children, require the use of aids in order to interpret test items. Aids may include auditory amplification devices, visual magnification devices, auditory tape of questions, or markers to maintain the student's place on a page. These children may also be allowed to have questions read to them or have questions signed to them.

Techniques That Modify Manner of Response

Students may be allowed to use aids to respond or to provide their responses in a different format.

- *Use of aids.* Students may be allowed to provide their answers to questions in a manner other than the conventional one. Techniques may include use of a tape recorder, use of a typewriter, use of a communication device, use of a word processor, or use of amanuensis (a secretary).
- *Revised format.* Some disabled students may be unable to record their responses to test questions on conventional answer forms and therefore require a change in the test format. They may be allowed to record answers directly in the test booklet or write cues (a stop sign, arrows) directly on the answer form. In addition, the pages they see may have increased spacing between questions or problems or larger answer blocks.

Techniques That Modify Process Used to Derive Response

Some students possess the innate ability to process mathematical information, but cannot use paper and pencil to make computations. Others may not be able to memorize arithmetic facts but can solve difficult word problems. When these problems occur they may be allowed to use a calculator, use an abacus, or use arithmetic tables.

Special Education Teacher's Role in Implementing Alternate Techniques

As the special education teacher, you are likely to play a crucial role in the implementation of alternate testing techniques, getting involved in any of the following ways.

As evaluator, you gain a clear understanding of a child's strength and weakness areas, learning style, and the effects of the disability on the child. You can use this information to analyze the need for modifications that can be substantiated by the results of the evaluation.

Special education teachers in self-contained classrooms come in direct contact with the students during classroom instruction. This experience provides a strong basis for recommending specific changes or additions to the testing modifications listed on a student's IEP.

As the special education teacher sitting on the eligibility committee, you provide the background experience that can help the team recommend appropriate testing modifications that may become part of an initial IEP, change an IEP during an annual review, or modify testing techniques as the result of a report from an outside agency.

You can help parents of students with disabilities understand alternate testing techniques and available options.

You may serve as a consultant to other teachers, parents, and administrators and offer advice on testing modifications.

You may monitor the implementation of assigned modifications for a particular student to ensure that the student's rights are being followed.

Chapter 12

The Special Educator's Role in the Annual Review Process

The annual review is a legal responsibility of the district. All classified students who reside in a school district must be given an annual review by the eligibility committee. The students' classification and educational program are reviewed, including related services provided, adding or removing test modifications, parental concerns or requests, academic progress, transportation needs, goals and objectives for the coming school year, and possible declassification.

Several people attend this review meeting. Although the specific individuals vary from district to district, they are likely to include the director of special education services or assignee, the school psychologist, parent of the child, guidance counselor (if at the secondary level), an assigned teacher (at the secondary level this may be the classroom teacher in a self-contained class, the resource room teacher, or one of the child's special education teachers), the classroom teacher (at the elementary level), a speech or language therapist, and even the child herself, if the team feels that the child could benefit from the discussion or may be able to shed light on a concern or recommendation being considered. Any other individual deemed necessary may also attend.

Special education teachers play an important role in the annual review process because they provide a great deal of the needed information. Many of the recommendations, changes, or additions the committee approves will result from the information the teacher reports during the annual review. Clearly, this is an important meeting because it will determine the child's educational direction and objectives for the coming year.

Special educators attending the annual review should be prepared with the following information: any pre- and poststandardized test scores indicating the child's academic progress for the year, a copy of the child's report card clearly outlining grades and attendance for the year, suggested goals and objectives for the coming year, an evaluation indicating whether the child benefited from the modifications allowed on his or her IEP and the probable reasons why they were or were not beneficial (if applicable), recommendations for additional test modifications (if applicable), recommendations for additional related services and the reasons why (if applicable), recommendations for reduction of related services and the reasons why, samples of the child's work over the course of the year, and a review of the child's social progress for the year.

Armed with this information, the special educator should be able to present a professional judgment of the child's progress and needs for the coming year.

Chapter 13

The Special Educator's Role in the Triennial Evaluation

Often, one of the responsibilities for the special education teacher is to participate in the triennial evaluation. As already suggested, this is a complete and updated evaluation required every three years for all children classified as having a disability by the eligibility committee. This is a very important component of the special education process, because the factors that accounted for the child's classification and placement are reviewed.

There are several phases to the triennial evaluation, and they may involve many professionals from a variety of disciplines. The special education teacher's tasks may include retesting the child's achievement skill areas, retesting the child's perceptual skill areas, analyzing the results and comparing the similarities in patterns to past evaluation results, and writing a detailed and comprehensive updated report of the findings that will be shared with the eligibility committee as well as the staff and parents.

It should be noted that a new release for testing is not required by law. If the committee requests new tests, the school may proceed with this process without a new release. However, the parents must be informed that the testing will take place. An example of that communication to parents follows.

PARENT NOTICE OF TRIENNIAL EVALUATION

To Parents/Guardian of ______________________________

Date ____________

Dear Parent,

Please be advised that the eligibility committee has arranged for a comprehensive reevaluation of your child that, according to state regulations, is required every three years.

The school psychologist will be available to review all the results with you when the reevaluation is completed. If you have any questions, please don't hesitate to call the school psychologist or me.

A Statement of Parents' Rights is enclosed for your information.

Sincerely,

The reevaluations to be done are:

____

Parents have certain rights in the triennial process. It is a good idea to become familiar with these rights because you will undoubtedly be asked about them from time to time and should always make sure parents are provided with a statement of these rights prior to the evaluation. This is one of their due process rights. An example of a statement of parents' rights follows.

STATEMENT OF PARENTS' RIGHTS

Dear Parents:

It is important that you be aware of, and understand, that you have the following rights in accordance with Section ___ of the Regulations of the Commissioner of Education:

1. To inspect all school files, records, and reports pertaining to your child. Such reports shall be available for duplication at reasonable cost.
2. To obtain an independent educational evaluation at public expense if you disagree with the evaluation obtained by the school district. However, the school district may initiate a hearing to show that its evaluation is appropriate. Such services may be obtained at: ____________.
3. To obtain free or low cost legal services at no cost to the school district. Such services may be obtained at: ____________.
4. To appeal the recommendations of the eligibility committee and request, in writing, an impartial formal hearing to determine the appropriateness of the proposed placement to change the program.

The impartial formal hearing will be conducted in accordance with the following rules:

- The board of education or trustees shall appoint an impartial hearing officer to conduct the hearing. The hearing officer shall be authorized to administer oaths and to issue subpoenas in connection with the administrative proceedings before him or her.
- A written or electronic verbatim record of the proceedings before the hearing officer shall be maintained and be made available to the parties.
- At all stages of the proceeding, where required, interpreters of the deaf or interpreters fluent in the dominant language of child's home shall be provided at district expense.
- The impartial hearing officer shall preside at the hearing and shall provide all parties an opportunity to present evidence and testimony.
- The parties to the proceeding may be represented by legal counsel or individuals with special knowledge or training with respect to the problems of children with disabilities, and may be accompanied by other persons of their choice.
- Unless a surrogate parent shall have previously been assigned, the impartial hearing officer shall determine whether the interests of the parents are opposed to or inconsistent with those of the child, or whether for any other reason the interests of the child would best be protected by assignment of surrogate parent, and where he or she so determines, the impartial hearing officer shall designate a surrogate parent to protect the interests of such child.

- The hearing shall be closed to the public unless the parent requests an open hearing.
- The parents, school authorities, and their respective counsel or representative shall have an opportunity to present evidence and to confront and question all witnesses at that hearing. Each party shall have the right to prohibit the introduction of any evidence the substance of which has not been disclosed to such party at least five days before the hearing.
- The parents shall have the right to determine whether the child shall attend the hearing.
- The impartial hearing officer shall render a decision, and mail a copy of the decision to the parents and to the board of education, not later than forty-five calendar days after the receipt by the board of education of a request for a hearing or after the initiation of such hearing by the board. The decision of the impartial hearing officer shall be based solely upon the record of the proceeding before the impartial hearing officer, and shall set forth the reasons and the factual basis for the determination. The decision shall also include a statement of such a decision by the commissioner in accordance with subdivision ____________________ (will vary for each state) of the hearing officer. The board of education shall mail a copy of such decision, after deleting any personally identifiable information, to the Office of Children with Handicapping Conditions, State Education Department, for the use of the state advisory panel.
- A review of the decision of a hearing officer rendered in accordance with subdivision ____________________ (will vary for each state) of this section may be obtained by an appeal to the commissioner. The written decision of the commissioner, a copy of which will be mailed to the parent and board of education, shall be final.

Although the special education teacher is likely to be responsible for updating the child's achievement and perceptual level records, other professionals involved in the triennial evaluation may include the psychologist, speech and language therapist, school nurse, social worker, guidance counselor, classroom teachers, and parents. However, if you are designated case manager for this process, it is important to remember that these reviews are required to be completed no later than three years from the previous date of testing. Therefore, be sure to maintain an updated list each year of all students who will be up for a triennial evaluation in that year. Begin early enough so that you meet the legal deadlines. Beginning early will never be a problem, but being late could create some concern from administrators as well as parents. The following checklist will help you ensure that you have included all the necessary materials in the final packet.

TRIENNIAL REVIEW REQUIRED MATERIALS CHECK LIST

Evaluations:

____________________ New psychological evaluations

____________________ New pyschoeducational evaluation

____________________ New speech/language evaluation(s), if applicable

____________________ Outside reports, if applicable

Academic data:

________________ Most recent report card

________________ Classroom teacher reports

Developmental data:

________________ New social and developmental history

Other required information and procedures:

________________ Parent letter of triennial review sent

________________ Medical update

Chapter 14

The Special Educator's Role in Transition Services

Special educators at the secondary level have a distinct and crucial responsibility. Beginning around age thirteen or fourteen, the law mandates that schools begin to prepare children with disabilities to make the transition to adult life. To accomplish this task, the schools must develop a transition plan covering all these students' needs to ensure that when they leave, everything they need will be ready for them. The goal is to make their transition to the adult world more positive and secure. You will need to assist both parents and students in this journey. This chapter will review many of the aspects involved in the process.

As most adults know from their own experience, the period known as adolescence is probably the most difficult and unsettling in a person's development. It is a time of physical, emotional, and social upheaval. Until their child leaves secondary school, parents feel that they are responsible for controlling and protecting that child. This protective guidance normally involves educational, medical, financial, and social input. When the child leaves this setting there is a personal struggle on the part of the parents in "letting go." There is always a normal amount of apprehension associated with a child's entry into the adult world. After all, the greater responsibility for proper adjustment now falls on the child, while the parent's role diminishes.

Because planning for the future of a child with disabilities is even more stressful, with great fear of the unknown, parents may have a tendency to delay addressing the issues and instead focus only on the present. However, the belief among professionals is that working through these fears and thinking about the child's future interests will ensure the best outcome. Regardless of the nature and severity of the disability, parents will go through a transitional process during the school years that will provide a foundation for the adult world. This transitional process will include many facets of planning for the future and should be fully understood by everyone concerned each step of the way. Planning for the future is an investment in a child's well-being.

What Are Transition Services?

Transition services aim to provide students and their families with the practical skills and knowledge they will need to make a successful transition to adult life. Although these services are available in each of the following areas, not every student with disabilities will need to receive all of them. Available are employment services, living arrangement services, recreation and leisure activities, transportation and travel training, financial and income advising services, postsecondary or continuing education, assistive technology, and medical and health services.

The Individualized Transitional Education Plan (ITEP)

If you are working in a secondary school, you will be directly involved in the development of your students' Individualized Transitional Education Plan (ITEP). The ITEP is a part of the IEP, and it is an important document in determining a child's future. The ITEP should address the following issues:

- A statement of transition services should focus on the child's preferences, interests, and needs. The beginning date for the service should be provided.
- Annual goals and objectives for the following areas: legal-advocacy (guardianship), independence or residential (private residence or group home), recreation-leisure (sports activities), financial and income (banking and checking accounts), medical-health (health insurance, physician selection), employment (sheltered workshop or competitive employment), transportation (public or private), postsecondary or continuing education (college or vocational training), other support needs (such as clergy, fraternal organizations).
- Long-term adult outcomes in the ITEP should include statements about the child's performance in employment, postsecondary education, and community living. This will only pertain to children around sixteen and older.
- The ITEP must describe a coordinated set of activities. It must demonstrate the use of various strategies, including community experiences, adult living objectives, and instruction. If one of these activities is not included in the ITEP in a particular year, then the document must explain why it is not reflected in any part of the student's program. Activities of daily living and functional vocational evaluation activities should also be included.
- A list of participants involved in the planning and development of the ITEP should be provided.

Transition Checklist

The following is a checklist of transition activities that families may wish to consider when preparing the ITEP with the IEP team. The student's skills and interests will determine which items are relevant and whether these issues should be addressed at IEP transition meetings. The checklist can also help identify who should be part of the IEP transition team. Responsibility for carrying out the specific transition activities should be determined at the IEP transition meetings.

Four to Five Years Before Leaving the School District

- Identify the student's personal learning styles and the accommodations that will be necessary for him or her to be a successful learner and worker.
- Identify career interests and skills, complete interest and career inventories, and identify the additional education or training that will be required to succeed in these areas.
- Explore options for postsecondary education and admission criteria.
- Identify interests and options for future living arrangements, including supports.

- Teach the student to communicate effectively his or her interests, preferences, and needs.
- Teach the student to explain his or her disability and what accommodations are necessary.
- Help the student learn and practice informed decision-making skills.
- Investigate assistive technology tools that can increase the student's community involvement and employment opportunities.
- Broaden the student's experiences with community activities and help him or her form friendships.
- Pursue and allow the student to use transportation options.
- Investigate money management and identify necessary skills.
- Acquire identification card for the student and foster the ability to communicate personal information.
- Identify and begin teaching skills necessary for independent living.
- Help the student learn about and practice personal health care.

Two to Three Years Before Leaving the School District

- Help the student to identify community support services and programs (vocational rehabilitation, county services).
- Invite adult service providers, peers, and others to the IEP transition meeting.
- Match career interests and skills with vocational coursework and community work experiences.
- Gather more information on postsecondary programs and available support services; make arrangements for accommodations to take college entrance exams.
- Identify health care providers and teach the student about sexuality and family planning issues.
- Determine the need for financial support (Supplemental Security Income, state financial supplemental programs, Medicare).
- Teach and allow the student to practice appropriate interpersonal, communication, and social skills for different settings (employment, school, recreation, with peers, and so on).
- Explore legal status with regard to decision making before the age of majority (wills, guardianship, special needs trusts).
- Help the student begin a résumé and update it as needed.
- Allow the student to practice independent living skills, such as budgeting, shopping, cooking, and housekeeping.
- Identify needed personal assistant services, and if appropriate, help the student learn to direct and manage these services.

One Year Before Leaving the School District

- Help the student apply for financial support programs (Supplemental Security Income, vocational rehabilitation).
- Help make up a postsecondary school plan and arrange for accommodations.

- Allow the student to practice effective communication by developing interview skills, asking for help, and identifying necessary accommodations at postsecondary and work environments.
- Teach the student to specify desired job; help him or her obtain paid employment with supports as needed.
- Train the student to take responsibility for arriving on time to work, appointments, and social activities.
- Train the student to assume responsibility for health care needs (making appointments, filling and taking prescriptions, and so on).
- Make sure the student registers to vote and, if male, for selective service.

Vocational Assessments

As your students approach the age of thirteen or fourteen, some will be evaluated to determine their skills, needs, and vocational options. This will be part of their transition plan and may lead to a work-training situation during school and a future vocation after school ends. Although you may not be directly involved in doing these evaluations, you should be familiar with the process in order to help parents and students through it.

Level I Vocational Assessment

The Level I assessment takes a look at the child from a vocational perspective. A trained vocational evaluator or knowledgeable special education teacher should be designated to collect the Level I assessment data. The information gathered for analyses includes existing information from cumulative records; student, parent or guardian, and teacher interviews; special education eligibility data; a review of the child's aptitudes; achievements; interests; behaviors; and occupational exploration activities.

The informal student interview involved in a Level I assessment should consider the child's vocational interest, interpersonal relationship skills, and adaptive behavior.

Level II Vocational Assessment

The Level II assessment follows the first one and is based on the analyses already obtained. Once the child reaches twelve years of age, this may be recommended by the eligibility committee at any time to determine a student's vocational skills, aptitudes, and interests. The same knowledgeable staff members involved in prior assessments should be involved. Collected data should include writing ability, interest inventory, motor skills (dexterity, speed, tool use, strength, coordination), spatial discrimination, verbal reading, perception skills (visual-auditory-tactile), speaking skills, numerical skills (measurement, handling money), comprehension (task learning, problem solving), and attention span (staying on task).

Level III Vocational Assessment

A Level III assessment is a comprehensive vocational evaluation that involves real or simulated work experiences. It becomes the basis for vocational counseling. Unlike with Level I and Level II assessments, a trained vocational evaluator only should administer or supervise this assessment. Level III assessment options include the following:

- Vocational evaluations, including aptitudes and interests that are compared to job performance to predict vocational success in specific areas. Work samples must be valid and reliable.
- Situational vocational assessments that occur in real work settings. This on-the-job assessment considers what has been learned and how well.
- Work study assessments. These are progress reports from supervisors or mentors that provide information on the child's job performance. A standard observational checklist may be employed.

Training and Work Options

Once all the evaluations and assessments are complete, students will be presented with a variety of training and work options depending on the results. There are many options available. The following three options may apply to most of the students you will work with but do not constitute all the options available.

Competitive Employment

Competitive employment is defined as a full-time or part-time job in the open labor market with competitive wages and responsibilities. Competitive employment is employment that the individual maintains with no more outside support than a coworker without a disability would receive. The key word here is *maintains.* Although a student may make use of transition services available in the community to prepare for and find competitive employment, these services are temporary. Once that individual has the job, support from outside agencies is terminated, and the individual maintains, or does, the job on her own.

The types of jobs that are normally considered competitive employment are as vast in number as they are varied. Waitress, service station attendant, clerk, secretary, mechanic, professional driver, factory worker, computer programmer and manager, teacher's aide, teacher, health care worker, lawyer, scientist, and engineer are just some examples of people who are competitively employed. As can be seen by these examples, the amount of training an individual needs varies considerably from job to job. Some jobs are entry-level and require little or no specific training. Others require vocational preparation and training, and still others require extensive academic schooling.

Supported Employment

Working at a job has two elements: finding the job and keeping the job. The student may require little or no help with one or both aspects or may require a great deal of help. As we have seen, the school system in partnership with the vocational rehabilitation agency, an outside state agency whose job it is to rule the student transition to adult life through such options as job training and vocational assessment, will help students find a job.

When an individual needs long-term or ongoing help in keeping a job it is called *supported employment.* These are paid jobs in a business in the community. Supported employment is right for adults who traditionally have not been considered part of the workforce; need long-term support to be employed; have one or more disabilities, such as mental retardation, autism, mental illness, traumatic brain injury, physical disabilities, severe learning disabilities or severe behavioral challenges; or requires intensive, repetitive, or adaptive assistance to learn new tasks.

Sheltered Employment

Sheltered employment options are ones in which individuals with disabilities work in a self-contained unit, segregated from workers who do not have disabilities. Sheltered employment options usually range along a continuum from adult day programs to work activity centers to sheltered workshops. In adult day programs, individuals generally receive training in daily living skills, social skills, recreational skills, and prevocational skills. Work activity centers offer individuals similar training but may also provide training in vocational skills. In sheltered workshops, individuals perform subcontracted tasks such as sewing, packaging, collating, or machine assembly and are usually paid on a piece-rate basis. People do not usually advance to the workshop until they have demonstrated certain mastery levels. Sheltered employment options are generally supported by federal or state funds and are operated by private, nonprofit corporations governed by a board of directors.

Traditionally, sheltered employment options were thought to be the only options possible for individuals with severe disabilities. There is now evidence from supported employment models that individuals with severe disabilities can work in community settings if provided adequate support. With the emergence of supported employment, many facilities began to modify their sheltered employment programs to provide workers with integrated options. Advocates of this trend away from sheltered employment point to the advantages of supported employment, which include higher wages, more meaningful work, and integration with workers who do not have disabilities.

Travel Training

Many students need training in getting from one place to another in the community. Travel training is short-term, comprehensive, intensive instruction designed to teach students with disabilities how to get around safely and independently on public transportation. The goal is to teach students to travel independently to a regularly visited destination and back. Travel trainers are specially trained in this area. In a quality travel training program, they work with one student at a time. Students learn travel skills while following a particular route, generally to school or a worksite, and are taught the safest, most direct route. The trainers follow the route with the student and instruct the student in dealing with problems such as getting lost or taking a detour around a construction site. They teach the student to make decisions, deal with the consequences of decisions, and maintain appropriate safety and behavior standards. Travel trainers are responsible for making sure the student experiences and understands the realities of public transportation.

The term *travel training* is often used generically to refer to a program that provides instruction in travel skills to individuals with any disability except visual impairment. Individuals who have a visual impairment receive travel training from orientation and mobility specialists, usually under the jurisdiction of the state commission for the blind. Travel trainers need to understand how different disabilities affect the ability to travel independently and devise customized strategies to teach travel skills that address the specific needs of these people.

A travel trainer usually begins training a student at the student's residence. In this way, he can observe the student in a familiar environment, reassure the family through daily contact, and assess the student's home environment at regular travel times for potential problems.

Medical and Financial Options

Many of the children and families you will work with will require medical and other forms of assistance. As a special educator you will not be required to provide these forms (for example, Social Security), but should be familiar with the options available and the differences between them.

Medicaid

Medicaid is a federal-state program that helps pay health care costs for nonelderly people who are financially needy or who have a disability. Individual states usually determine who is eligible for Medicaid and which health services will be covered. Most people do not qualify for Medicaid until the majority of their money has been spent. It is important to realize, however, that some individuals whose incomes are not in the lowest category, but who have substantial medical expenses, do qualify for Medicaid. These individuals, who either have incomes higher than the Aid for Families with Dependent Children (ADFC) cut-off or have very high medical bills that reduce their incomes below the level established for "categorically needy," are termed "medically needy." Once Medicaid covers an individual, that person is entitled to receive the following minimal services: physician services, laboratory and X-ray services, outpatient hospital services, skilled nursing facilities (persons over age twenty-one), family planning services, medical diagnosis and treatment (persons under age twenty-one), home health services, and in-patient hospital services.

In many states Medicaid will also pay for some or all of these: dental care; medically necessary drugs; eyeglasses; prosthetic devices; physical, speech, and occupational therapy; private-duty nursing; care from alternative medical providers, such as chiropractors and acupuncturists; in-patient psychiatric care; and diagnostic, preventive, screening, and rehabilitative services.

Medicare

Medicare is a federally funded system of health and hospital insurance for U.S. citizens age sixty-five and older, for younger people receiving Social Security benefits, and for persons needing dialysis or kidney transplants for the treatment of end-stage renal disease. Usually, Medicare beneficiaries can receive medical care through physicians of their own choosing or through health maintenance organizations and other medical plans that have contracts with Medicare.

Eligibility for Medicare does not depend on income; almost everyone age sixty-five and older is entitled to it. Workers are not required to retire when they reach sixty-five in order to be covered. Coverage under Medicare is restricted to reasonable and medically necessary treatment in a hospital; skilled nursing home, meals, and regular nursing care services; costs of necessary special care; and home health services and hospice care for terminally ill patients. For more detailed information, a good starting point is the official Web site for Medicare.

Supplemental Security Income (SSI)

The SSI program is targeted to individuals who are both in financial need and blind or disabled. People who are on SSI usually get food stamps and Medicaid, too. The evaluation process for eligibility varies depending on whether the applicant is under or over age eighteen. When a child reaches the age of eighteen, the Social Security Administration no longer considers the income and resources of parents when determining eligibility for benefits.

Under the SSI program, individuals over age eighteen may receive monthly payments if they have little or no income or resources, such as savings accounts; are considered medically disabled or blind; and either do not work or earn less than a certain amount, defined by the Social Security Administration as Substantial Gainful Activity (SGA).

Social Security Disability Insurance (SSDI)

The SSDI program is somewhat different from SSI because it considers the employment status of the applicant's parents. "SSDI benefits are paid to persons who become disabled before the age of twenty-two if at least one of their parents had worked a certain amount of time under Social Security but is now disabled, retired, and/or deceased" (National Association of State Directors of Special Education, 1992, p. 9). As with SSI, eligibility for SSDI generally makes an individual eligible for food stamps and Medicaid benefits as well.

In the past, the amount of benefits an individual might receive from either or both of these programs would be substantially reduced or even eliminated by income earned at a job (Krebs, 1990). Recent legislation, however, has made big changes in both the SSI and SSDI programs to encourage people receiving these benefits to try to work and become independent. These changes are called *work incentives,* because they make it possible for individuals with disabilities to work without immediate loss of benefits.

Food Stamps

The food stamp program provides financial assistance by enabling recipients to exchange the stamps for food. It is a major income supplement for income if an individual with a disability meets the income requirements. This program is federally funded through the Department of Agriculture's Food and Nutrition Service (NFS). It is administered by state and local social service agencies. In most cases, if an individual is eligible for SSI, food stamps will be available, too. For more information, contact your local department of social services.

In sum, whatever the financial status of the family at the time their disabled child turns eighteen, they should have a thorough understanding of that child's financial entitlements. For a complete list of organizations that help with transition and vocational skills, see Appendix I.

Chapter 15

Assistive Technology and the Special Educator

With the increase in technology in society today, its use is nowhere more evident than in the classroom. Special educators are required to assess, use, purchase, and monitor their students' progress with a variety of assistive technology devices and software. If you know what is available for children with different disabilities, it can enhance their performance in the classroom and in many cases even the playing field so that they can function in a regular inclusion class in a regular school. Further, all IEPs contain a section on assistive technology. In many cases this will be an integral part of the child's education plan, along with modifications and accommodations. Because special education teachers are actively involved in writing IEPs, you will be called on to recommend assistive technology devices for your students. Resources are available to assist all consumers in making decisions, including periodicals; disability, parent, and professional organizations; national technology centers; and private companies. The assistive technology maze can become less complex and confusing if you know where to go for help.

Today, a nonverbal child can speak with the help of an electronic communication aid. A student with learning disabilities can master math facts using a computer game. A child with vision problems can benefit from an inexpensive device that enlarges printed words on the computer screen. And for more severe vision problems, there are speech synthesizers that can be used with computers to convert typewritten words or text into an electronic voice.

For children with a physical disability, special devices will allow them to input information into the computer without using the conventional keyboard. Instead, they may use a single switch or some type of voice recognition system. Other alternative input devices can be used simply by touching the computer screen or points on a touch-sensitive tablet that correspond to points on the computer screen.

Assistive technology has increased enormously the ability of those with disabilities to lead independent lives. Computer-based environmental control units allow users to turn on lights and appliances and open doors from a wheelchair. Augmentative communication devices enable those who cannot speak to voice thoughts and needs by using touch- or light-activated keyboards coupled to synthetic speech systems. Screen reading programs for the blind, screen magnification systems for those with low vision, and special ability switches that permit the mobility-impaired to use a computer are only a few examples of the technology by which the individuals gain access to the computer screen and keyboard.

Defining Assistive Technology Devices

Computers were designed to perform at maximum efficiency when used by the nondisabled. But almost everyone employs some type of adaptive technology when using the computer. For example, we may wear eyeglasses or wrist supports or simply adjust the brightness of the screen display or the height and angle of the monitor. In contrast, assistive technology usually refers to a device or piece of equipment that increases the independence of a person with disabilities. Assistive technology for the disabled, of course, is not new. For instance, the wheelchair has long been an indispensable assistive device for those with impaired mobility.

The distinction between adaptive technologies employed by the nondisabled and assistive technologies for the disabled blurs at times. Some of the assistive technologies designed for the disabled have proven so ergonomically sound that they have been incorporated as standard features. One such example is the placement of the keyboard on-off switch, which was designed so that people with motor impairments would not have to reach to the back of the machine to turn the power on and off.

According to the Technology-Related Assistance for Individuals with Disabilities Act of 1988 (Public Law [PL] 100–407, August 19, 1988), assistive technology is "any item, piece of equipment, or product system, whether acquired commercially or off the shelf, modified or customized, that increases, maintains, or improves functional capabilities of individuals with disabilities."

Assistive technology devices can be anything from a simple tool with no moving parts (for example, a toothbrush with a built-up handle) to a sophisticated mechanical or electronic system (a robotic arm). Simple, mechanical devices are often referred to as low-tech devices, while computer-driven or complex assistive technology may be called high-tech. However, many people in the assistive technology field have argued that this complexity-based classification is not a useful one because there is no clear division between simple and complex. With the passage of the Rehabilitation Act Amendments of 1992 (PL 102–569), assistive technology devices and assistive technology services are now included as part of rehabilitation technology.

Assistive Technology for the Visually Impaired

Special education teachers working with students with visual impairments need to be aware of the types of assistive technology devices available. This assistance is crucial for a child with this disability if she is to have a good chance of succeeding with the demands of the curriculum. The technology available to computer users who are blind or have low vision is extensive. The choice of the appropriate technology depends on a number of factors. Among them are the cause of the visual loss, the extent of loss of visual acuity, the quality of peripheral vision, and any other physical or mental limitations that might affect use of a computer.

Following are examples of assistive devices designed to help those with visual disabilities.

- *Speech and Braille.* Software is available that gives audio cues to on-screen visual images such as icons, windows, menus, and cursor location (the numeric keypad replaces the need for a mouse); other programs convert text to Braille and formats printing on a Braille embosser. Another item that may assist your students is a synthetic speech system. This contains two parts: the synthesizer does the speaking, and the screen access program tells the synthesizer what to say.

- *Magnification devices.* Often students can be helped if the presentation of the material is magnified. There are several things that can be done to enlarge the images on the screen. One solution is software that magnifies the screen image up to sixteen times its regular size. Other magnification solutions range from monitors that display images in multiple resolutions to magnification lenses that attach to the outside frame of the monitor. Special education teachers may also want to consider software that reads text aloud, so that instead of looking at the words on the computer, the student can listen to them. Many companies that provide assistive technology software and devices can be found on the Web (see, for example, http://www.Atto.buffalo.edu). Systems also exist that offer the ability to scan hard-copy text into a PC that then magnifies it on the computer screen.
- *Optical character recognition systems.* Optical character recognition (OCR) technology offers blind and visually impaired people the capacity to scan printed text and then have the computer translate it to synthetic speech or save it on the computer. OCR technology usually contains three essential elements: scanning, recognition, and text reading. Current-generation OCR systems provide very good accuracy and formatting capabilities at prices that are up to ten times lower than a few years ago.

Assistive Technology for the Hearing Impaired

Many devices are available for students with hearing impairments to assist them in their daily lives. Special education teachers of children with hearing impairments should be aware of these devices and share the information with the parents of these children.

FM Trainers

Many deaf and hard-of-hearing children can participate fully in regular classroom education with the aid of FM (listening) systems. These devices allow the teacher or other speaker to talk into a small microphone that transmits their voice directly to the child's hearing aid. This reduces the impact of poor acoustics and classroom noise and allows the child to hear what she needs. The federal government has understood the value of this service and set aside a part of the radio spectrum (216–217 MHz) for use by these devices.

Alerting Devices and Systems

Various alerting and alarm systems that signal deaf and hard-of-hearing people include security systems, baby cry alarms, smoke alarm systems, doorbell alerting systems, paging devices, telephone signaling systems, and wake-up alarms.

The signal may be visual (a flashing light), auditory (an increase in amplification), or vibrotactile (a vibrator). For instance, if an alarm clock is wired to a vibrotactile device under the pillow, the user is literally shaken awake. Auditory signals are sometimes used in conjunction with either visual or vibratory signals.

Telephone Aids

Amplification devices include a specially wired telephone handset with an amplification device and portable amplifiers that attach to a phone. Such volume control handsets may provide up to 30 percent additional power for the listener who has a hearing loss. These devices may be used with or without an individual's hearing aid.

Text telephones (TTY) and telecommunication devices (TDD) enable deaf and hard-of-hearing people to have conversations by typing messages that are sent through the telephone network. Although these devices are helpful, they offer a rather slow means of communication, especially when compared to computers.

Telecaption adapters are sometimes referred to as television decoders. They attach to the television and enable deaf and hard-of-hearing people to read captions on their television screens.

Assistive Technology for Individuals with Mobility Impairments

Most children with mobility disabilities have assistive devices or will be in need of them at some time in their educational career.

Many devices are available to help people with impaired mobility to use the computer. Although a standard keyboard and mouse are the input devices of choice for most people, other devices have been developed. Among the most frequently used are modified and alternate keyboards, ability switches, and headpointers and joysticks. The computer reads the input from these methods just as if it had been received through the standard keyboard. Descriptions of three of these devices follow.

Specialized Keyboards

There are dozens of different kinds of keyboards for your students to choose from depending on their personal abilities and preferences. Any of a number of them may be appropriate. The right keyboard may be the kind that looks like a traditional keyboard, but has large, touch-sensitive keys to help make typing easier. Another has only seven keys and uses a typing technique called "chording," originally designed for one-handed typists.

Some adjustable keyboards split into two sections and conform to the natural position of a child's arms to make typing comfortable. There are also switch-operated, on-screen keyboards that let a person type with almost any part of the body and "smart" keyboards that allow a person to customize each key's position, size, and function.

Mouse Alternatives

Your students may need a different kind of pointing device than a mouse. There are many from which to choose: head-controlled mice, trackballs (in effect a mouse turned upside down), joysticks, mice of different sizes and speeds, writing pads that function as mice, touch-sensitive screens that act as mice, and even remote-controlled mice.

Input Systems

Keyboards and mice are traditionally used to control personal computers. Although your students may not be able to use these devices, there are a number of alternatives, including voice recognition systems that allow a person to control the computer by talking to it; on-screen keyboards that facilitate typing without physically touching the keys; and head-controlled keyboards and mice that let a person type using head movements.

Assistive Technology Screening Evaluations

Special educators are sometimes asked to determine a child's need for an assistive technology device. Although many school districts employ outside agencies to carry out an assistive technology evaluation, some may use the special education staff for this purpose.

The following report outlines the areas that need to be covered. If you are asked to do this evaluation and you know the type of assistive technology device necessary (for example, a word processor), then secure three or four different types and evaluate the child on each device to see which one helps her perform best. You may want to consider the following factors in making the decision: the abilities of a child; her interests and preferences, the family's culture and value system, the environment in which it will be used, the functional tasks for participating in daily routines, available materials and technologies, the barriers to the child's participation, and ongoing intervention and evaluation.

Here is an example of a report of an assistive device technology evaluation.

ASSISTIVE DEVICE TECHNOLOGY EVALUATION

Name: John Smith
Address: 42 Bryant Ave.
Date of birth: January 5, 1989
Grade: 9th
School: Harwood Middle School
Parents' names: Bill/Martha

Teacher: Mrs. Stewart
Phone: 456–9876
Referred by: MDT
Date of evaluation: March 2003
Date of report: April 2003
Chronological age at time of evaluation: 14 years 3 months

Purpose of Evaluation

The school district has requested an assistive technology evaluation for John. This evaluation will focus on the use of technology to remediate, enhance and/or provide John with options for improving his note-taking skills.

Background History

John is a fourteen-year-old student who is in a ninth-grade inclusion program at the local high school. He is classified as learning disabled with attention deficit disorder. John has previously attended the Nassau County Day School. His academic levels of performance have been described as average for reading and math and well below average for writing.

Present Computer Availability

John reported that he currently has six computers at home, five being Macintosh and one being a PC with Windows XP. John informed us that he uses the computer at home for downloading music from the Internet and e-mailing friends on AOL. In school there are Gateway PCs available for use in the computer lab and one also in his guided studies class.

Evaluation Observations

John was evaluated in a closed room office situation for approximately one hour. He understood the purpose of our meeting and was very cooperative and willing to participate in all of the tasks asked of him. Several of his teachers were available to provide input with respect to his academic goals and objectives as well as their individual class writing requirements. During this functional assessment, informal measures were used to evaluate academic skills and his ability to use various assistive technology devices. The following is a summary of his performance:

Handwriting skills: John, who is right-hand dominant and prefers printing to cursive writing, filled in a simple form that displayed sizing, spacing, and spelling errors. He was asked to provide several handwriting samples of near, far point, and auditory copying. He was asked to copy a paragraph taken directly from his earth science textbook while on his desk, from the board, and as if it were being dictated in a class note-taking situation.

His far point copying sample displayed missing words six out of a text of fifty. It appeared he would look up at the board and from memory write the words down, thus making frequent gross spelling errors and word reversals. The individual timed results are attached; however, all of the samples were replete with sizing, spacing, and spelling errors.

Keyboarding skills: John was given a Macintosh PowerBook G3 laptop computer to type selections with. John was then asked to type the original paragraph, which took slightly longer than his near and far point copying samples.

He is a two-handed typist whose keyboarding skills are in the "hunt and peck" method and although he is quick, he is not particularly accurate. John has revealed that he has not had formal keyboarding training and has just picked it up as he has used the computer. John was able to maneuver the desktop with minimal assistance and displayed basic text editing skills related to word processing such as deleting, inserting, moving and copying letters, words and phrases, spell-check, saving and printing his work.

Co:Writer is a word prediction program that encourages students in language development. Its knowledge of grammar and language rules helps students select the right words for their sentences and compositions. When any letter is typed, a suggestion list appears to help the writer select the correct word. The program does eventually help to predict the user's most frequently used words and prompts the user with the appropriate grammar. John did not like the auditory feedback aspect of this program and because of its inherent nature of prediction it was too slow and presented too many distractions for him.

Write:OutLoud is an easy-to-use talking word processor that also has a talking spell-checker. It greatly benefits students who need to listen as they write as well as students who need to review their writing auditorially for reinforcement and proofing. John found typing letters, words, or sentences with the speech function of this program on too distracting. John was instructed that this function can be shut off and used only upon completion of an entire document being typed so that it is read back all at once. He did express an interest in the audible spell-check feature as well as having an entire document read back.

John was then asked to use AlphaSmart 3000. This device is a portable word processor that students can take class notes with and later on transfer their notes to any word processing application on a Macintosh or PC. John was again able to navigate the keyboard and understand the concepts of using spell-checker, creating individual files, one for English, one for science, and so on, and then eventually transferring this information to his home or resource room computer.

Academic and cognitive skills: John's current levels of functioning have been described as average academically with the exception of writing, and in line with characteristic ADD identifiable behaviors. John showed us his notebooks and Ms. Benson, his guided studies teacher, described how she uses color-coding and outlines to assist John in overcoming his organizational problems as well as clarifies his class work and homework assignments on a daily basis.

Occupational Therapy Observations

John demonstrated poor organizational skills and tends to rush through his handwriting of class notes, and so on, at times, using his own abbreviation system. During the evaluation process, "breaks" were given as John demonstrated difficulty focusing on the task at hand following an approximate ten-minute block of time. It was, however, easy to refocus him and bring him back to task. At this time he does not receive occupational therapy services.

Summary

John is a student who has a classification of learning disability and attention deficit disorder and whose learning differences present obstacles to accessing his academic environment and achieving his academic goals. John requires the support he currently receives each day to reach these goals and objectives on a daily basis.

Compensatory Strategies

- Simple outlines or templates should be provided by the teacher wherever possible.
- Encourage the use of organizational guides such as notebooks, appointment books, and structured study guides to reinforce his current organizational skills.
- Provide more time for all written tasks.
- Allow the use of a tape recorder for individualized homework or class work assignments when appropriate.
- Use of a calculator will assist in mathematical and computational problems.

Recommended Technology

A keyboarding program such as Mavis Beacon Teaches Typing is a structured typing tutorial program that would improve John's keyboarding skills and is currently used at his school.

A portable word processor such as the AlphaSmart 3000 would allow John to type notes and keep them organized in electronic folders while eventually being able to be uploaded to a full-sized word processing program on either a Macintosh or PC. A list of these devices is attached with appropriate contact numbers. All are available on a loaner basis from each company for your individual assessment.

Write:OutLoud could prove to be a useful tool for John in his writing as it would provide spelling and auditory reinforcement for him.

Follow-up and reassessment should be part of an ongoing technology plan, if technology is determined to be a viable option for John by those able to assess and monitor his progress.

Jane Berman
Assistive Technology Specialist

PART FOUR

WORKING AS A SPECIAL EDUCATION TEACHER

Chapter 16

Getting Ready for School

As we have seen in earlier parts of the book, as a special educator you are likely to be hired into one of three settings: resource room, self-contained special class, or inclusion setting. This chapter will discuss the steps that should be taken to ensure the welfare of your children, create the proper educational setting, and find the right information to make your job easier and more rewarding. We explain when information is best suited to one particular setting. Generally, however, the information we provide here is relevant to all three settings.

Learn as Much as Possible About Your Students Before School Begins

The very first step to take in setting up a classroom is getting to know your incoming students. It is important to find out as much information about each student as possible. Schools have a wealth of available materials on each child if you know where to look. Information on children with disabilities can be found in several documents. We have talked about the first ones at length in earlier parts of this book. The *permanent record folder*, which contains all the basic information on the child, is usually stored in the main office. *Past teachers' reports* may be in the permanent record folder or may be part of the child's report card forms. *Past report cards* show a pattern of performance including strength and weakness areas. These are likely to be contained in the permanent record folder. *Group achievement scores*, if accurate, also show patterns of strengths and weaknesses. However, it is important not to draw conclusions from low scores unless other information backs up the same impressions, such as classroom performance and teachers' reports. Sometimes children who are having academic problems do not try so hard as they could for fear of failure. Consequently, the resulting scores may not reflect true achievement levels.

It is also a good idea to find out the *number and types of schools attended.* A review of the past school names on the report cards found in the permanent folder will give you this information. Be sure to note what kind of schools they were. Perhaps this is the first year for some to attend a mainstreamed school. These children may require added attention and support in the transition. Next, *medical records* can be gathered from the school nurse's office. Pay close attention to vision and hearing levels, medications, allergies, and any other medical issues that might need attention in the classroom.

The most recent *Individualized Education Program (IEP)* is a crucial piece of information, but is usually not kept in the permanent record folder. It may be found among the records in the office of pupil personnel services, the psychologist's file on the child, or the special education folder on the child. This file normally travels from teacher to teacher. However, it may also be included in a main file in the office of the special education coordinator for your building.

Health alerts may be found on the front page of the IEP. Find out as much as possible about any conditions noted. You want to sound knowledgeable when speaking with parents about their child's special health issues.

Also be sure to find out as much as possible about each child's specific disability *classification*. You may already be knowledgeable about the disability but it never hurts to learn more. This knowledge base can only gain you respect from staff and parents. (A very good source for learning about all kinds of classification disabilities is NICHCY.org.)

Look for the classroom and test *modifications* that the child is entitled to have; these are listed in the IEP. Investigate each modification thoroughly to understand what is involved. Think about the possible reasons why the child was granted this modification in the first place. You will need to understand these modifications fully. If you will be working with other teachers, then you will be communicating and explaining them to all the child's teachers.

Sometimes a child is entitled to some classroom *accommodation*, such as special furniture, filters for lighting, acoustic enhancements, and so on. Again investigate and become knowledgeable about each accommodation.

The IEP will also contain a section on *related services* that the child is entitled to have while in school. (See the section on this later in this chapter.)

Some children may be entitled to *assistive technology*, such as a word processor. This too should be noted on the IEP. Find out everything you can about this technology. There are numerous sites that you can visit to gain information; for more on assistive technology, see Chapter Fifteen.

It is important to determine, if possible, the *ability level* of the child. Ability level is measured in many ways, as we have already seen earlier in this book. This information can usually be found in one of the following places:

- *The permanent record folder.* Look for a group IQ test or a test that offers a score labeled School Abilities Index, or SAI; this has replaced the term IQ in some districts. These group measures may offer some insight. Again, be careful about depending on low scores alone to gauge ability, as mentioned previously.
- *The psychologist's office.* Look up the last triennial report; it should have some measure of ability noted.
- *The IEP.* The IEP may describe ability level. This information may be listed under the Wechsler Scales of Intelligence or the Stanford Binet Test of Intelligence.
- *Past teacher's comments about the child's ability levels.*

You may also want to meet your students individually before school begins to get to know them on a personal basis. If you can begin a week before the school year starts, send a letter home to the students introducing yourself and inviting them in to help you set up the classroom or just to come in and get to know each other. This may alleviate many fears on the part of the children and offer you greater insights into their needs. Keep this meeting very informal. If parents bring the child, let them know that they too will soon be receiving an invitation to come in and meet with you. This is discussed at length later in this chapter.

Meet with Your Assistant Teacher or Aide Before School Begins (Resource Room and Self-Contained Classroom)

Most special educators in resource rooms and self-contained classrooms have one or more paraprofessionals, aides, or assistant teachers to help them. The best way to get the most from these assistants is to encourage them to take responsibility for getting results in the classroom. To do this, you need to involve them in almost every activity—from duplicating worksheets to supervising the children, planning, grading, keeping records, and teaching. Of course, the level of responsibility will vary among the three positions, depending on their training and job description. Try to get a copy of each individual's job description from central administration or the principal. The job description is usually compiled when hiring for a position. It provides an excellent starting place for discussion and will help you set the right expectations. There are a few commonsense things you can do to help everyone do their best.

Allow your support team to use their abilities and talents; give them the chance to make and try suggestions. Let them see that you appreciate initiative. Make sure they realize that they are essential to the success of the students with whom they work.

Treat your aides, paraprofessionals, and assistant teachers as "second teachers" in the classroom. Encourage them to look around, see what needs to be done, and do it. However, be aware that there could be liability issues if the children are left with an aide, paraprofessional, or assistant teacher who is not a licensed certified teacher. If a child gets hurt or problems arise while you are not in the room, for example, there could be problems. Meet with your supervisor and discuss this matter to see what your guidelines and responsibilities are in these cases.

Make your support team aware of the IEP goals for each student. They will grow personally and professionally if you trust them and let them know you appreciate what they do. For example, short written notes of thanks are a really good practice. You might write: "I want to thank you for being so positive when talking to the students."

First-year teachers are often unsure how to use their helpers. If these individuals are idle, resources are being underutilized. Aides, teaching assistants, and paraprofessionals can perform numerous duties, as we already noted. Working with students, however, whether individually or in small groups, is their most important function.

If problems arise with someone on your team, it may be helpful to meet with the school psychologist, your coordinator of special education, or the principal to find a way to resolve the problems. It is advisable to act promptly in these instances—the longer you wait to talk about a challenging situation, the more difficult it often becomes.

Meet with Your Team Teacher Before School Begins (Inclusion Classroom Only)

A key component in the success of an inclusion classroom is the relationship between the special education teacher and the regular education teacher. Many questions and issues need to be discussed to prevent misconceptions, frustration, or dissension.

Before school begins, talk about your roles and clearly define the professional responsibilities so that there is no confusion. Talk about similarities and differences in teaching styles and how that might affect the students and the presentation of information. Even if your teaching styles are different, they may complement each other.

Also, talk about the delivery systems to be used in the classroom; there are several different methods for instruction and assistance in an inclusion setting. Alternative delivery systems are management systems that provide support for students and maximize learning while presenting the core curriculum. The goal is to develop many creative ways of working together for the benefit of all students. Because there are many different approaches, it is best to find one on which you and your team teacher agree. Here are some examples that you may want to consider.

Team Teaching

Cooperative teaching, sometimes called coteaching, is an educational approach in which general and special educators, as well as specialists from other programs, are simultaneously present in the general education classroom, sharing responsibility for some specific classroom instruction. This approach allows the successful integration of the teaching because the classroom teacher is teamed with the specialist.

General and special educators jointly plan how to teach academic subject content to all students. The general education teacher is responsible for the entire class, while the special educator is responsible for implementing the IEP goals for the special education students.

Complementary Teaching

In this approach the general education teacher assumes primary responsibility for teaching specific subject matter, while the specialist has responsibility for teaching academic survival skills necessary for the special education students to access and master the core curriculum. The content may be delivered in the classroom and complemented when the special education students are pulled out of the classroom to another setting. The critical difference between complementary instruction and a traditional pullout program is that the two professionals prepare instruction together and deliver it in the general classroom. Specific types of complementary instruction include these:

- *One teaches, one observes.* In this approach one teacher leads the lesson while the other gathers specific predetermined information—such as writing skills, attention to task, and attention span—on certain students. It is important that both teachers switch off roles so that more than one perception is used in making academic decisions for students.
- *One teaches, one supports.* Here the regular education teacher is responsible for teaching the curriculum while the role of the special education teacher is to move among all children with a disability and answer questions, monitor class notes, explain the material and assignments, and work closely with the students to help level the playing field for them.
- *Station teaching.* One teacher presents half the content to half the students while the other teaches the other half of the content to the rest of the class. The student groups are then switched and each teacher repeats his or her lesson.

- *Parallel teaching.* In this type of arrangement, the teachers divide the class into two heterogeneous groups and each teacher presents a lesson to half the class. Sometimes a third independent study group can be established as well to reduce the number of students in each group.
- *Alternate teaching.* Here, the two teachers divide the whole group into one large group and one small one. This system allows the use of remediation with the small group of students, who might require more individual attention.

Set Up Your Classroom Design (Resource Room and Self-Contained Classroom)

How you set up the physical structure of your classroom is a personal choice. There are several designs to consider.

In the *station-oriented* model, the room is divided into stations that contain specific content area materials. For example, there might be a reading center, math center, computer center, writing center, and so on, to which specific children go to work on their specific IEP goals.

In the *child-oriented* model, the room is arranged so that the children are separated. This avoids distraction and helps increase concentration. In this setting, the teacher moves from student to student. Because most of the work is individualized, the teacher and the assistants can work on specific areas of weakness for a particular child.

In the *teacher-centered* model, the teacher's work table or area is the center of the room. In this way, the teacher can work with several children at a time and monitor their progress. If the teacher feels one child needs less distraction, she can move the child to another part of the room to work with or without an assistant teacher.

Set Up Your Classroom Design (Inclusion Classroom)

In this instance there is really very little classroom setup to do. In elementary inclusion classes, the regular education teacher will set up the room. In this case assist the teacher, making suggestions if you feel they will better serve the population of children with disabilities—for example, suggest setting up a quiet corner or study carrel to avoid distractions. At the high school level, there may be even less to do in setting up the room because many teachers will be using the same room. However, again, assist the teacher and suggest anything that you feel might help your students.

Communicate and Interact with Parents (Resource Room, Self-Contained Classroom, and Elementary-Level Inclusion Classroom)

Your first goal in working with parents is to help them participate in meetings, conferences, and other interactions in a way that is meaningful and respectful. Consequently, the first order of business is to introduce yourself to the parents of the children with whom you will be working. You can do this by sending home an introductory letter in which you inform parents of your background and experience, your hopes and goals, and your desire to collaborate with and keep them informed of their child's progress throughout the year. On the elementary level you may want to invite them in to meet with you individually, and then in late September hold a group meeting for all parents. It is a good idea to meet individually first in case one parent among them is very angry at the system, school, and so on. You do not want to take the chance that this parent might use the group meeting as a platform for his personal issues. By meeting with such parents alone first you may be able to reassure them or defuse their concerns. Because the caseloads in these settings are smaller, this plan should be realistic.

When you meet with the parents, be sure to discuss the following issues so that everything is clear from the outset: parents' role and responsibilities, parental expectations, parents' involvement with homework, and means of communication between home and school and between school and home, such as by phone, letter, progress reports, or e-mail.

Communicate and Interact with Parents (Secondary-Level Inclusion Classroom)

The secondary school setting does not lend itself to individual meetings with parents because special education teachers may be working with class totals of over one hundred students, both with and without disabilities, every day. But communication with the parents of children with disabilities is still necessary. You may still want to send home an introductory letter, but not suggest an individual meeting before school begins. Instead, you can learn more about each child from the parents by including a questionnaire, checklist, or both. Friend (2002) provides the following series of questions, which can serve as a structure for such a questionnaire or checklist:

1. What is your child's favorite class activity?
2. Does your child have any worries about class activities? If so, what are they?
3. What are your priorities for your child's education this year?
4. What questions do you have about your child's education in my class this year?
5. How could we at school make this the most successful year ever for your child?
6. Are there any topics you want to discuss that may require a conference? If so, please let me know.
7. If a conference is requested, would you like other individuals to participate? If so, please give me a list of their names so that I can invite them.
8. If a conference is requested, would you like me to have particular school information available? If so, please let me know.
9. If you have any questions that I may be able to answer by phone, you can reach me between 7:30 and 8:10 A.M. and between 3:00 and 3:30 P.M. at the following number ______. If you prefer you can reach me by e-mail at _______. (Providing your e-mail address is optional, and of course you will provide the hours that suit your schedule best.)

In your initial letter to the parents, be sure to clarify the same issues as indicated earlier for the other settings: parents' role and responsibilities, parental expectations of the school and their child, parents' involvement with homework, and means of communication between home and school and between school and home.

Communicate with Related Service Providers

It is imperative that you maintain close communication with every related service provider involved with your students (for example, occupational therapist, speech language therapist, and so on). You want to maintain the most up-to-date information in case you are questioned by parents, students, or administrators. To set up these lines of communication, take the following steps.

First, send out letters to the related service providers for each child, introducing yourself and asking for a time to get together. Outline your objectives for this meeting, including coordination of services, avoiding scheduling conflicts, and communication and IEP development.

At the meeting, discuss goals of the service, expectations, communication with parents, and establish a schedule of collaboration meetings for the upcoming school year to discuss the child's progress.

If you are designated as the case manager for the IEP, which is a strong possibility, find out how you will get the information that you will need from these service providers as you help develop the new IEP at the annual review meeting.

Also find out as much as you can about the child's specific problem, cause (etiology), and outcome (prognosis) from the service provider.

Communicate with Classroom Teachers (Resource Room Only)

As a resource room teacher, one of your most important responsibilities after assisting children is dealing with the classroom teachers. Your main role here will be to help adapt the curriculum, monitor modifications, prepare adapted materials for the children to use in the classroom, provide information and suggestions on the children's disabilities, and provide alternate curriculum materials suited to their skill levels. Many of these curriculum concerns are discussed in the next chapter, "Curriculum Considerations for Special Educators."

The first thing you should do as a new teacher in a school is place a letter in the classroom teachers' mailboxes introducing yourself, offering some background information, and listing the names of the children you wish to discuss. Explain that you will personally contact the teachers for a convenient time to meet to discuss any issues pertaining to the children receiving resource room services. A similar letter, adapted accordingly, should be sent even by teachers who are not new to a school.

During this personal meeting with the classroom teachers, there are several objectives. First, define your responsibilities and the resources you can provide to the teacher, including information on the disability, ideas for adapting materials, and more suitable materials for the children's skill levels.

Discuss scheduling the children's time in the resource room to avoid the possibility of fragmentation. As was explained earlier, fragmentation occurs when a child leaves the classroom to go to the resource room in the middle of a lesson and returns in the middle of another. It can be detrimental to many children who are already confused by the demands of the curriculum. Work with the classroom teachers to find a convenient time that will ease the transition for the child to and from the room.

Discuss the children's classroom and test modifications outlined in the IEP and leave the teachers with a written statement of these modifications. Discuss how these should be implemented in the classroom. Also, go over the children's IEPs step by step so that the teachers are fully aware of what the eligibility committee has determined.

Discuss any curriculum concerns that the teachers may have and offer alternatives and options. (The next chapter discusses these subjects.)

Finally, talk about how to coordinate parent communication: how often to hold parent meetings or send home communications, such as progress reports, and what kind of information will be reported to parents.

Communicate with the Classroom Teachers with Whom Your Students Will Be Mainstreamed (Self-Contained Classroom Only)

At times during the school year you may consider mainstreaming a child in your class into the regular education program. Mainstreaming can be anywhere from five minutes to five hours or more, depending on the needs and tolerances of the child. When the mainstreaming team (a group of school staff members—a psychologist and the classroom teacher where the child will be mainstreamed—and the parent and child) decides to move a child for a portion of the school day into the regular education program, several issues need to be discussed with the mainstream teacher. This communication is crucial, because the regular education teacher may have serious concerns or apprehensions about this arrangement. Be sure to cover the following:

- Define your responsibilities and the resources you can provide the teacher when the child is in that classroom, including specific information on the child's disability, with Internet sites and names of books or articles the teacher may want to research; adaptive materials that could be used in the classroom to increase the child's chances of completion and success and avoid frustration; finding more suitable materials for the child's skill levels; monitoring progress; meeting with the child before and after the mainstream experience to alleviate any concerns that might arise; meeting with the teacher on a regular basis to answer any questions and solve any issues that need to be addressed.
- Discuss the child's classroom and test modifications outlined on the IEP and leave the teacher with a written statement of these modifications. Discuss how these should be implemented in the classroom.
- Go over the child's IEP step by step so that the teacher is fully aware of what has been determined by the eligibility committee.

- Discuss any curriculum concerns that the teacher may have and offer alternatives and options. (See the next chapter for more on this.)
- Talk about how to coordinate parent communication. Discuss how often to hold parent meetings or send home communications, such as progress reports, and what kind of communication will be reported to parents.
- Discuss specific goals you have for the child—academic, behavioral, social, and emotional—and how you will go about determining whether the situation is working for the child and for the teacher.

In conclusion, in this chapter we have reviewed how to begin the school year as a special education teacher in a resource room, a self-contained classroom, or an inclusion setting. If you follow these suggestions, it should increase your chances of success and help establish your position in a positive manner with students, other teachers, and parents.

Chapter 17

Curriculum Considerations for Special Educators

Children and adults are exposed to a variety of stressors on any given day. When children are stressed, it may manifest itself in dysfunctional behavior at school. All problems create tension, and the tension must be relieved either verbally or behaviorally. If a child is unable to communicate his feelings, as is the case with most children, that tension will exhibit itself in symptomatic behavior. Although such behavior does not always indicate a serious problem, if it is frequent, intense, and long-lasting, it usually does.

Teachers are confronted with symptomatic behavior every day. If they do not understand the nature of the symptoms, they will treat them like problems. Treating a fever like the problem will never cure the infection. Although it is true that teachers need not "cure" the problem, they do need to recognize symptom patterns of a more serious condition so that they can make the proper referrals.

If a teacher understands the nature of the symptomatic behavior and makes the proper referrals for guidance, then a more serious problem can be averted. However, even if correctly identified, a child's symptomatic behavior may take a while to dissipate. It is during this time that teachers can use certain techniques to calm the child, provide suitable boundaries, reduce classroom frustration, and so on, while the real problem is being resolved. Later chapters in this part of the book provide you with such techniques.

Stress Factors Affecting Children

First, however, we will discuss eight important factors that can cause stress in a child's life. If intense enough, any of them can create classroom symptoms resulting in academic, behavioral, or social dysfunction.

Academic Factors

Academic deficits impair a child's ability to function in the classroom. Factors that can contribute to academic dysfunction include developmental reading disorders, developmental math disorders, developmental writing disorders, developmental spelling disorders, poor prior teaching, lack of basic skills, inconsistency during critical periods of skill development, problems in concept formation, and lack of reinforcement.

Environmental Factors

Environmental factors are the circumstances at home or in the community that have a profound impact on a child's ability to function in school. They include home issues such as parental abuse, parental fighting, separation, divorce, family illness, economic hardships, a parent's loss of job, moving to a new neighborhood, serious sibling rivalry, family mental illness, relatives residing in the home, alcoholism, and drug abuse. Environmental factors may also originate in the community, such as problems with neighbors, poor reputation in the neighborhood, isolation of the family from neighbors, and problems with the law.

Intellectual Factors

Sometimes a child's difficulties in school are the result of intellectual factors. Some of the factors included in this category are undetected limited intellectual ability and undetected gifted intellectual capacity.

Language Factors

Language is the foundation for all communication, problem solving, integrating, analyzing, and synthesizing knowledge. Therefore, deficits in language can have a profound impact on an individual's ability to learn and function competently and confidently as he interacts in the world.

Language development difficulties, too, can result in classroom symptoms. These difficulties may be in nonverbal language, oral language (that is, listening and speaking), written language (that is, reading and writing), pragmatic language (using language for a specific purpose such as asking for help), phonology, audiology, word retrieval, articulation, receptive aphasia, expressive aphasia, and bilingualism.

Medical Factors

Numerous medical factors may contribute to a child's academic dysfunction. Although a serious medical condition is likely to have already been identified by the child's pediatrician or parent, this is not always the case, especially with very young children. Certain more common medical problems that may impair a child's ability to function adequately in the classroom include attention deficit disorder, vision problems, hearing problems, neurological problems, muscular problems, and coordination problems.

Perceptual Factors

Perceptual issues can impair a child's ability to function in the classroom. Although perceptual deficits are often misunderstood or undiagnosed, they account for a large number of high-risk children. Most of us take perception for granted, but for some children it represents a very difficult, frustrating, and deflating experience. If you can identify symptoms that may be caused by serious perceptual deficits, it can reduce a child's frustration, both inside and outside the classroom.

Psychological Factors

Psychological factors that may contribute to a child's dysfunction in school include clinical depression, mental illness, anxiety, eating disorders, personality disorders, schizophrenia, phobias, obsessive compulsive disorders, psychosexual dysfunction, substance abuse, sleep disorders, brief situational disturbances or adjustment reactions, conduct disorders, separation anxiety, and oppositional defiant disorders.

Social Factors

Social factors may contribute to a child's stress and consequently interfere with learning. Although social status is a crucial factor at many ages, it becomes particularly crucial as children approach adolescence. Social pressures and peer influence sometimes create an imbalance in a child's functioning, and this often results in lower available energy for school because of the intense need for energy to cope with his social world or social conflicts. Such social factors include peer rejection, preoccupation with boyfriend or girlfriend, low social status, social victimization, scapegoating, social intimidation, bullying behavior, social control issues (the need to be in control), peer competition, social isolation, and social overindulgence.

Adapting the Curriculum for Students with Disabilities

When you work with a population of students with disabilities, you will have to learn how to adapt and modify the curriculum so that the students have a better chance of success and task completion. The Ministry of Education of British Columbia (1995), for example, suggests the following ways to adapt the science curriculum.

When a student with special needs is expected to achieve or surpass the learning outcomes established in the science curriculum, regular grading practices and reporting procedures are followed. For students not expected to achieve the learning outcomes, adaptations and modifications must be noted in the Individualized Education Program. In this way, instructional and assessment methods may be adapted to meet the needs of all students.

To help students with special needs achieve success in science, you may want to try the following:

- *Adapt the environment:* Change where the student sits in the classroom, make use of cooperative grouping.
- *Adapt presentations:* Provide students in advance with organizers of key scientific concepts, demonstrate or model new concepts, adapt the pace of activities.
- *Adapt materials:* Use large-print activity sheets, use overlays on text pages to reduce the quantity of print that is visible, highlight key points on the activity sheet.
- *Adapt assistance:* Use peers or volunteers to assist students with special needs, use students with special needs to assist younger students in learning science, use teacher assistants to work with small groups of students as well as with an identified student with special needs, use consultants and support teachers for problem solving and to assist in developing strategies for science instruction.
- *Adapt assessment:* Provide various ways for students to demonstrate their understanding of scientific concepts, such as performing experiments, creating displays and models, and tape recording observations.
- *Expand assessment tools* such as paper-and-pencil tests to include such options as oral tests, open-book tests, and tests with no time limits. Keep work samples on NCR paper. Use computer programs that provide opportunities for scientific practice and recording results.

- *Provide opportunities for extension and practice:* Require small amounts of work to be completed at a given time. Simplify the way questions are worded to match the students' level of understanding. Provide functional everyday examples, such as building structures to develop an understanding of forces.

If you are working in a regular school district, you will likely come into contact with high-incidence disabilities, including learning disabilities, mental retardation, emotional disabilities, and other health impaired children, such as those with attention deficit hyperactive disorder. This section deals with curriculum adaptations for these specific disabilities.

Learning Disabilities

Although not all techniques work with all students, teachers should nevertheless try as many of them as possible. These techniques should create a better learning environment for children with learning disabilities.

Make adjustments in the type, difficulty, amount, and sequence of materials:

- Give shorter but more frequent assignments.
- Shorten the length of the assignments to ensure a sense of success.
- Hand out copies of textbook chapters so that the children can use a highlighter pen to underline important facts.
- Make sure that the children's desks are free from all unnecessary materials.
- Correct the children's work as soon as possible to allow for immediate gratification and feedback.
- Allow children several alternatives in both obtaining and reporting information—tapes, interviews, and so on.
- Break assignments down into smaller units. Allow the children to do five problems at a time, or write five sentences, so that they can feel success, receive immediate feedback if they are doing the assignment incorrectly, and direct their energy to more manageable tasks.
- Hold frequent, if short, conferences with the children to allow them to ask questions, clear up confusion, create a sense of connection, and avoid the feelings of isolation that often occur if the work is too difficult.

Adjust space, work time, and grouping:

- Permit these children to work in a quiet corner or a study carrel when requested or necessary. This should not be a permanent situation because isolation may have negative consequences. However, these children will be less distracted working under these conditions.
- Try moving such children closer to you for more immediate feedback.
- Try to separate them from other students who may be distracting.
- Alternate quiet and active time to maintain levels of interest and motivation.
- Make up a work contract with specific times and assignments so that the children have a structured idea of their responsibilities.

- Keep work periods short and gradually lengthen them as the students begin to cope.
- Try to match each learning disabled student with a peer helper to help with understanding assignments, read important directions, do oral drills, summarize important textbook passages, and work on long-range assignments.

Also, consider adjusting presentation and evaluation modes. Some students learn better by seeing (they are visual learners), some by listening (auditory learners), some by feeling (tactile learners), and some by a combination of approaches. Make adjustments to determine the best functional system of learning for your students with learning disabilities. This will vary from child to child and is usually included in the child's last evaluation.

For children who are primarily auditory learners, offer adjustments in the mode of presentation as follows:

- Give verbal as well as written directions on assignments.
- Place assignment directions on tape so that students can replay them when they need to.
- Give students oral rather than written tests.
- Have students drill on important information using a tape recorder, reciting information into the recorder, and playing it back.
- Have students drill aloud to themselves or to other students.
- Have the children close their eyes to try and hear words or information.

For children who are primarily visual learners, adjust the mode of presentation as follows:

- Have students use flash cards printed in bold bright colors.
- Let students close their eyes and try to visualize words or information in their heads, to see things in their minds.
- Provide visual clues on the chalkboard for all verbal directions.
- Encourage students to write down notes and memos to themselves concerning important words, concepts, and ideas.

Retardation

What is a mental disability?

A student can be defined as having a mental disability if she exhibits certain learning, social, and behavioral patterns to a marked extent and over a prolonged period of time. Such patterns may include a consistently subaverage intellectual level; impaired adaptive functioning in such areas as social skills, communication, and daily living skills; consistently slow rate of learning with a resultant level of development resembling that of a younger child; and delays in most areas of development.

Some common characteristics of a mild mental disability that you may observe over a period of time include academic underachievement, difficulty with abstract concepts, difficulty generalizing learned concepts to new situations, social isolation or withdrawal, poor social relationships, anxious and worried behavior, including excessive fears and phobias, frustration even when confronted with a simple task, resistance to change, and short attention span.

Students who are mildly mentally disabled learn in the same way as normal students. However, adaptations and a variety of techniques need to be employed. Consequently, certain areas should be targeted as priorities for these children in the classroom. These target areas are functional academics, general work habits, and career awareness. Teachers should try to focus on one area at a time.

Functional Academics

In general, design practice activities in any basic skill that relates to the children's daily life problems. Provide materials that are commensurate with their skill levels. Provide activities that will reinforce independent work. If the activity is too hard, these children may become too dependent on teacher supervision.

When it comes to reading, provide activities that focus on reading for information and leisure. Provide activities that require the children to become more aware of their surrounding environment. For example, having them list the names of all food stores in the community, or all hospitals, and so on, will increase their familiarity with their surrounding environment. Have them collect food labels and compare them. Allow the children in your class to look up the names of all their families in the phone book. (Use the smaller local guide for this activity.) Develop activities that will allow them to become familiar with menus, bus and train schedules, movie and television timetables, or job advertisements.

To develop handwriting and spelling skills, have the children make a list of things to do for the day. Have one child run a messenger service in the classroom so that he can write the messages and deliver them from one student to another. Provide activities for older children that incorporate daily writing skills necessary for independence, such as social security forms, driver's license applications, bank account applications, and so on.

In math, have the children buy something at the school store. Have them make up a budget for their allowance. Encourage them to cook at school or at home so that they can become more familiar with measurements. Have them record the daily temperature. Involve them in measuring the height of classmates. Have older children apply for a loan or credit card. Show the children how to use a daily planning book. Provide activities that teach the children how to comparison-shop. Provide them with a pretend amount of money and a toy catalogue, and have them purchase items and fill out the forms.

General Work Habits

This skill area is composed of many skill areas that are necessary to allow the children to succeed in a regular classroom. They include the following:

- *Work completion.* Reward activities contingent upon successful completion of work. Have the children maintain a performance chart on the number of tasks completed each day. Evaluate the length and level of an assignment to make sure it is within the ability level of these children. Give shorter but more frequent assignments. Build a foundation of success by providing a series of successful assignments. In this way they can gain a sense of confidence.

- *Attendance and punctuality.* Communicate the importance of being on time to class. Be clear about your expectations for attendance and punctuality. Have the children maintain a record of attendance and on-time behavior. Develop a pretend time clock that they have to punch in when entering the classroom. Encourage punctuality by scheduling a favorite activity in the morning. Have the children sign a contract establishing consequences for tardiness and rewards for on-time behavior.
- *Working with others.* Provide these children with small group activities that are geared to their ability levels. Use peer tutors so that relationships can be established. Have the children participate in many group activities that require sorting, pasting, addressing, folding, simple assembly, and so on. Provide them with some simple job that requires other students to go to them. For example, put one child in charge of attendance and have him check off the children when they report in. Help them start a hobby and then form a hobby club involving other students. Put a child on a team that takes care of the class pet or is involved in some other class activity. (Calling it a team will make the child feel more connected.) Speak with the school psychologist and see if she can run a social, hobby, or project-oriented group in your classroom.

Career Awareness

Career awareness is a skill that can be adapted to the classroom curriculum in many ways. Many of the skills already mentioned will enhance your students' career skills.

Emotional Disabilities

It may not be necessary to adapt the curriculum for students with emotional disabilities. These children's issues more than likely can be addressed through the classroom management techniques that are described in the next chapter. If you wish to adapt the curriculum, however, you may take some of the suggestions described in the other disability areas of this chapter.

Attention Deficit Hyperactive Disorder (ADHD)

Classroom teachers of children with ADHD can adjust certain factors to accommodate the individual curriculum to the needs of these children. They need the most help in organizational skills and academic skills.

Organizational Ability

Children with ADHD usually keep very disorganized notes, notebooks, desks, and lockers. Make it a weekly task to have these children organize these areas. Make it part of their contract. The routine will also make them feel better about themselves.

Ask the parents to help organize their child at night. Have them develop a checklist so that the child's clothes, books, assignments, and so on are ready for the next morning. The stress and disorganization of the morning should be avoided at all costs. This will also make the child feel more secure when going to school.

Prepare a copy of your homework assignments and hand it to these children at the end of the day. This will alleviate a great deal of stress for these children, especially if they are disorganized and frequently forget to copy the homework. The goal here is to create a comfortable environment. In this case, having the children accomplish the homework is more important than having them surmount the difficulty of copying down the assignment.

Avoid giving multiple directions or multiple assignments. Allow these children to finish one assignment or direction at a time before going on to the next.

Reinforce the use of word processing, typing, spell-checkers on the computer, and use of the computer in general. This device can be very motivating and the end product (that is, a typed report) will make these children feel good about themselves.

Academic Skills

Allow these children to use graph paper while doing math. In this way they will have a structured environment in which to place numbers. Use very large graph paper so that they have little difficulty placing one number in each box. This will keep them organized and focused.

Allow them to use a calculator or basic math tables when doing their assignments. The goal here is for successful accomplishment of the assignment. If they become frustrated because they can't recall the facts, they may give up.

Do not use bubble sheets. Allow these children to answer questions directly in the test booklet or on a piece of paper. Reducing the amount of movement during academic tasks is more beneficial because ADHD children have difficulty refocusing.

Use manipulative materials as often as possible. Also, use books on tape, or ask the parents to tape-record a chapter of your textbook so that their child can read and listen at the same time.

Window out single math problems so that the child only sees one at a time. This can be accomplished by cutting out a square on a piece of paper that the child can move from one problem to the next. When she does this, all the other problems will be covered.

Allow older children to have a sheet with the formulas already printed. Asking them to memorize may reduce their ability to accomplish the task. The less they have to worry about, the more likely they may be to finish.

Determine what your goal is when presenting an assignment. Once you have done this, pave all the roads for the children up to that point. For example, if your goal is to see if the children can find the circumference of a circle, provide them with the formulas, definitions, and examples. These materials will reduce frustration and confusion and will increase chances of success.

Have these children do five problems, two questions, and so on, at a time. Then have them come up for immediate feedback. Numerous successful tasks can only add to their confidence levels. This will also prevent them from progressing too far while making the same error.

Use unison reading when you have these children read aloud. This means that both you and the child have the same book and read out loud together. The added sensory feedback and pacing will keep these children focused.

Try to use interactive CD reading programs. The multisensory stimulation will keep these children focused. However, make sure the program does not require them to do too many tasks at one time because this could overload them.

Tips for Teachers Working with Children with ADHD

- Learn as much as you can about ADHD. See Appendix H at the back of this book for the names of organizations that can help you identify behavior support strategies and effective ways to support the student educationally. Some strategies follow here as well.
- Figure out what specific things are hard for your students. For example, one student with ADHD may have trouble starting a task, whereas another may have trouble ending one task and starting the next. Each student needs help in a different area.
- Post rules, schedules, and assignments. Clear rules and routines will help a student with ADHD. Have set times for specific tasks. Call attention to changes in the schedule.
- Show students how to use an assignment book and a daily schedule. Also teach study skills and learning strategies, and reinforce these regularly.
- Help students channel their physical energy—for example, let them do some work standing up or at the board. Be sure to provide regularly scheduled breaks.
- Give step-by-step directions, and make sure that these students are following the directions. Give directions both verbally and in writing. Many students with ADHD also benefit from doing the steps as separate tasks.
- As noted earlier, let these students work on a computer.
- Work together with the students' parents to create and implement an educational plan tailored to meet their needs. Regularly talk to the parents about how their child is doing at home and at school.
- Have high expectations for these students, but be willing to try new ways of doing things.
- Be patient. Maximize these students' chances for success by presenting tasks with a high success rate.

Chapter 18

Classroom Management Techniques for Children with Disabilities

In this chapter we offer some practical information on a variety of disabilities you may find in your classroom: personality problems, emotional problems, ADHD, autism, traumatic brain injury, physical disabilities, and visual and hearing problems.

A Review of Different Personality Problems

The classroom techniques we suggest are not intended to replace therapeutic treatment. Guidance counselors, nurses, doctors, school psychologists, and outside agencies should provide therapeutic treatment. Regardless of the resources used, however, the classroom teacher bears the brunt of these children's personality issues. If your attitude and actions are intelligent, constructive, and immediate, you can be a tremendous help.

Keep in mind that there are many overlapping characteristics in the personality types described here. Also, every child does not evidence all the symptoms listed. Look for a pattern of behavior. Remember, too, that there is always something to like about every child.

The Aggressive Child

- *Symptoms.* The aggressive child looks for trouble, wants his own way, is always on the defensive, blames others for inappropriate behavior, is quarrelsome, disrupts class and routine procedures, destroys property, is resentful, defiant, rude, sullen, or insolent, defies authority, or may bully other children.
- *Possible reasons for behavior.* This child may have domineering, overstrict parents, or weak overindulgent parents who give into the child's every whim. He may fear expressing feelings to his parents—and thus take it out on other children. He may feel a lack of affection from his parents. He may be unhappy in his relations with others. He may be masking intense feelings of vulnerability or inadequacy.
- *Suggestions.* Direct this child's energy to keep him busy. Give him large-muscle activities to do. Give him leadership responsibilities. Place him on a daily progress report so that positive changes are seen immediately. Reprimand in private. Attempt to reach or make friends with the child. Meet with him more often on a one-to-one basis. Give simple but definite standards of conduct. Hold conferences

with parents and the student. Let him work with modeling clay to release frustrations. Recommend individual or group in-school counseling. Shape positive behavior with success-oriented tasks. Try to reward or compliment when he least expects it.

- *Things to keep in mind.* Improvement will usually be slow, especially if symptoms are historic. The child's parents may not recognize or may deny the problem. There will be relapses even with improvement. Arguing will not solve the problem. Think over your own feelings and actions toward the child, and be sure his actions are not just "normal" misbehaving.

The Withdrawn Child

- *Symptoms.* This child talks in a very soft voice, sits quietly most of the time, has difficulty carrying on a conversation, withdraws and hangs back, has few if any friends, has difficulty making decisions, may be fearful of adults, tires without apparent reason, and avoids contact with people.
- *Possible reasons for behavior.* The family may behave in the same way. The child may fear failure and therefore not try anything. She may come from an overly critical home, her parents may be perfectionists. She may have low energy levels resulting from depression. She may be extremely overprotected (learned helplessness).
- *Suggestions.* Praise, notice, and talk with her. Find occasions for errands, first with no oral message and later with very simple messages. Always call on her when volunteering. Have a smile ready for her any time you catch her eye. Use puppets and have the child talk for the puppet. Try to get her interested in collecting things, such as baseball cards, coins, and so on. Give routine tasks with automatic rotation, such as leading the pledge or taking the lunch count. Try to get her involved in a group with other shy children in the school.
- *Things to keep in mind.* This child will need to know exactly what to do in each situation. Pushing her into the limelight may make the problem worse. Make sure other children do not always do things for the child or come to her rescue; courage follows success. Improvement will be slow and growth may be gradual. The child may have some health problem or hidden physical abnormality.

The Underachieving Child

- *Symptoms.* The underachieving child avoids effort—dawdles over writing assignments. She does messy, incomplete work. She waits for help and does not try to solve problems, tends to be listless and careless, seldom volunteers, gives many excuses for failure to complete work. She is slow in starting a task or assignment—can't find pencil or paper, for example, and is slow in doing or finishing anything. She daydreams, lacks concentration on work.
- *Possible reasons for behavior.* There may be frustration that the work is too difficult. There may be inappropriate parental expectations. The child may experience too many failures and too few successes, receive little praise and much criticism. In contrast, she may lack challenging school work. There may be health or physical deficiencies or the behavior may be a cover-up for lack of ability. Finally, she may stay up too late or not get restful sleep.

- *Suggestions.* Praise the child for each effort. Study her home life—talk to parents. Help develop a skill or hobby at which she might succeed. Overlook minor failures. Study results of diagnostic tests for clues, adjust work to her ability level, time her assignments and try to have her beat her own record. See that she starts work more promptly by helping her through transitions. Use shorter but more frequent assignments.
- *Things to keep in mind.* Praising good work promotes activity. Laziness is not normal—it is a symptom. A lazy child has some sort of problem. Laziness may disappear during later stages of development. Laziness is not necessarily an indication of intelligence. Make sure the student's work meets certain standards before acceptance.

The Frightened Child

- *Symptoms.* The frightened child panics easily or gets frustrated, shows anxiety, withdraws, may tremble at the slightest provocation, may be moody, may be overly afraid of being hurt, rarely takes chances, may be extremely emotional, fears criticism, or requires constant reassurance.
- *Possible reasons for behavior.* This child's parents may also have fears and openly express them. Perhaps there has been a death or an injury to someone close to them. They may be overly protective parents. There may be a history of unfortunate or traumatic experiences. Or the child may be given constant and harsh punishments, there may be slow physical development, or there may be bullying playmates.
- *Suggestions.* Try a variety of creative activities to release the child's fears. Have the child write an article on "Things That Make Me Afraid." Reassure him whenever he shows fear. Suggest to the parents that they seek outside consultation if the pattern is historical. Give him work at which he can succeed; build up his confidence by using a variety of success-oriented tasks. Praise him for his accomplishments. Explain that others also have fears. Check his health record. Organize a group of children who suffer from the same condition.
- *Things to keep in mind.* The child's fears may be imaginary. As his teacher, your own reactions are important because they affect the child. Fears melt before affection. Fears also diminish with maturity. It is natural for most people to fear some things.

The Slow Learning Child

- *Symptoms.* This child may have a short attention span, may not be able to generalize, may feel insecure, may consistently achieve below grade level, may have a low intellectual ability, may withdraw and not participate. She also likely seldom volunteers in class, has trouble getting started, and has trouble finishing assignments.
- *Possible reasons for behavior.* There may be a familial pattern of slow learners, a lack of environmental stimulation in the home, or possible learning disabilities, especially if greater potential is indicated despite a low intellectual quotient. Frequent illness may be causing gaps in critical stages of learning. There may be

rejection by parents or playmates, poor nutrition, or severe emotionality interfering in cognitive functioning.

- *Suggestions.* Provide many learning materials at her level of ability. Ask for an evaluation using individual tests, such as intellectual and academic. Give her many opportunities for success and to feel a sense of achievement. Try to get her interested in hobbies or extracurricular activities. Provide a place to work where distractions are at a minimum. Investigate her physical and health condition. Praise her whenever possible and build up her good qualities. Have her work with a peer tutor. Make the parents aware of her limitations so that they do not add to the problem with inappropriate demands.
- *Things to keep in mind.* Parents often reject the idea that their child is a true slow learner. However, requiring more of this child than she can do will cause frustration. Improvement in academic achievement will always be slow. Expect the child to achieve only up to her ability. Be careful that she doesn't get "lost in the crowd."

It is important to remember, too, that the learning disabled child and the slow learner exhibit many of the same behaviors. However, there are distinct differences between these two groups. A true slow learner presents an intellectual pattern in the low average range—usually an IQ between approximately 75 and 89. This pattern is consistent with past evaluations and does not indicate any further potential indicated by the scatter of the scores. A child with learning disabilities may also score in the low average range, but his pattern indicates greater potential, probably well within the average or even the above-average range.

A true slow learner will never perform at grade level in all areas. The underlying assumption with learning disabled children is that they will attain grade-level performance with support and modifications. A learning disabled child shows a marked discrepancy between intellectual potential and academic achievement. A slow learner will have academic percentiles very close to his intellectual ability.

Classroom Management Techniques for Children with Emotional Issues

What is emotional disturbance?

A student may be defined as having an emotional disability if he or she exhibits certain behavior patterns to a marked extent and over a prolonged period of time. Such patterns are as follows:

- An inability to learn on a consistent basis that cannot be explained by intellectual capability, hearing and vision status, or physical health anomalies
- An inability or unwillingness to develop or maintain satisfactory interpersonal relationships with peers, teachers, parents, or other adults
- Extreme overreactions to minimally stressful situations over a prolonged period of time
- A generally pervasive mood of sadness or depression
- A tendency to develop somatic complaints, pains, or excessive fears associated with home, school, or social situations

Some common characteristics of emotional disorders that you may observe over a period of time include academic underachievement, social isolation or withdrawal, excessive lateness, excessive absences, frequent trips to the nurse, negativism, open defiance to authority or rules, extreme distractibility, poor social relationships, feelings of hopelessness, verbal aggression, confrontational behavior, inappropriate classroom behaviors, impulsive behavior, rigid behavior patterns, anxious and worried behavior, excessive fears and phobias, frustration even when confronted with a simple task, and resistance to change.

Because the behavior of emotionally disabled children can vary from withdrawal, in the case of depression, to aggressive tendencies, in the case of a conduct disorder, you need to be aware of techniques to employ in a variety of situations. However, certain basic behaviors should be targeted as priorities when dealing with emotionally disabled children in the classroom. These behaviors include attendance and tardiness; challenges to authority, inappropriate verbalizations, and outbursts; incomplete class work; difficulty remaining seated; developing social relationships; and following directions and paying attention.

Although many or all of these behaviors may be exhibited by the emotionally disabled child, try to focus on one target pattern at a time. Patience, fairness, willingness to confront inappropriate behaviors, a sense of conviction in maintaining boundaries, and a sense of fair play in establishing consequences are all qualities required by the teacher in these situations.

Problems with Attendance and Tardiness

Reward these children for being on time. The reward can be extra free time, a token (if a token economy is being used), a congratulatory note home, a verbal compliment, and so on. (*Token economy* refers to the use of tokens, such as stars, points, candy, to reinforce various behaviors.) Work with the parents on rewarding on-time behavior. Plan a special activity in the morning. Use a chart to visually describe a child's pattern of punctuality and lateness; this will reduce the child's level of denial and may make him more aware of his behavior. Encourage and help these children to start a club in their area of greatest interest and make participation contingent on a positive pattern of attendance. Use a point system for on-time attendance; the points may be later turned in for class privileges. Set up a buddy system if the children walk to school to encourage on-time behavior. Set up a nightly contract for the children, listing all the things they need to do to make the morning easier to manage. Have the parent sign it and reward their child when he brings it in.

Challenges to Authority, Inappropriate Verbalizations, and Outbursts

Arrange a time-out area in the classroom. In this case, the amount of time spent in the area is not so significant as your ability to begin the time-out and end it. Therefore, make the time-out period a duration that you can control. Structure a time when these children are allowed to speak to you freely without an audience around. In this way, they will have an opportunity to speak their concerns rather than act them out. It will also allow you to deflect any confrontations to that specific time. Approach these children as often as possible and ask them if there is anything bothering them that they would like to speak about. Offering them the opportunity, even if they refuse, may reduce their need for "spotlight" behaviors in front of the class.

Provide an emotional vocabulary so that the children can label their feelings. Tension is expressed either verbally or behaviorally. Providing them with the proper labels may reduce their frustration. Move these students away from those who might set them off. Preempt their behavior by waiting outside before class and telling them in private what you expect during class. Also make them aware of the rewards and consequences of their actions. Offer other options and indicate that any inappropriateness is their decision. Making the children aware that behavior is their responsibility allows them to realize that not doing something inappropriate is also in their control. Establish clear classroom rules stating rewards and consequences. Always praise students for complying with rules and carrying out directions without verbal resistance.

Incomplete Class Work

Write a contract with these children in which they can determine their rewards for completing class work. Give shorter but more frequent assignments. Do not force the children to write if their handwriting is beyond correction; compensate with a word processor or typewriter. Correct assignments as soon as possible and hand them back for immediate gratification. Reward students for handing in neat, complete assignments in a timely manner. Help students become organized by keeping very little in their desk, using a bound book for writing rather than a loose-leaf binder where pages can fall out and add to disorganization; provide large folders for the children to keep work in; and so on. Have students mark their own work. Be very specific in explaining what you mean by "neat," "organized," and so on. Abstract labels have different meanings to different people. Say, "Please be neat. By neat, I mean . . . ."

Remaining Seated

Try to find a pattern in when these children get up out of their seats. Once this is determined you can arrange to have them run an errand, come up to your desk, and so on, at such times. In this way you will channel the tension and remain in control. Use an external control, like an egg timer, so that the children have an anchor to control their behavior. Praise other students or hand out rewards to everyone for remaining seated and following the rules. Give children a written copy of the rules, explaining what will result in a reward or positive feedback. Also give them a list of the behaviors that will lead to negative consequences. Close proximity to these children will help them stay in their seats. Seat them close to your desk or stand near them during a lesson.

Developing Social Relationships

Role-playing different scenarios with another student during private time will allow the children to get feedback from peers. Provide these children with a "toolbox" of responses and options for typical social situations. Speak with the school psychologist about including these children in a group. Arrange for a peer to guide them through social situations; these children may be more willing to model peer behavior. Start them in a small group activity with only one child, then slowly increase the size of the group as they become more comfortable. Arrange for goal-oriented projects where a group of students must work together to accomplish a task. At first limit this to only two children. Have an emotionally disabled child and a responsible peer organize team activities or group projects. Some children rise to the occasion when placed in a leadership role. Praise these students as often as realistic when they are not exhibiting aggressive or inappropriate social behavior.

Following Directions and Paying Attention

Use a cue before giving the children directions or important information. Give one direction at a time and make it as simple as possible. Have them chart their own patterns of behavior in relation to attention and direction. Physical proximity may assist them in focusing on your directions; keep them close to you. Praise them when they follow directions or pay attention. However, be aware that some emotionally disabled students have a hard time accepting praise, especially in front of a group, so you may want to give this praise in private. Provide optional work areas that may have less distractions. Randomly question the children and try to have them participate as often as possible to increase their interest in the lesson. Make sure the materials being presented are compatible with their learning levels. In this way you can avoid frustration that is also a cause of inattention. Use a variety of visual and auditory techniques, such as an overhead projector, tape recorder, or computer, to enhance the lesson and stimulate attention.

Classroom Management Techniques for Children with Attention Deficit Hyperactive Disorder

Children with ADHD need help in particular in the following areas: social interaction, inattentiveness, impulsiveness, and emotional expression.

Social Interaction

Identify appropriate social behavior and reinforce it when exhibited. Sit with the children and set up a social contract that clearly outlines what goals they would like to accomplish. Be sure to name the behaviors that are required to attain these goals. Use verbal and written praise whenever possible; this type of praise gives the children the feedback they need to understand their own behavior. Expose the children to small group interactions at first; placing a child with ADHD in a large group may be detrimental. Allow the group to be goal-oriented and interdependent so that the children can accomplish some simple tasks and feel successful. Use peer interaction and cooperative learning for certain academic tasks that do not require sitting for long periods of time. Try to identify strengths in each child that can be publicly announced or praised; in this way the other students will develop a more positive perception of that child. Role-play social situations with the child emphasizing the use of specific skills. In this way the child can develop a "toolbox" of skills that can be applied at a later time.

Inattentiveness

You may want to have these children finish all assignments in school. There are times when they are so inattentive that sending homework home to be accomplished may result in more stress, especially in parental interaction. Always allow them extra time for completing assignments. Sometimes the time constraints set up by teachers are arbitrary and do not reflect the "real" time required by children with ADHD. Try to give shorter but more frequent assignments. Remember, confidence comes with repeated successful experiences, and the ADHD child will have a greater chance of success with shorter assignments. If a child has problems listening and taking notes, then have a "buddy" take notes using carbon paper. A copy will then be available for the ADHD child and the stress of listening and writing will be reduced. Also, try to stand in close proximity to the student while lecturing.

Impulsiveness

Be realistic about your expectations for the children's behaviors. Choose your guidelines wisely. Try to ignore minor incidents and focus on the more intrusive or inappropriate ones. Shape appropriate behavior by reinforcing positive responses or actions. Do not hesitate to set up specific consequences for inappropriate actions. In this way these children will have to work at being more consciously aware of their behavior. Build in periods of time when they can leave their seat for some activity such as collecting homework, getting some material for you from the closet, and so on. Try to offer immediate gratification for appropriate behavior. If you wait too long to reward, you may lose the desired effect. Assign a monitoring "buddy" to offer feedback and hints about appropriate and inappropriate behaviors; this may be especially helpful during recess and lunch. Try to preempt behavior especially during changes in the schedule; inform these children about five minutes before the change and explain your expectations of what is appropriate behavior during this change.

Emotional Expression

Be aware of the children's frustration "aura." If you can recognize when an ADHD child is about to lose focus, it may prevent inappropriate behavior and feelings of failure. Do not be afraid to discuss this with the children so that both the children and you can identify the factors that lead to their frustration. Offer them an emotional vocabulary. Tension and frustration come out either verbally or behaviorally. Although ADHD children may not be able to control certain behaviors, the added tension resulting from stress should be reduced through venting. Having the proper labels enhances a child's ability to communicate feelings.

Teach students the concept of healthy anger. Offer them the rules of healthy anger—for example, deal with the situation as close to when it happens as possible, deal directly with the person with whom you are angry, never use the word "you" when conveying feelings of anger (using "I," "me," "we," or "us" is preferred). Try to empower ADHD children by focusing on all the parts of their life over which they have control. Children with ADHD frequently feel out of control and helpless. This feeling can lead to depression and victimization. Empowering them with simple jobs; simple hobbies; choices of food, clothing, room arrangement; and so on gives them a feeling of some control over their environment and may help to balance their feelings of powerlessness.

Classroom Issues for Children with Autism

There are several methods of educating young children with autism. The most well-known strategies are applied behavior analysis and TEACCH. Some school districts offer just one strategy. However, it is good to be familiar with all of them, because some children you work with respond better to one than another. Also, be aware that the practitioners of one strategy may criticize those who use another method. Do your own research and draw your own conclusions.

Many children with autism benefit from physical, speech, or occupational therapies at school. An occupational therapist can help the child improve poor hand skills, as well as address the sensory problems commonly found in autistic spectrum disorders.

Applied Behavior Analysis (ABA)

ABA generally assumes that appropriate behavior—including speech, academic skills, and life skills—can be taught using scientific principles. ABA assumes that children are more likely to repeat behaviors or responses that are rewarded, and less likely to continue behaviors that are not reinforced. Eventually, the teacher reduces the "reinforcers" so that the child can learn without them.

The most well-known form of ABA is *discrete trial instruction.* Discrete trials are used to teach a variety of skills, such as eye contact, imitation, fine motor skills, academic skills, and language. Students start with learning small skills, and gradually learn more complicated skills as each smaller one is mastered.

If a therapist is trying to teach imitation, for example, she may give a command, such as "Do this," while tapping the table. The child is then expected to tap the table. If the child succeeds, he receives positive reinforcement, such as a raisin, a toy, or praise. If the child fails, then the therapist may say, "No." The therapist then pauses before repeating the next trial, ensuring that each trial is separate or discrete. The therapist also will use a prompt—such as helping the child tap the table—if the child continues to respond incorrectly.

Some people incorrectly assume that ABA is synonymous with the method developed by Dr. O. Ivar Lovaas, a pioneering researcher in the psychology department at UCLA. Lovaas describes one form of ABA. In 1987, he published a study showing that almost half of the nineteen preschoolers involved in intensive behavioral intervention—forty hours per week of one-on-one therapy—achieved "normal functioning." It should be noted that many years ago, Lovaas described using mild physical punishment during therapy sessions. He no longer advocates such punishment, and modern behavior therapists do not use it.

One drawback to ABA is that children in intensive home therapy programs may not have time to socialize with children their age. Also, some school districts do not pay for ABA, and it can be expensive for parents to fund.

Treatment and Education of Autistic and Related Communication Handicapped Children (TEACCH)

TEACCH, developed at the University of North Carolina, is often less intensive than ABA. A TEACCH classroom is usually very structured, with separate, defined areas for each task, such as individual work, group activities, and play. It relies heavily on visual learning, a strength for many children with autism. The children use schedules made up of pictures or words to order their day and to help them move smoothly between activities. (Children with autism sometimes find it difficult to make transitions between activities and places.) Children may sit at a workstation and be required to complete certain activities, such as matching pictures. The finished assignments are then placed in a container. Children may use picture communication symbols—small laminated squares that contain a symbol and a word—to answer questions and request items from their teacher. The symbols help relieve frustration for nonverbal children while helping those who are starting to speak to recall and say the words they want.

One drawback: social interaction and verbal communication may not be heavily stressed. Also, more research is needed into the effectiveness of TEACCH, especially in comparison to ABA. In contrast to the outcome studies of ABA published by Dr. Lovaas, there have not been any comprehensive, long-term studies of the effectiveness of TEACCH in treating and educating children.

Floor Time

Dr. Stanley Greenspan, a child psychiatrist based in the Washington, D.C., area, has written extensively about a strategy of teaching children with autism through the use of interactive play and relationships. The child's actions are assumed to be purposeful. It is the parent's or caregiver's role to follow the child's lead and help him or her develop interaction and communication. For example, the child may enjoy tapping a toy car against the floor. During a "floor time" session, the parent may imitate the action, or put his car in the way of the child's car, thereby bringing about an interaction. From there, the parent encourages the child to develop more complex play schemes and incorporate language.

School systems may incorporate this strategy into their programs, but they generally do not make this their primary means of educating young children with autism. This approach may work best in conjunction with a program like ABA. Floor time lacks the controlled research studies of ABA or even TEACCH, but it is being used by teachers and some parents to complement the other approaches.

Sensory Integration

One common symptom of autism is an unusual response to the senses of hearing, sight, touch, smell, and movement. According to the National Information Center for Children and Youth with Disabilities (2003), children with pervasive developmental disorders (PDD) such as autism "may seem underresponsive or overresponsive to sensory stimuli. Thus, they may be suspected of being deaf or visually impaired. It is common for such young children to be referred for hearing and vision tests. Some children avoid gentle physical contact, yet react with pleasure to rough-and-tumble games. Some children carry food preferences to extremes, with favored foods eaten to excess. Some children limit their diet to a small selection."

The theory of sensory integration was developed by occupational therapist A. Jean Ayres, Ph.D. Occupational and physical therapists who are also trained in "sensory integration" techniques offer a range of activities designed to help the child process the information he receives from his senses in a more typical manner. Children with autism and PDD may qualify for free physical and occupational therapy at their schools or through their state's early intervention program. Also, parents and caregivers can learn sensory activities to do at home with the child. This therapy is almost never offered as a sole treatment for autism or PDD; instead, it may be a piece of a larger educational program. It can be expensive if not covered by insurance or provided by the school or early intervention.

Classroom Issues for Children with Traumatic Brain Injury (TBI)

Although TBI is very common, many medical and education professionals may not recognize it for what it is. Often students with TBI are thought to have a learning disability, emotional disturbance, or mental retardation. As a result, they don't receive the type of educational help and support they really need.

When children return to school after this kind of injury, their educational and emotional needs are often very different from before. Their disability has happened suddenly and traumatically. They can often remember how they were before the brain injury. This can bring on many emotional and social changes. The child's family, friends, and teachers also recall what the child was like before the injury. These other people in the child's life may have trouble changing or adjusting their expectations of the child.

Planning for the Child's Return

Therefore, it is extremely important that you help the child's return to school along with the parent. You may want to inform parents ahead of time about special education services at the school. The school will need to evaluate the child thoroughly. This evaluation will let the school and parents know what the student's educational needs are. The Individualized Education Program will then be developed to address those educational needs. It is important to remember that the IEP is a flexible plan. It can be changed as the parents, the school, and the student learn more about what the student needs at school.

Tips for Teachers Working with Children with TBI

- Find out as much as you can about these children's injuries and their present needs. Find out more about TBI in general. (See the list of resources and organizations in Appendix H at the back of this book.)
- Give these students more time to finish schoolwork and tests.
- Give directions one step at a time. For tasks with many steps, it helps to give the students written directions.
- Show the students how to perform new tasks. Give examples to go with new ideas and concepts.
- Have consistent routines. This helps the students know what to expect. If the routine is going to change, let students know ahead of time.
- Check to make sure that they have actually learned the new skill. Give them lots of opportunities to practice the new skill.
- Show them how to use an assignment book and a daily schedule. This helps them get organized.
- Realize that these students may tire quickly. Let them rest as needed.
- Reduce distractions.
- Keep in touch with parents. Share information with each other about how the students are doing at home and at school.

Classroom Techniques for Children with Physical Disabilities

In the past, students with severe or multiple disabilities were routinely excluded from public schools. Since the implementation of Public Law 94–142 (the Education of the Handicapped Act, now called the Individuals with Disabilities Education Act, or IDEA), public schools now serve large numbers of students with severe and multiple disabilities. Educational programming is likely to begin as early as infancy. At that time, as well as later on, the primary focus is on increasing the child's independence.

Needs Assessment

Educational programs have to incorporate a variety of components to meet the considerable needs of individuals with severe or multiple disabilities. Programs should assess needs in four major areas: domestic, leisure-recreational, community, and vocational. These assessments help identify functional objectives (objectives that will result in the learner's increased skill and independence in dealing with the routine activities of his life). Instruction should include expression of choice, communication, functional skill development, and age-appropriate social skills training.

Related Services

Related services are of great importance, and a multidisciplinary approach is crucial. Appropriate professionals such as speech and language therapists, physical and occupational therapists, and medical specialists need to work closely with classroom teachers and parents. Because of problems with skill generalization, related services are best offered during the natural routine in the school and community rather than removing a student from class for isolated therapy.

Classroom Arrangement

Frequently, classroom arrangements must take into consideration students' needs for medications, special diets, or special equipment. Adaptive aids and equipment enable students to increase their range of functioning. In recent years, computers have become effective communication devices. Other aids include wheelchairs, typewriters, headsticks (headgear), clamps, modified handles on cups and silverware, and communication boards. Computerized communication equipment and specially built vocational equipment also play important roles in adapting working environments for people with serious movement limitations.

Integration with Nondisabled Peers

Integration with nondisabled peers is another important component of the educational setting. Attending the same school and participating in the same activities as their nondisabled peers are crucial to the development of social skills and friendships for people with severe disabilities. Integration also benefits nondisabled peers and professionals through positive attitude change.

Community-Based Instruction

Beginning as early as the elementary school years, community-based instruction is an important characteristic of educational programming. To increase the student's ability to generalize (transfer) skills to appropriate situations, this type of instruction takes place in the actual setting where the skills will be used. As students grow older, increasing time is spent in the community; high school students may spend as much as 90 percent of their day there. Programs should draw on existing adult services in the community, including group homes, vocational programs, and recreational settings.

In light of the Vocational Rehabilitation Act (1973) and the practice of supported employment, schools are now using school-to-work transition planning and working toward job placement in integrated, competitive settings rather than sheltered employment and day activity centers.

Classroom Issues for Children with Visual Impairments

The effect of visual problems on a child's development depends on the severity, type of loss, age at which the condition appears, and overall functioning level of the child. Many children who have multiple disabilities also have visual impairments resulting in motor, cognitive, or social developmental delays.

A young child with visual impairments has little reason to explore interesting objects in the environment, and thus may miss opportunities to have experiences and to learn. This lack of exploration may continue until learning becomes motivating or until intervention begins.

If the child cannot see parents or peers, she may be unable to imitate social behavior or understand nonverbal cues. Visual handicaps can create obstacles to a growing child's independence. Many factors need to be considered or reviewed when working with a child with visual impairments.

Check the school records to see when the children were first evaluated. If they were assessed very early, find out if they benefited from early intervention programs. Also explore the IEPs through the years (if the child is older) to see what technology was used. Technology in the form of computers and low-vision optical and video aids enable many partially sighted, low vision, and blind children to participate in regular class activities. Large-print materials, books on tape, and Braille books are also available.

Students with visual impairments may need additional help with special equipment and modifications in the regular curriculum to emphasize listening skills, communication, orientation and mobility, vocation-career options, and daily living skills. Students with low vision or those who are legally blind may need help in using their residual vision more efficiently and in working with special aids and materials. Students who have visual impairments combined with other types of disabilities have a greater need for an interdisciplinary approach and may require greater emphasis on self-care and daily living skills.

Classroom Issues for Children with Hearing Impairments

Hearing loss or deafness does not affect a child's intellectual capacity or ability to learn. However, children who are either hard of hearing or deaf generally require some form of special education services in order to be adequately educated. Such services may include regular speech, language, and auditory training from a specialist; amplification systems; the services of an interpreter for students who use sign language; favorable seating in the class to facilitate lip reading; captioned films or videos; assistance of a notetaker (a person who takes notes for the student with a hearing loss, so that the student can fully attend to the instruction); instruction for the teacher and peers in alternate communication methods, such as sign language; and counseling. It may also be helpful to learn sign language or have an assistant who knows sign language.

Children who are hard of hearing will find it much more difficult than children who have normal hearing to learn vocabulary, grammar, word order, idiomatic expressions, and other aspects of verbal communication. For children who are deaf or have severe hearing losses, early, consistent, and conscious use of visible communication modes (such as sign language, finger spelling, and cued speech), or amplification and aural-oral training can help reduce this language delay. By age four or five, most children who are deaf are enrolled in school on a full-day basis and do special work on communication and language development. If a child is receiving outside assistance or related services from an audiologist, then it is important for teachers and audiologists to work together to teach the child to use his or her residual hearing to the maximum extent possible, even if the preferred means of communication is manual. Because most deaf children (over 90 percent) are born to hearing parents, help parents find programs that provide instruction for parents on implications of deafness in the family.

People with hearing loss use oral or manual means of communication or a combination of the two. Oral communication includes speech, lip reading, and the use of residual hearing. Manual communication involves signs and finger spelling. Total communication, as a method of instruction, is a combination of the oral method plus signing and finger spelling.

There are now many helpful devices available to individuals with hearing loss, including those who are deaf. Text telephones (known as TTs, TTYs, or TDDs) enable them to type phone messages over the telephone network. The Telecommunications Relay Service (TRS), now required by law, makes it possible for TT users to communicate with virtually anyone (and vice versa) via telephone. The National Institute on Deafness and Other Communication Disorders Information Clearinghouse (www.nidcd.nih.gov) makes available lists of TRS numbers by state.

PART FIVE

WHAT SPECIAL EDUCATION TEACHERS NEED TO KNOW AND DO ABOUT . . .

Chapter 19

Common Disorders Seen by Special Educators

In the course of their experience, special educators are likely to encounter a wide variety of special education conditions. Many are caused by intellectual, social, emotional, academic, environmental, or medical factors. It is important to have at least a basic understanding of the more common conditions that your students may present. Your knowledge can be helpful to parents, doctors, other students in the class, and the affected students themselves. Understanding the nature of certain disorders will enhance your total understanding of the children and all the factors that play a role in their educational development.

This chapter covers the more common disorders that you are likely to encounter as a special education teacher. A description of each disorder, symptoms associated with the disorder, educational implications (that is, more classroom management techniques), possible treatment options, and other factors specific to the disorder are discussed.

The most common reference on psychological disorders used by professionals today is the *Diagnostic and Statistical Manual of Mental Disorders®* (4th edition, 2002). The DSM-IV-TR has been updated several times in scope and format from its original publication as DSM-I in 1952. For a more thorough understanding of the disorders reviewed in this part of the book, you may want to purchase this manual as a reference source. The list presented here represents only a cross section of the conditions that you may encounter in the classroom. Further disorders can also be found in the DSM-IV®-TR (American Psychiatric Publishing, 1994).

You can also visit the Web sites or contact the organizations listed at the end of each section.

Developmental Disorders

Mental Retardation

Description

This disorder is characterized by severe delayed development in the acquisition of cognitive, language, motor, or social skills. The general characteristics of this diagnostic category are consistent and significant subaverage intellectual performance, significant deficits in the development of adaptive functioning, and onset prior to age eighteen.

Etiology

There are several possible contributing factors to this disorder, including heredity, prenatal damage (that is, damage prior to birth, such as maternal alcohol consumption), chromosomal changes, perinatal problems (problems occurring at the time of birth, such as premature delivery), malnutrition, postnatal problems (problems occurring after birth, such as infections), trauma, and environmental or sensory deprivation during critical stages of development.

Types

Several subtypes are classified by educational or psychological terminology. They are as follows:

Type	*Range*	*Approximate IQ Range*
Educable mentally retarded	Mild	55–77.5
Trainable mentally retarded	Moderate	35–55
Severely mentally retarded	Severe	25–35
Profoundly mentally retarded	Profound	Below 25

Educational Implications

The more severe the category, the greater the possibility of associated features being present, including seizures and visual, auditory, or cardiovascular problems. Other educational implications involve poor social skills, severe academic deficits, and possible behavioral manifestations such as impulsivity, low frustration tolerance, aggressiveness, low self-esteem, and in some cases self injurious behavior. However, a child with mental retardation can do well in school but is likely to need individualized help.

For children up to age three, services are provided through an early intervention system. Staff work with the child's family to develop the Individualized Family Services Plan (IFSP). The IFSP describes the child's unique needs. It also describes the services the child will receive to address those needs. The IFSP emphasizes the unique needs of the family, so that parents and other family members will know how to help their young child with mental retardation. Early intervention services may be provided on a sliding-fee basis, meaning that the costs to the family will depend on their income. In some states, early intervention services may be provided at no cost to parents.

For eligible school-aged children (including preschoolers), special education and related services are made available through the school system. School staff work with the child's parents to develop the Individualized Education Program (IEP), which describes the child's unique needs and the services that have been designed to meet those needs. Special education and related services are provided at no cost to parents.

Many children with mental retardation need help with adaptive skills—that is, skills needed to live, work, and play in the community. Teachers and parents can help a child work on these skills at both school and home. Some of these skills are communicating with others; taking care of personal needs (dressing, bathing, going to the bathroom); looking out for one's health and safety; home living (helping to set the table, cleaning the house, or cooking dinner); social skills (manners, rules of conversation, getting along in a group, playing a game); reading, writing, and basic math; and as they get older, workplace skills.

Classroom adaptations help most students with mental retardation. Some common adaptations follow.

- Learn as much as you can about mental retardation. The organizations listed at the end of this section will help you identify specific techniques and strategies to support the student educationally.
- Recognize that you can make an enormous difference in this student's life! Find out what the student's strengths and interests are, and emphasize them. Create opportunities for success.
- If you are not part of the student's IEP team, ask for a copy of the IEP. The student's educational goals will be listed there, as well as the services and classroom accommodations he is to receive. Talk to other specialists in your school as necessary. They can help you identify effective methods of teaching this student, ways to adapt the curriculum, and how to address the student's IEP goals in your classroom.
- Be as concrete as possible. Demonstrate what you mean rather than just giving verbal directions. Rather than just relating new information verbally, show a picture. And rather than just showing a picture, provide the student with hands-on materials and experiences and the opportunity to try things out.
- Break longer, new tasks into small steps. Demonstrate the steps. Have the student do the steps, one at a time. Provide assistance as necessary.
- Give the student immediate feedback.
- Teach the student life skills such as daily living, social skills, and occupational awareness and exploration, as appropriate. Involve the student in group activities or clubs.
- Work together with the student's parents and other school personnel to create and implement an educational plan tailored to meet the student's needs. Regularly share information about how the student is doing at school and at home.

Possible Least Restrictive Educational Setting

Least restrictive educational settings for these students range from inclusion or self-contained classrooms in a regular school with mainstreaming options (for educable students) to residential school and institutionalization (for profoundly retarded individuals).

Organizations

The Arc of the United States (formerly the Association for Retarded Citizens of the United States)

1010 Wayne Avenue, Suite 650

Silver Spring, MD 20910

(301) 565-3842

E-mail: Info@thearc.org

Web sites: http://www.thearc.org; http://www.TheArcPub.com

American Association on Mental Retardation (AAMR)
444 North Capitol Street NW, Suite 846
Washington, DC 20001
(202) 387-1968; (800) 424-3688
Web site: http://www.aamr.org

Division on Mental Retardation & Developmental Disabilities (MRDD)
Council for Exceptional Children (CEC)
1110 North Glebe Road, Suite 300
Arlington, VA 22201-5704
(888) 232-7733; (703) 620-3660; (703) 264-9446 (TTY)
E-mail: cec@cec.sped.org
Web site: http://www.mrddcec.org

Autism

Description

This is a very serious developmental disorder characterized by severe impairment in the development of verbal and nonverbal communication skills, marked impairment in reciprocal social interaction (a lack of responsiveness to or interest in people), and almost nonexistent imaginative activity. Also known as infantile autism or Kanner's syndrome.

Etiology

The condition is usually reported by most parents before the age of three. The condition is, in almost all cases, lifelong. The condition is thought to result from a wide range of prenatal, perinatal, and postnatal conditions, including maternal rubella and anoxia during birth, which affects brain function.

Gender

The condition is more common in males, at a ratio of approximately three or four to one.

Educational Implications

Children with this disorder normally exhibit poor social skills and impaired cognitive functioning and language. The onset of puberty may increase oppositional or aggressive behavior. Other complications may include seizures and low intellectual development.

The following list of teacher suggestions for working with children with autism is adapted from *Teaching Tips for Children and Adults with Autism* (Grandin, 2002):

- Avoid long strings of verbal instructions. People with autism have problems with remembering the sequence. If the child can read, write the instructions down on a piece of paper.

- Many children with autism are good at drawing, art, and computer programming. These talent areas should be encouraged. Talents can be turned into skills that can be used for future employment.
- Many autistic children get fixated on one subject, such as trains or maps. The best way to deal with fixations is to use them to motivate schoolwork. If the child likes trains, then use trains to teach reading and math.
- Use concrete visual methods to teach number concepts.
- Many autistic children have problems with motor control in their hands. Neat handwriting is sometimes very hard for them. This can frustrate the child. To reduce frustration and help the child to enjoy writing, let him type on the computer. Typing is often much easier.
- Some autistic children learn reading more easily with phonics, and others learn best by memorizing whole words. Children with echolalia often learn best if flash cards and picture books are used so that the whole words are associated with pictures. It is important to have the picture and the printed word on the same side of the card. When teaching nouns the child must hear you speak the word and view the picture and printed word simultaneously. For example, to teach the verb *jump*, hold up the card with the word "jump" written on it, and jump up and down while saying the word.
- Children with autism need to be protected from sounds that hurt their ears. The sounds that will cause the most problems are school bells, PA systems, buzzers on the scoreboard in the gym, and the sound of chairs scraping on the floor. In many cases these children can tolerate the bell or buzzer if it is muffled slightly by stuffing it with tissues or duct tape. Scraping chairs can be silenced by placing slit tennis balls on the ends of the legs or installing carpet.
- Some autistic people are bothered by visual distractions and fluorescent lights. They can see the flicker of the sixty-cycle electricity. To avoid this problem, place such children's desks near a window or try to avoid using fluorescent lights. If the lights cannot be avoided, use the newest bulbs you can get.
- Some hyperactive autistic children who fidget all the time will become calmer if they are given a padded, weighted vest to wear. Pressure from the garment helps to calm the nervous system. For best results, the vest should be worn for twenty minutes and then taken off for a few minutes. This prevents the nervous system from adapting to it.
- Some individuals with autism will respond better and have improved eye contact and speech if a teacher interacts with them while they are swinging on a swing or rolled up in a mat. Sensory input from swinging or pressure from the mat sometimes helps to improve speech. Swinging should always be done as a fun game. It must *never* be forced.
- Some autistic children and adults can sing better than they can speak. They may respond better if words and sentences are sung to them. Some children with extreme sound sensitivity respond better if the teacher talks to them in a low whisper.

- Some nonverbal children and adults cannot process visual and auditory input at the same time. They are *monochannel.* They cannot see and hear at the same time. They should not be asked to look and listen at the same time. They should be given either a visual task or an auditory one. Their immature nervous system is not able to process simultaneous visual and auditory input.
- Some children and adults with autism can learn more easily if the computer keyboard is placed close to the screen. This enables them to see the keyboard and screen at the same time. Some individuals have difficulty remembering if they have to look up after they have hit a key on the keyboard.
- Some nonverbal children and adults will find it easier to associate words with pictures if they see the printed word and a picture on a flash card. Some individuals do not understand line drawings, so working with real objects and photos first is recommended. The picture and the word must be on the *same* side of the card.
- Some autistic individuals do not know that speech is used for communication. Language learning can be facilitated if language exercises promote communication. If the child asks for a cup, then give him a cup. If the child asks for a plate when he actually wants a cup, give him a plate. He needs to learn that when he says words, concrete things happen. It is easier for individuals with autism to learn that their words are wrong if the incorrect word results in their being given an incorrect object.
- Many individuals with autism have difficulty using a computer mouse. Try a roller ball (or tracking ball) pointing device that has a separate button for clicking. Autistics with motor control problems in their hands find it very difficult to hold the mouse still during clicking.
- Parents have indicated that the closed captions on the television have helped their children to learn to read. The children were able to read the captions and match the printed words with spoken speech. Similarly, recording a favorite program with captions on the tape would be helpful because the tape can be played over and over again and stopped.
- Some autistic individuals do not understand that a computer mouse moves the arrow on the screen. They may learn more easily if a paper arrow that looks exactly like the arrow on the screen is taped to the mouse.
- Children and adults with visual processing problems can see flicker on TV-type computer monitors. They can sometimes see better on laptops and flat panel displays, which have less flicker.
- Individuals with visual processing problems often find it easier to read if black print is printed on colored paper to reduce contrast. Try light tan, light blue, gray, or light green paper.

Possible Least Restrictive Educational Setting

Most children with this condition require the most restrictive educational setting possible. The student-teacher ratios are usually six to one or two or smaller because of the close supervision required. Those who are not capable of maintaining this type of setting may have to be institutionalized. Interestingly, in rare cases an individual may improve to the point of being able to complete formal education or even attain an advanced degree.

Organizations

Autism Hotline
Autism Services Center
P.O. Box 507
Huntington, WV 25710-0507
(304) 525-8014
Web site: http://www.autismservices.com

Autism National Committee
P.O. Box 6175
North Plymouth, MA 02362-6175
Web site: http://www.autcom.org

Autism Society of America
7910 Woodmont Avenue, Suite 300
Bethesda, MD 20814
(800) 328-8476; (301) 657-0881
E-mail: info@autism-society.org
Web site: http://www.autism-society.org

Indiana Resource Center for Autism (at Indiana University)
Indiana Institute on Disability and Community
2853 East 10th Street
Bloomington, IN 47408-2696
(812) 855-6508; (812) 855-9396 (TTY)
Web site: http://www.iidc.indiana.edu/~irca

Developmental Arithmetic Disorder

Description

This is a serious marked disability in the development of arithmetic skills. Often called dyscalculia, the condition cannot be explained by mental retardation, inadequate teaching, or primary visual or auditory defects and may be consistent throughout school.

Age of Onset

It usually becomes apparent between age six (first grade) and ten (fifth grade).

Educational Implications

Children with this condition exhibit seriously impaired mathematical ability, which may require classroom modifications like extended time on tests, use of a calculator, flexible setting for tests, and revised test format. These children may have poor self-esteem, social self-consciousness, and academic avoidance, which may increase secondary problems.

In comparison to remediation studies in the reading disability area, little research has been done on remediation in the math disability area. Part of the difficulty is that little is really known about the nature and course of math disabilities—and it is hard to develop effective remedial techniques for a disorder that is not well understood. Nonetheless, this is an area of great need and an area in which we can probably begin to develop remedial programs, at least for basic counting and arithmetic.

Possible Least Restrictive Educational Setting

Children with this disorder may receive assistance through special education services like a resource room or a consultant teacher, and are usually able to maintain placement in a regular class setting.

Organizations

See the section "Developmental Reading Disorder."

Developmental Expressive Writing Disorder

Description

This disorder is characterized by a serious impairment in the ability to develop expressive writing skills that significantly interferes in the child's academic achievement. This condition is not the result of mental retardation, inadequate educational experiences, visual or hearing defects, or neurological dysfunction.

Age of Onset

Considering the nature of the disorder and the levels of impairment, the age of onset can range from age seven (second grade) for the more severe types to age ten or eleven (fifth grade) for the less severely impaired.

Symptoms

Symptoms associated with this disorder include an inability to compose appropriate written text coupled with serious and consistent spelling errors, grammatical or punctuation errors, and very poor organization of thought and text.

Educational Implications

Teachers should be aware that these children may exhibit a series of symptoms, including avoidance, procrastination, denial, and possibly disruptive behaviors when written assignments are involved in order to cover up the seriousness of their disorder.

Luttinger and Gertner (2003) indicate that the process of writing includes prewriting activities, the writing itself, and postwriting activities. Prewriting begins with planning, which includes analyzing the purpose of the writing and generating and organizing ideas.

To help children develop prewriting skills, teach the child to recognize types of recurring patterns and structures that relate to types of text. Explain that narrative text (for example, a temporally ordered story) differs from expository text. Teach the child to include elements that match the identified text structure. Discussion and interaction appear to benefit the development of prewriting planning skills. You may also model brainstorming or think-aloud techniques.

Be aware that accommodations and modifications to the child's learning environment will be necessary and most likely will appear on the child's IEP. These could include seating closer to the board and your desk; a scribe or peer to assist with note-taking (for example, using a buddy system, teacher-prepared notes, technologies such as tape recording and laptop computers); extended time for class and standardized tests where writing is required; alternate expressive options such as oral reports, dioramas, video presentations, and so on; use of a word processor; and voice recognition software.

Especially in later grades when the need for producing longer written assignments and note-taking increases, these accommodations can have an important positive effect.

Possible Least Restrictive Educational Setting

Children with this disorder may receive assistance through special education services like a resource room or a consultant teacher, and are usually able to maintain placement within a regular class setting.

Organizations

See the list under "Developmental Reading Disorder."

Developmental Reading Disorder

Description

The more common features of this disorder include a marked impairment in the development of the child's decoding and comprehension skills, which significantly interfere in the academic performance. Like some other developmental disorders, this condition is not the result of mental retardation, inadequate educational experiences, visual or hearing defects, or neurological dysfunction. This condition is commonly referred to as dyslexia.

Age of Onset

This disorder is usually observed in children as young as six (first grade). Diagnosis of such a serious impairment in the later grades may result from the child's ability to compensate with high intellectual ability or poor educational diagnostics.

Symptoms

Typical symptoms of this disorder include a slow, halting reading pace, frequent omissions, loss of place on a page, skipping lines while reading without awareness, distortions, substitutions of words, and a serious inability to recall what had been read.

Educational Implications

Early diagnosis of this disorder is crucial to avoid serious secondary symptoms of poor self-esteem, behavior disorders, and educational failure. Be sure to pay attention to the possible symptoms exhibited by children with this disorder so that you can assist in early identification of high-risk children. Also be aware of the various reading techniques used to assist children with this disorder.

Several accommodations can facilitate learning among children with a developmental reading disorder, including taped textbooks available through Recording for the Blind and Dyslexic; extended time on tests; peer tutoring; use of a notetaker (for students who have trouble listening in class and taking notes); use of a scribe during test-taking (for students who have trouble writing but who can express their answers verbally to the scribe, who writes down the responses); use of a reader during test-taking (for students who have trouble reading test questions); tape-recording class lectures; and testing in a quiet place (for students who are easily distracted). These children can also be given oral examinations, large-print type, and have questions read for them during tests.

Possible Least Restrictive Educational Setting

Children with this disorder may receive assistance through special education services like a resource room or a consultant teacher, and they are usually able to maintain placement within a regular class setting.

Organizations

International Dyslexia Association
8600 LaSalle Road
Chester Building, Suite 382
Baltimore, MD 21286-2044
(410) 296-0232; (800) ABCD123
E-mail: info@interdys.org
Web site: http://www.interdys.org

Learning Disabilities Association of America (LDA)
4156 Library Road, Suite 1
Pittsburgh, PA 15234-1349
(412) 341-1515; (412) 341–8077
E-mail: ldanatl@usaor.net
Web site: http://www.ldaamerica.org

National Center for Learning Disabilities
381 Park Avenue South, Suite 1401
New York, NY 10016
(212) 545-7510; (888) 575-7373
E-mail: http://www.ld.org

National Institute of Child Health and Human Development (NICHD)
National Institutes of Health
Building 31, Room 2A32
Bethesda, MD 20892-2425
(301) 496-5133; (800) 370-2943
E-mail: NICHDClearinghouse@mail.nih.gov
Web site: http://www.nichd.nih.gov

Developmental Expressive Language Disorder

Description

This disorder is characterized by a serious impairment in the child's ability to develop expressive language. This condition is not the result of mental retardation, inadequate educational experiences, visual or hearing defects, or neurological dysfunction.

Symptoms

Common symptoms associated with this disorder are limited use of vocabulary, shortened sentences, slow rate of language development, simplified sentence structure, and omissions of sentences.

Age of Onset

The more serious forms of this disorder are usually diagnosed by age three; less severe forms may not be noticed until much later in development.

Educational Implications

As many as from 3 percent to 10 percent of school-aged children suffer from this disorder, which may greatly hamper a child's social interaction skills as well as academic performance.

The Kaufman Children's Center (2003) suggests that teachers try the following strategies to improve expressive language:

- *Gain attention.* Be sure to get the child's attention before giving instructions. This can be done by calling the child's name or giving a gentle touch.
- *Monitor comprehension.* Periodically ask the child questions related to the subject under discussion.
- *Rephrase.* Restate what has been misunderstood rather than repeating the information. Reduce the complexity of the message as well as the vocabulary level.
- *Use brief instructions.*
- *Pre-tutor.* Familiarize these children with new vocabulary and concepts to be covered in class. Note that parents can be particularly helpful in this activity.
- *List key vocabulary.* Before dealing with new material, write key vocabulary on the chalkboard. Then center the discussion on these words.

- *Write instructions.* Write assignments on the board. Assign another child as a "buddy" to this disabled child to make sure the child is made aware of assignments handed out during the day.
- *Use visual aids.* Jot key words on the chalkboard, or provide simple written or picture outlines. This may be useful in presenting information.
- *Provide individual help.* One-to-one teacher tutoring will help fill in the gaps in understanding.
- *Provide breaks.* Children with auditory processing problems need frequent breaks. They put out more effort in paying attention and discriminating information than other children. Therefore, they must have a chance to relax. Once a child is fatigued, further instruction will lead to frustration for both you and the child.

Possible Least Restrictive Educational Setting

Children with this disorder may receive assistance through special education services like a resource room, a consultant teacher, or services from a speech therapist, and are usually able to maintain placement in a regular class setting.

Organizations

American Speech-Language-Hearing Association (ASHA)
10801 Rockville Pike
Rockville, MD 20852
(301) 897-5700 (V/TT); (800) 638-8255
E-mail: webmaster@asha.org
Web site: http://www.asha.org/

Learning Disabilities Association of America (LDA)
4156 Library Road
Pittsburgh, PA 15234-1349
(412) 341-1515; (412) 341-8077
Email: ldanatl@usaor.net
Web site: http://www.ldaamerica.org

Division for Children with Communication Disorders
Council for Exceptional Children (CEC)
1920 Association Drive
Reston, VA 22091-1589
(703) 620-3660
Web site: http://www.cec.sped.org

Behavior Disorders

Attention Deficit Hyperactive Disorder (ADHD)

Description

Children with this disorder exhibit behaviors of inattention, hyperactivity, and impulsiveness that are significantly inappropriate for their age levels. These behaviors may be severe and have an adverse affect on the child's academic achievement.

Etiology

The condition is six to nine times more common in males than females and several conditions may contribute to the development of the disorder. These may include neurological factors and central nervous system dysfunction as well as environment, abuse, and neglect.

Symptoms

The symptoms of this disorder should be present for a minimum of six months and may include some of the following: constant fidgeting, difficulty remaining seated, excessive talking at inappropriate times, inability to listen, carelessness, disorganization, difficulty sustaining a focus on tasks or play activities, distractibility, and difficulty in following instructions.

Educational Implications

Be aware of the academic as well as the social difficulties experienced by students with this disorder. Social rejection is common and may contribute to low self-esteem, low tolerance for frustration, and possibly aggressive or compulsive behavior patterns.

These students often do best with teachers who are positive, upbeat, flexible, and highly organized problem-solvers. Praise liberally and be willing to "go the extra mile" to help students succeed; this can be enormously beneficial to students with ADHD. The following adaptations can also be helpful with children with ADHD:

- *In general:* Provide more direct instruction and as much one-on-one instruction as possible. Use guided instruction. Teach and practice organization and study skills in every subject area. Lecture less. Design lessons so that students have to respond actively—get up, move around, go to the board, move in their seats. Design highly motivating and enriching curriculum with ample opportunity for hands-on activities and movement. Eliminate repetition from tasks or use more novel ways to practice. Design tasks of low to moderate frustration levels. Use computers in instruction. Challenge but don't overwhelm. Change evaluation methods to suit these children's learning styles and strengths. Pair them with a study buddy or learning partner who is an exemplary student. Provide frequent feedback. Structure tasks. Monitor independent work. Schedule difficult subjects at these students' most productive times. Use mentoring and peer tutoring. Provide frequent and regularly scheduled breaks. Use timers for specific tasks. Call attention to schedule changes. Maintain frequent communication between home and school. Do daily and weekly progress reports. Teach conflict resolution and peer mediation skills.

- *To support planning:* Teach these students to use assignment pads, day planners or time schedules, task organizers, and outlines. Teach study skills and practice them frequently in all subjects.
- *To increase organization:* Allow time during the school day for locker and backpack organization. Allow time for students to organize materials and assignments for homework. Have students create a master notebook—a three-ring binder—in which they can organize (rather than stuff) papers. Limit the number of folders used, and have these students use hole-punched paper and clearly label all binders on spines. Monitor notebooks. Have daily and weekly organization and clean-up routines. Provide frequent checks of work and systems for organization.
- *To improve follow-through:* Create work completion routines. Provide opportunities for self-correction. Accept late work. Give partial credit for work that is partially completed.
- *To improve self-control:* Prepare students for transitions. Display rules. Give behavior prompts. Enforce clear consequences. Provide students with time to de-stress. Allow doodling or other appropriate, mindless motor movement. Use activity as a reward. Provide close supervision.
- *To assist with working memory:* Focus on one concept at a time. List all steps. Write all work down. Use reading guides and plot summaries. Teach note-taking skills—let these students use a study buddy or teacher-prepared notes to fill in gaps. List all key points on the board. Provide summaries, study guides, outlines, and lists. Let these students use the computer.
- *To assist with memory retrieval:* Teach these students memory strategies (grouping, chunking, mnemonic devices). Practice sorting main ideas and details. Teach information and organization skills. Make necessary test accommodations: allow open-book tests; use word banks; use other memory cues; test in preferred modality—for example, oral or fill-in-the-blank tests; give frequent quizzes instead of lengthy tests.
- *For difficulty in beginning tasks:* Repeat directions. Increase task structure. Highlight or color-code directions and other important parts of assignments. Teach the students keyword-underlining skills. Summarize key information. Give visual cues. Have the class start tasks together.
- *For difficulty in sticking with and finishing tasks:* Add interest and activity to tasks. Divide larger tasks into easily completed segments. Shorten overall tasks. Allow the students a choice in tasks. Limit lecture time. Call on these students often.

Possible Least Restrictive Educational Setting

Children with mild forms of this disorder may be able to maintain a regular class placement with the intervention of medication. More serious cases may require more restrictive settings, especially if the children have associated oppositional or conduct problems. In such cases, special schools or residential settings may be the least restrictive settings possible.

Organizations

CHADD—Children and Adults with Attention Deficit Hyperactivity Disorder
8181 Professional Place, Suite 150
Landover, MD 20785
(301) 306-7070; (800) 233-4050
E-mail: national@chadd.org
Web site: http://www.chadd.org

National Attention Deficit Disorder Association
1788 Second Street, Suite 200
Highland Park, IL 60035
(847) 432-2332
E-mail: mail@add.org
Web site: http://www.add.org

Conduct Disorder

Description

This condition is characterized by a persistent pattern of behavior that intrudes and violates the basic rights of others without concern or fear of implications. This pattern is not selective and is exhibited in the home, at school, with peers, and in the community. Other behaviors present with this condition may include vandalism, stealing, physical aggression, cruelty to animals, and fire setting.

Etiology

The age of onset is usually before puberty for males and after puberty for females. Although the causes are varied, they often include parental rejection, harsh discipline, early institutional residence, inconsistent parenting figures as experienced in foster care, and so on.

Gender

Empirical studies indicate that 9 percent of males and 2 percent of females suffer from this disorder.

Types

Several subtypes of this disorder are classified by educational or psychological terminology. They are as follows:

Type	*Description*
Solitary aggressive type	Aggressive behavior toward peers and adults
Group type	Conduct problems mainly with peers as a group
Undifferentiated type	For those not classified in either of the previous groups

Educational Implications

Children with this condition may be physically confrontational to teachers and peers, have poor attendance, have high levels of suspension thereby missing a great deal of academic work, and exhibit other forms of antisocial behavior.

Suggestions for dealing with this disorder are listed under "Oppositional Defiant Disorder."

Possible Least Restrictive Educational Setting

Children with this condition may be educated in a special class in a regular school if the condition is mild. However, most of these students are educated in a more restrictive program housed in a special school, a residential school, or an institution if the antisocial behavior is extreme.

Organizations

See organizations listed under "Oppositional Defiant Disorder."

Oppositional Defiant Disorder

Description

This disorder is usually characterized by patterns of negativistic, hostile, and defiant behaviors with peers as well as adults. It is considered less serious than conduct disorder because of the absence of serious behaviors that violate the basic rights of others. These children usually exhibit argumentative behaviors toward adults, which may include swearing and frequent episodes of intense anger and annoyance. These symptoms are usually considered to be more serious and intense than those exhibited by other children of the same age.

Age of Onset

The behaviors associated with oppositional defiant disorder usually appear around age eight and usually not later than early adolescence.

Educational Implications

Children with this disorder may have low frustration tolerance, frequent temper outbursts, low sense of confidence, and an unwillingness to take responsibility for their actions, consistently blaming others for their own mistakes or problems. They may also exhibit behaviors associated with attention deficit hyperactive disorder.

Millette (1996) suggests the following when dealing with children with oppositional disorders:

- Set rules; make them simple and straightforward. Trying to reason with or lecture to an oppositional child, especially one who is very verbal, is usually counterproductive. Many oppositional children love a good debate or even a bad one, and this will end up with you a sputtering and frustrated teacher.

- Avoid power struggles. These are situations where, even if you win, you lose. Do not give the child a chance to feel martyred. You will still feel frustrated and often feel you have sunk to the child's level. You are the adult and you can remain in authority without engaging in a power struggle. If you have a tendency to engage in power struggles with children or other adults, take a good look at what makes you tick.
- Be consistent. Do not give a child the opportunity to play one adult authority figure against another or to be able to point out that you said something different last week.
- Communicate. This will help with the previous item, and it will also help with general school behavior. Let other teachers, guidance counselors, and parents know your rules and vice versa. Let them know what you think works best for the child.
- Make the child accountable. When the child is with another caregiver (this could include other teachers as well), they may give a different interpretation of your rules (for example, "My teacher lets me do my homework in school"). Let the child know that other caregivers know your rules and that they let you know what the child says and does while with them.
- Write things down and let these children know that this is part of your communication system. They may conclude that there is no way to get away with anything. It may even become a greater incentive for them to learn to read and write.
- Remember, oppositional disorder is often a "cut-your-nose-off-to-spite-your-face" situation, because of these children's tendency to hold onto behaviors that are often destructive to their own interests or relationships. It is often chronic and can last for several years. If it continues into adulthood, passive-aggressive personality disorder may result. You must be patient, yet deliberate.

Possible Least Restrictive Educational Setting

Children with this condition may be educated in a special class in a regular school if the condition is mild. However, most students with this disorder are educated in a more restrictive program housed in a special school, residential school, or institution if the antisocial behavior is extreme.

Organizations

American Academy of Child and Adolescent Psychiatry
Public Information Office
3615 Wisconsin Avenue, NW
Washington, DC 20016
(202) 966-7300
Web site: http://www.aacap.org

Center on Positive Behavioral Interventions and Supports
1235 College of Education at University of Oregon
1761 Alder Street
Eugene, OR 97403-5262
(541) 346-2505
E-mail: pbis@oregon.uregon.edu
Web site: http://www.pbis.org

Federation of Families for Children's Mental Health
1101 King Street, Suite 420
Alexandria, VA 22314
(703) 684-7710
E-mail: ffcmh@ffcmh.org
Web site: http://www.ffcmh.org

National Alliance for the Mentally Ill (NAMI)
Colonial Place Three
2107 Wilson Boulevard, Suite 300
Arlington, VA 22203-3754
(703) 524-7600; (703) 516-7227 (TTY); (800) 950-6264
E-mail: helpline@nami.org
Web site: http://www.nami.org

National Clearinghouse on Family Support and Children's Mental Health
Portland State University
P.O. Box 751
Portland, OR 97207-0751
(800) 628-1696; (503) 725-4040
Web site: http://www.rtc.pdx.edu/

National Mental Health Association
2001 N. Beauregard Street, 12th Floor
Alexandria, VA 22311
(703) 684-7722; (800) 969-6642; (800) 433-5959 (TTY)
E-mail: infoctr@nmha.org
Web site: http://www.nmha.org

National Mental Health Information Center
P.O. Box 42490
Washington, DC 20015

(800) 789-2647; (301) 443-9006 (TTY)
E-mail: info@mentalhealth.org
Web site: http://www.mentalhealth.org

Antisocial Personality Disorder

Description

This disorder is characterized by a pattern of irresponsible and antisocial behavior. The condition is usually first seen in childhood or early adolescence and continues throughout the child's development. The diagnosis is usually made after the age of eighteen and the individual must have had a history of symptoms before the age of fifteen indicative of a conduct disorder.

Symptoms

It is common for these individuals to exhibit symptoms such as lying, stealing, truancy, fighting, vandalism, and physical cruelty to animals or people. They usually do not adhere to financial obligations, repeatedly perform antisocial acts that may be grounds for arrest, and fail to conform to social norms.

Educational Implications

The situation for the classroom teacher can be serious with this type of disorder. Because these individuals have little or no regard for the personal rights of others, any antisocial act can occur, even ones that may place you in danger. Medication may help reduce tension, and therapy may have limited success.

Schools can take a lot of approaches to prevent antisocial behavior and to address it when it does occur. According to NICHCY (2003), best practice indicates the following:

- Assessment of the student's behavior must be linked with interventions that follow the student through whatever placements the student has. Multiple interventions are necessary for improving the behavior of most students. Any positive effect of a single strategy, especially when the intervention is short-term, is likely to be temporary. Just as behavior problems and risk factors come in packages, so too should interventions.
- To produce lasting effects, interventions must address not only the behavior that led to disciplinary action but a constellation of related behaviors and contributing factors.
- Interventions must be sustained and include specific plans for promoting maintenance over time and generalization across settings. Focusing on the student's behavior while placed in any short-term setting, such as an interim alternative educational setting, is not sufficient. Interventions need to follow the student to his or her next placement (and elsewhere).
- A combination of proactive, corrective, and instructive classroom management strategies is needed. Interventions must target specific prosocial and antisocial behaviors and the "thinking skills" that mediate such behaviors. Such a

combination provides an atmosphere of warmth, care, support, and necessary structure. Interventions must be developmentally appropriate and address strengths and weaknesses of the individual students and their environment.

- Parent education and family therapy are critical components of effective programs for antisocial children and youth. Interventions are most effective when provided early in life. Devoting resources to prevention reduces the later need for more expensive treatment.
- Interventions should be guided by schoolwide and districtwide policies that emphasize positive interventions over punitive ones. Interventions should be fair, consistent, culturally and racially nondiscriminatory, and sensitive to cultural diversity.
- Interventions should be evaluated as to their short-term and long-term effectiveness in improving student behavior. Both the process and outcome of each intervention should be evaluated.
- Teachers and support staff need to be well-trained in assessment and intervention. Staff working with students who have behavior problems will require ongoing development and support services.
- Effective behavioral interventions require collaborative efforts from the school, home, and community agencies. Helping children and youth must be a shared responsibility.

Possible Least Restrictive Educational Setting

Children or individuals who are determined to have this disorder may no longer be part of the educational system. If already classified as disabled, they would probably be placed in a very restrictive educational setting until the age of twenty-one. However, they may well have already been arrested by that time.

Organizations

Beach Center on Disability at University of Kansas
Haworth Hall, Room 3136
1200 Sunnyside Avenue
Lawrence, KS 66045
(785) 864-7600 (V/TTY)
Web site: http://www.beachcenter.org

Center for Effective Collaboration and Practice
(Improving Services to Children and Youth with Emotional and Behavioral Problems)
American Institutes for Research
1000 Thomas Jefferson Street, NW, Suite 400
Washington, DC 20007
(202) 944-5400
E-mail: center@air.org
Web site: http://cecp.air.org

Center on Positive Behavioral Interventions and Supports
1235 College of Education at University of Oregon
1761 Alder Street
Eugene, OR 97403-5262
(541) 346-2505
E-mail: pbis@oregon.uoregon.edu
Web site: http://www.pbis.org

Disorders of Childhood and Adolescence

Anorexia Nervosa

Description

Children with this condition show a marked disturbance and unwillingness to maintain a minimal body weight for their age and height. An extremely distorted sense of body image exists, and intense fears and worries about gaining weight become obsessive. It is not uncommon for bulimia nervosa (discussed later) to be an associated feature. In more severe cases death may occur.

Etiology

Studies seem to indicate that anorexics are usually perfectionist, high-achieving females.

Gender

Ninety-five percent of the cases of anorexia nervosa are among females.

Symptoms

Children with this disorder may also exhibit self-induced vomiting, use of laxatives, reduction of food intake, preoccupation with becoming fat, and noticeable increase in the frequency and intensity of exercise. In females, absence of menstrual cycles is common as the child's weight decreases and the body chemistry changes.

Educational Implications

Be aware of frequent absences because of medical complications. These children are usually high-achievers, but because of their medical conditions may find it difficult to keep up with their studies.

Levine (1994) suggests the following tips for teachers who are involved with students with eating disorders:

- Do not cast a net of awe and wonder around the existence of an eating disorder. Keep the focus on the reality that eating disorders result in *IMAD:*
  I*nefficiency in the fulfillment of academic, familial, occupational, and other responsibilities*

Misery in the form of food and weight obsession, anxiety about control, guilt, helplessness, hopelessness, and extreme mood swings

Alienation in the form of social anxiety, social withdrawal, secrecy, mistrust of others, and self-absorption

Disturbance of self and others through loss of control over dieting, body image, eating, emotions, and decisions

- Do not oversimplify. Avoid thinking or saying things such as "Well, eating disorders are just an addiction like alcoholism," or "All you have to do is start accepting yourself as you are."
- Do not imply that bulimia nervosa, because it is often associated with "normal weight," is somehow less serious than anorexia nervosa.
- Do not be judgmental—that is, don't tell the child that what she is doing is "sick" or "stupid" or "self-destructive."
- Do not give advice about weight loss, exercise, or appearance.
- Do not confront her as part of a group of people.
- Do not diagnose: keep the focus on IMAD and the ways that the behaviors are affecting the child's life and well-being.
- Do not become the person's therapist, savior, or victim. In this regard, do not "promise to keep this a secret no matter what."
- Do not get into an argument or a battle of wills. If the person denies having a problem, simply and calmly: Repeat what you have observed—that is, your evidence that there is a problem. Repeat your concern about the person's health and well-being. Repeat your conviction that the circumstance should at least be evaluated by a counselor or therapist. End the conversation if it is going nowhere or if you or the child becomes too upset. This impasse suggests that she needs to consult a professional.
- Take any actions necessary to carry out your responsibilities or to protect yourself.
- If possible, leave the door open for further conversations.
- Do not be inactive during an emergency. If the child is throwing up several times per day, or passing out, or complaining of chest pain, or is suicidal, get professional help immediately.

Possible Least Restrictive Educational Setting

Children with this disorder can be maintained in the regular school setting unless the condition becomes severe enough to warrant hospitalization. In some cases, if the child is at home and unable to attend school, homebound instruction is utilized.

Organizations

National Eating Disorders Organization

603 Stewart Street, Suite 803

Seattle, WA 98101

(206) 382-3587

Web site: http://www.nationaleatingdisorders.org

Anorexia Nervosa and Related Eating Disorders, Inc.
The Center for Eating Disorders
St. Joseph Medical Center
7620 York Road
Towson, MD 21204–7582
Web site: http://www.eating-disorders.com

American Anorexia/Bulimia Association, Inc.
Web site: http://www.aabainc.org/

Bulimia Nervosa

Description

This condition is characterized by recurrent episodes of uncontrolled consumption of large quantities of food (binging) followed by self-induced vomiting (purging) and use of laxatives or diuretics over a period of at least two months.

Etiology

Some research indicates that obesity during the teenage years might be a predisposing factor for bulimia in later life.

Symptoms

The individual with bulimia nervosa exhibits symptoms characterized by binging and purging, use of laxatives and diuretics, obsessive preoccupation with body shape and weight, and a feeling of lack of control over food consumption during binge episodes.

Educational Implications

It is likely you will not even know that one of your students is bulimic. Individuals hide this "secret" well and may not divulge the problem to anyone, not even a best friend. This is usually a private disorder until the person feels so out of control that she seeks help and support. Consequently, try to be aware of frequent trips to the bathroom, especially in the morning after breakfast or after lunch. Changes in skin color and look may give some indication of a problem. If you suspect anything, let the nurse investigate this further. (Also see the educational implications section under "Anorexia Nervosa" for further suggestions.)

Possible Least Restrictive Educational Setting

Unlike children with anorexia nervosa, those with bulimia nervosa seldom suffer incapacitating symptoms except in rare cases when the eating and purging episodes run throughout the day. Consequently, in most cases these children can be maintained in the regular school setting unless the condition becomes severe enough to warrant hospitalization.

Organizations

See organizations listed under "Anorexia Nervosa."

Selective Mutism

Description

This disorder is characterized by persistent refusal to talk in one or more primary social situations, including school, despite the ability to comprehend spoken language and to speak. The resistance to speak is not a symptom of any other major disorder.

Etiology

The possible causes for such a condition vary from maternal overprotection, immigration, mental retardation, and hospitalization or trauma before the age of three.

Symptoms

Some symptoms associated with this disorder besides the refusal to speak include excessive shyness, social isolation, compulsive behavior, temper tantrums, negativism, clinginess, and withdrawal.

When in school or other anxiety-provoking settings, behavioral characteristics may vary, with some children being much more withdrawn than others. Some children with selective mutism stand motionless and expressionless, and may demonstrate awkward or stiff body language. Some may turn their heads, avoid eye contact, chew or twirl their hair, or withdraw into a corner. Over time, some learn to cope and participate in certain social settings by performing nonverbally or by talking quietly to a select few.

Children with selective mutism tend to have difficulty initiating and may be slow to respond even when it comes to nonverbal communication. This can be quite frustrating to the children themselves and lead to falsely low test scores and misinterpretation of their cognitive abilities. Such scores will need to be reviewed for their accuracy.

Educational Implications

This condition may create a difficult situation for the classroom teacher. You will not be able to measure certain language or social levels, will have to deal with social concerns and comments from classmates, and will have a difficult time encouraging these children to participate in necessary class activities or group projects. If you have such a child in your classroom, contact the school psychologist as soon as possible. Individual and family counseling is highly suggested for such a disorder. Children with selective mutism are usually treated with cognitive behavior therapy (CBT) and behavioral therapy—that is, desensitization and positive reinforcement, administered by trained professionals in this technique. As a classroom teacher you would not be directly involved in CBT but might be asked to carry out some of the professionals' recommendations in the classroom.

According to the Selective Mutism Group, CBT therapists help children change their thoughts (the cognitive part) and their actions (the behavioral part). CBT therapists recognize that anxious children tend to exaggerate the frightening aspects of certain situations, so they help the children gain a more realistic perspective in order to decrease anxiety.

Consider the following when working with a student with selective mutism:

- Reduce the child's anxiety by not forcing him to speak. It is important that you do not blame the child. No matter how frustrated you may become, remember that this is not something the child wants. Consider it a "speech block."
- Encourage the child to develop independent skills. Give the child classroom responsibilities. Although these children may not speak, they are usually still very capable.
- Improve communication. Help reinforce speech in school by providing rewards and incentives. But do not force the child to speak. Say, for example, "If you can smile at me, I will give you a star." Develop a step-by-step process toward actual speech. For example, the steps could be as follows: smile at the teacher, raise hand to say hello, whisper "hello" to teacher, say "hello" to teacher.
- Have the parent speak to the child in the school environment. Have the parent ask the child questions about what is going on in school. By getting the selectively mute child to talk, you are also reducing his sensitivity to the unfamiliar environment at school.
- Do not reinforce the gains that a selectively mute child receives. In many cases, and without awareness, parents, siblings, other teachers, and classmates have accommodated the child's mute behavior by doing things for him and treating him as if he is really mute.
- Take the opportunity to encourage the child to do things for himself.
- Work closely with professionals, such as speech and language pathologists, psychologists, and psychiatrists. Seek their help and advice.

Possible Least Restrictive Educational Setting

This type of child can usually be maintained in the regular educational setting as long as he or she maintains sufficient performance levels. However, if the child's academic performance becomes discrepant, or if social and intellectual factors interfere in performance, then a more restrictive placement may have to be explored.

Organization

Selective Mutism Foundation, Inc.

P.O. Box 13133

Sissonville, WV 25360-0133

Web site: http://www.selectivemutismfoundation.org

Tourette's Syndrome

Description

This disorder is characterized by motor and vocal tics that may be exhibited in the form of grunting, coughs, barks, touching, knee jerking, drastic head movements, head banging, squatting, and so on.

Symptoms

The described symptoms may change as the child develops but the course of the disorder is usually lifelong. Associated features include obsessive compulsive disorder (OCD) and ADHD (attention deficit hyperactive disorder, discussed earlier). The condition is more common in males, and family patterns are also common. Coprolalia (vocal tic involving the expression of obscenities) is an associated symptom in about 33 percent of cases.

Educational Implications

If you have a student with Tourette's syndrome, be aware and sensitive to the social difficulties and confusion exhibited by the student's peers. Social rejection, isolation, and victimization are common and you need to step in to prevent these situations from occurring. In older students, be aware of the child's use of a great deal of energy in an attempt to control the tics because of social pressure; this may come at the cost of attention and consistent academic performance.

Possible Least Restrictive Educational Setting

Children with mild forms of this disorder can easily be maintained in a regular educational setting with supportive services. Because the condition does affect performance in many cases, these children are usually classified as disabled and receive special education services, including modifications. More severe cases that do not respond to medication may require a more restrictive setting. Medication, counseling, and special education services provide a good treatment plan. However, a child may have to try many medications before finding one that relieves the tics. Medications are also taken if OCD symptoms are associated.

If you have a student with this condition, contact the local Tourette's association in your area for further literature. The Center for Applied Research in Education (1995) suggests the following classroom strategies when working with children with Tourette's syndrome:

- Keep in mind that motor or vocal tics are occurring involuntarily.
- Try not to react with anger or annoyance.
- Try to be a role model for the other students on how to react to the Tourette's symptoms.
- Provide the child with opportunities for short breaks out of the classroom.
- Try to find a private place somewhere in the school where the child can "let out" the tics, since the effort to suppress the tics causes a buildup of tension.
- Allow the student to take tests in a private room so that he does not waste energy suppressing the tics, which will interfere with his concentration.
- Work with the student's classmates to help them understand the tics and to reduce ridicule and teasing. Secure audiovisual materials or pamphlets to provide information for your students and colleagues.
- If the student's tics are particularly disruptive, avoid having him recite in front of the class.

- Have the student tape-record oral reports.
- Keep in mind that students with Tourette's often have visual motor difficulties.
- Modify written assignments by reducing the number of problems presented to the child.
- Allow parents to copy down work so that the child can dictate his ideas to facilitate concept formation.
- Allow the student to write the answers directly on a test paper or booklet rather than use computerized scoring sheets.
- Allow the child untimed tests to reduce stress.
- Allow another child to take notes for the student so that he can listen to the lecture without the added stress of copying notes.
- Try not to penalize for spelling errors.
- Use a multisensory approach whenever possible.
- Avoid giving multiple directions at once.
- Use graph paper for math so that the student can place one number in each box.

Organization

Tourette's Syndrome Association
42-40 Bell Boulevard, Suite 205
Bayside, NY 11361-2820
(718) 224-2999; 888-4-TOURET (486-8738)
E-mail: ts@tsa-usa.org
Web site: http://tsa-usa.org

Functional Encopresis

Description

The primary symptom of this disorder is repeated involuntary or intentional passage of feces into clothing or other places that are inappropriate. The condition is not related to any physical condition, must occur for a period of six months on a regular basis, and be present in a child over the age of four for diagnosis to take place.

Educational Implications

Children with this disorder may experience social ridicule if the occurrences take place in school. You need to be sensitive to the condition and involve the school psychologist and parents. Try to intervene as quickly as possible if a pattern exists to avoid further embarrassment for the child and secondary complications such as avoidance.

If you have a child with this condition in your classroom, keep the following in mind:

- Keep your responses low-key.
- Have a change of clothes available at school, in the clinic or an alternative location.

- Plan a consistent response to events. Send the student to the clinic or other location to clean up and change clothes. While wearing latex gloves, place soiled clothes in a plastic bag. Call parent and make arrangements for soiled items to be returned home.
- Observe for consistent trigger events.
- Support the bowel-bladder retraining program that is recommended by the physician.

Possible Least Restrictive Educational Setting

Children with this condition should have no problem maintaining a regular educational setting unless the condition is associated with other disabilities that require special education placement. However, this condition may create social pressures and isolation for the child.

Organization

American Academy of Family Physicians
11400 Tomahawk Creek Parkway
Leawood, KS 66211-2672
Web site: http://www.aafp.org/

Functional Enuresis

Description

This disorder is characterized by repeated involuntary or intentional elimination of urine during the day or night into bed or clothes at an age when bladder control is expected. A frequency of at least two times per month must be present for the condition to be diagnosed between the ages of five and six and at least once a month for older children.

Etiology

In at least 75 percent of cases, the child has a first-degree biological relative who has or has had the condition.

Educational Implications

This condition may create social pressures and isolation for the child.

Possible Least Restrictive Educational Setting

Children with this condition should have no problem maintaining a regular educational setting unless the condition is associated with other disabilities that require special education placement.

Organizations

International Enuresis Research Center
Web sites: http://www.ierc.org; http://www.mdekf.aau.dk/ierc/ierc.htm

National Enuresis Society
Web site: http://www.peds.umn.edu/Centers/NES

Anxiety and Mood Disorders

Separation Anxiety Disorder

Description

This disorder is characterized by extreme anxiety associated with separation from someone with whom the child views as a significant other. Although this reaction is common among very young children on their first day of school, continuation of the anxiety for more than two weeks indicates a problem that needs to be addressed. Separation anxiety is frequently exhibited at school and at home. It should be noted that if symptoms of separation anxiety occur in an adolescent, other factors such as social or academic pressure may be the contributing cause.

Age of Onset

This condition may be seen in children as early as preschool age; onset in later developmental stages around adolescence is rare.

Educational Implications

Children with this disorder may require a great deal of your attention. The child may cling, be afraid to try new things, require a great deal of reassurance, and cry frequently. Panic attacks are common, and you may find that reasoning does not reduce the anxiety. Physical complaints are common and should never be ignored. However, once medical causes are ruled out, these "physical" symptoms are usually manifestations of the anxiety.

Watkins and Brynes (2001) suggest that teachers do the following:

- Introduce yourself to the child and invite the child to play with toys or have a snack.
- Offer to have the parent stay a while; leave the child alone briefly with the parent and then return.
- Suggest to the parent that he or she try role-playing with the child at home to rehearse the separation.
- Create a ritual for the parent leaving the child.
- If the child is in an absolute panic, ask the parent to stay until the child quiets down. Ask the parent to comfort the child in a firm, loving voice.
- Never criticize the child for feeling sad or anxious.

Possible Least Restrictive Educational Setting

Children with this disorder can usually be maintained in the regular class setting through the help of the school psychologist working with the child and parents. If the condition persists and the diagnosis changes—for example, if it deepens into major depression—then outside professional help may be required and a more restrictive program, sometimes even homebound instruction if attendance at school is not possible, may have to be instituted.

Organizations

See the organizations listed under "Oppositional Defiant Disorder," and also the following:

Anxiety Disorders Association of America
(Formerly the Phobia Society of America)
11900 Parklawn Drive, Suite 100
Rockville, MD 20852-2624
(301) 231-9350

Anxiety Disorders Education Campaign
National Mental Health Association
1021 Prince Street
Alexandria, VA 22314-2971
(800) 969-NMHA; (703) 684-7722; (800) 433–5959 (TTY)

Anxiety Disorders Education Program
National Institute of Mental Health
5600 Fishers Lane, Room 7-99
Rockville, MD 20857
88-88-ANXIETY (269–4389) (information on anxiety); 888-64-PANIC (64–72642) (information on panic attacks); (800) 421-4211 (information on depression)

Center for Help for Anxiety/Agoraphobia Through New Growth Experiences
128 Country Club Drive
Chula Vista, CA 91911
(619) 425-3992

Avoidant Disorder of Childhood and Adolescence

Description

This disorder results in the child withdrawing from social contact or interaction with an unfamiliar peer or adult to the point of becoming a significant factor in social development.

Symptoms

Symptoms include lack of assertiveness, low self-esteem, frequent embarrassment, narrow safety zone (areas or situations in her life in which she safely and comfortably operates), and a need to be socially involved only with family members or peers already known to the child.

Gender

This disorder may be found more commonly in females than males.

Educational Implications

Children with this disorder can maintain regular class placement as long as achievement levels do not present problems, possibly signifying some other condition. If you have this type of student in your classroom, be aware of social isolation, withdrawal from activity-based assignments, and a complete unwillingness to try new situations involving social interaction with unfamiliar peers.

Try the following strategies with such students:

- Do not try to force the child into new social interaction situations; this may only result in further withdrawal socially as well as verbally.
- Work alone with the child or along with familiar peers only for a while.
- Slowly increase the time that you allow the child to work with another student. Provide success-oriented tasks for the child and her working mate.
- Develop a trust relationship; your influence may then increase.
- Refer the child to the school psychologist. With the psychologist, explore individual outside counseling with a slow lead into small group counseling. However, be aware that the child may resist this.

Possible Least Restrictive Educational Setting

Children with this disorder can usually be maintained in the regular class setting through the help of the school psychologist working with the child and parents.

Organizations

See the organizations listed under "Separation Anxiety Disorder."

Overanxious Disorder

Description

The main feature of this disorder is an excessive level of anxiety or worry extending over a six-month or longer period of time.

Symptoms

Children with this disorder exhibit symptoms including constant need for reassurance, inability to relax, unrealistic worry about present or future events, frequent physical concerns, and self-consciousness. Physical concerns are common but should always be ruled out by a medical professional. In most cases of overanxious disorder, somatic (bodily) complaints are manifestations of inner tension and conflict.

Educational Implications

If you have a student with this disorder, be aware that she may have poor academic performance because of her constant worrying. Also try to reassure and compliment the child as much as possible when she is not drawing negative attention to herself.

You may want to consider the following strategies:

- Be enthusiastic about any change in routine or schedule. Provide these students with a five- or ten-minute notice before the change will take place. If you are excited and confident about the change, they will be too.
- Start daily routines that add to continuity. Let the children run consistent errands—collecting snack money daily or laying out materials. Such daily and consistent routines will anchor these children and give them something to look forward to when they come to school.
- Put aside extra time for chatting with these children on a daily basis. This personal sense of connection will comfort them.
- Go to these children as often as possible when they are not expecting it and compliment them, make a funny comment, or offer them some information. This will give them reassurance that you are thinking about them and watching out for them. Always personally say good-bye to these children at the end of the day and offer them some happy piece of information about the following day.
- Make sure the class activities are developmentally appropriate for these children: interesting and challenging but doable activities will help them feel comfortable in the classroom.
- Find out from the parents as much as you can about these children's interests or hobbies and try to connect them with other children with the same interests. Hold an orientation for children and parents. Small groups will make it easier for children to get to know each other. If you are dealing with an older child, have him work with much younger children so he can feel powerful and more in control.
- Set up an area for photos of parents and family members that children may "visit" throughout the day. Also include items that reflect the cultural experience of all children to help promote a sense of mutual respect and understanding. This will offer these children a better connection to the classroom.

Possible Least Restrictive Educational Setting

Most children with this disorder can be educated in a regular class placement unless the condition is coupled with more serious disabilities that require a more restrictive setting. Referral to the school psychologist is highly recommended.

Organizations

See the organizations listed under "Separation Anxiety Disorder."

Obsessive Compulsive Disorder (OCD)

Description

The main characteristics associated with this disorder are persistent obsessions (persistent thoughts) or compulsions (repetitive acts) that significantly interfere with the individual's normal daily social, educational, occupational, or environmental routines.

Symptoms

Typical obsessive symptoms include persistent thoughts, impulses, or images. Typical compulsive symptoms include repetitive and intentional behaviors. Although the individual is aware that these behaviors and thoughts are irrational, she is unable to control the outcome.

Educational Implications

Children and adolescents with this disorder have difficulty concentrating and maintaining consistent academic performance. They may also experience depression as a result of their difficulties, and medication may be prescribed to relieve the anxiety associated with this disorder.

Parker (2002) suggests the following tips for teachers dealing with children with obsessive compulsive disorder:

- Allow more time for completing tasks and tests. Other testing accommodations may include testing in an alternate location, providing breaks during testing, and allowing the student to write directly on the test booklet. In some cases you may need to allow these students to take tests orally.
- For students with compulsive writing rituals, consider limiting handwritten work. Common compulsive writing rituals include dotting *i*'s in a particular way or retracing particular letters ritualistically, counting certain letters or words, completely blackening in the circles on test forms, and so on. In such cases, a reasonable test accommodation would be to have the student circle her answers or record the answers directly on the test booklet.
- If the student's compulsions are not triggered by keyboarding, have the child use a word processor or notebook computer.
- If reading rituals and intrusive thoughts are severe, consider going to books on tape or recording the material for the student to listen to.
- Try to reduce triggers to compulsive rituals, if possible. If you know that a student will "have to" engage in a ritual if she sees the pencil sharpener, perhaps you can put the sharpener out of sight.
- Whenever it does not endanger the student or anyone else, accommodate situations over which she has little or no control. If she is late to school every day because her rituals are interfering with getting to school on time, it will only

make things worse if you discipline or punish her. Remember that the student is more frustrated with the situation than you are.

- Be aware of the peer problems or emotional needs of the student with OCD.
- Identify the child's strengths and talents, and be sure to point them out to her. Also try to compliment her in front of her peers; social problems are common in this population. If the student is being ridiculed for her rituals or obsessive fears, consider conducting a peer education program. Many videos are available on this topic.
- Consult often with the parent and the school psychologist.

Possible Least Restrictive Educational Setting

This type of child can usually be maintained in the regular educational setting as long as the child maintains sufficient performance levels. However, if the academic performance becomes discrepant, or if social and intellectual factors interfere in performance, then a more restrictive placement may have to be explored.

Organizations

Anxiety Disorders Association of America
8730 Georgia Avenue, Suite 600
Silver Spring, MD 20910
(240) 485-1001; (240) 485-1035
Web site: http://www.adaa.org

Association for Advancement of Behavior Therapy
305 Seventh Avenue
New York, NY 10001
(212) 647-1890
Web site: http://server.psyc.vt.edu/aabt/

Freedom From Fear
308 Seaview Avenue
Staten Island, NY 10305
(718) 351-1717
Web site: http://www.freedomfromfear.com

Madison Institute of Medicine
Obsessive Compulsive Information Center
7617 Mineral Point Road, Suite 300
Madison, WI 53717-1914
(608) 827-2470
Web site: http://healthtechsys.com/mimocic.html

Obsessive-Compulsive Foundation, Inc.
337 Notch Hill Road
North Branford, CT 06471
(203) 315-2190
E-mail: info@ocfoundation.org
Web site: http://www.ocfoundation.org/

Trichotillomania Learning Center
1215 Mission Street, Suite 2
Santa Cruz, CA 95060-3558
(831) 457-1004
E-mail: trichster@aol.com
Web site: http://www.trich.org

Dysthymia

Description

The essential feature of this disturbance among children and adolescents is chronic disturbance of moods involving depression or irritable mood for a period of one year.

Symptoms

Vegetative signs of depression include poor appetite, difficulty sleeping, low energy, general fatigue, low self-esteem, difficulty concentrating, and feelings of hopelessness.

Educational Implications

If you have this type of student in your classroom, you need to work closely with the school psychologist or private therapist, if the child is in treatment. You should also be aware that medication may be involved, so it will be helpful for you to gain an understanding of the side effects.

Possible Least Restrictive Educational Setting

Students with this disorder can usually be maintained in a regular setting or a more restrictive special education program, if the symptoms become more intense. The chronicity of this disorder rather than the severity usually accounts for a mild or moderate impairment. Consequently, hospitalization is rare unless suicide is attempted. See further suggestions under "Childhood Depression."

Organizations

See organizations listed under "Childhood Depression."

Childhood Depression

Description

This mood disorder among children resembles depression in adults, but shows up in different ways. In children, it is the persistent experience of a sad or irritable mood and loss of interest or pleasure in nearly all activities. These feelings are accompanied by a range of additional symptoms affecting appetite and sleep, activity level and concentration, and feelings of self-worth.

Symptoms

The symptoms of childhood depression, sometimes referred to as early onset depression, are persistent sadness and hopelessness; withdrawal from friends and from activities once enjoyed; increased irritability or agitation; missed school or poor school performance; changes in eating and sleeping habits; indecision, lack of concentration, or forgetfulness; poor self-esteem or guilt; frequent physical complaints such as headaches and stomachaches; lack of enthusiasm, low energy, or low motivation; drug or alcohol abuse; and thoughts of death or suicide.

An Australian study reported that 2.1 percent of girls and 3.7 percent of boys between the ages six and twelve experienced depression during the course of a year. Other studies report that between 4 percent and 8 percent of teenagers suffer from depression. Depression before puberty is more likely to occur in boys; it is more likely after puberty in girls.

Educational Implications

Teachers can help lighten depressed students' load by creating a comfortable classroom where these students know they are cared for and where there is no time limit on cheering up. Depression takes a lot of time to get over, and school does not have to be a negative place of responsibility.

Here are three tips for dealing with depressed students in the classroom:

- Do not ignore depressed students. It shows that you do not care and invites the student to give up, guaranteeing failure. Draw such students out in class discussion and do whatever it takes to stimulate their minds so that they don't, in turn, learn to ignore you.
- Let them know that you care, but without getting too personal. Help them to update any missing assignments, or set up extra study time; whether they accept your efforts or not depends upon the severity of the depression. The fact that you have proven you care may make all the difference in the world.
- Never give up on these students, regardless of how long it has been since they have made any effort in your class. Students can tell when a teacher no longer believes in them and expects them to fail, and it only ends up making the situation worse than necessary.

Possible Least Restrictive Educational Setting

Students with this disorder can be maintained in either a regular setting or a more restrictive special education program, if the symptoms become more intense. The severity of this condition will determine the ability of the child to maintain a regular school setting. Hospitalization is not uncommon in severe cases unless the condition can be controlled with medications.

Organizations

American Academy of Child and Adolescent Psychiatry
Public Information Office
3615 Wisconsin Avenue, NW
Washington, DC 20016
(202) 966-7300
Web site: http://www.aacap.org

American Psychiatric Association
1400 K Street, NW
Washington, DC 20005
(202) 682-6000
Web site: http://www.psych.org

American Psychological Association
750 First Street, NE
Washington, DC 20002-4242
(202) 336-5500
Web site: http://www.apa.org

Center on Positive Behavioral Interventions and Supports
1235 College of Education at University of Oregon
1761 Alder Street
Eugene, OR 97403-5262
(541) 346-2505
E-mail: pbis@oregon.uregon.edu
Web site: http://www.pbis.org

Depression and Related Affected Disorders Association
600 North Wolfe Street
Baltimore, MD 21287-7381
(410) 955-4647
Web site: http://www.med.jhu.edu/drada

Federation of Families for Children's Mental Health
1101 King Street, Suite 420
Alexandria, VA 22314
(703) 684-7710
E-mail: ffcmh@ffcmh.org
Web site: http://www.ffcmh.org

National Alliance for the Mentally Ill (NAMI)
Colonial Place Three
2107 Wilson Boulevard, Suite 300
Arlington, VA 22203-3754
(703) 524-7600; (703) 516-7227 (TTY); (800) 950-6264
E-mail: helpline@nami.org
Web site: http://www.nami.org

National Alliance for Research on Schizophrenia and Depression
60 Cutter Mill Road, Suite 404
Great Neck, NY 11021
(800) 829-8289
Web site: http://www.narsad.org

National Clearinghouse on Family Support and Children's Mental Health
Portland State University
P.O. Box 751
Portland, OR 97207-0751
(800) 628-1696; (503) 725–4040
Web site: http://www.rtc.pdx.edu/

National Council for Community Behavioral Healthcare
12300 Twinbrook Parkway, Suite 320
Rockville, MD 20852
(301) 984-6200
Web site: http://www.nccbh.org

National Depressive and Manic Depressive Association
730 N. Franklin, Suite 501
Chicago, IL 60601-7204
(800) 826-3632
Web site: http://www.ndmda.org

National Foundation for Depressive Illness Inc.
P.O. Box 2257
New York, NY 10116
(800) 239-1265
Web site: http://www.depression.org

National Mental Health Association
2001 N. Beauregard Street, 12th Floor
Alexandria, VA 22311
(703) 684-7722; (800) 969-6642; (800) 433-5959 (TTY)
E-mail: infoctr@nmha.org
Web site: http://www.nmha.org

National Mental Health Information Center
P.O. Box 42490
Washington, DC 20015
(800) 789-2647; (301) 443-9006 (TTY)
E-mail: info@mentalhealth.org
Web site: http://www.mentalhealth.org

Chapter 20

What Special Educators Need to Know About Medication

There may be times when the special education teacher will be exposed to a special student whose condition may require the use of medication. While it is not important to possess a deep knowledge of medications, it is important to understand the nature of the medication, the reason for its use, and the possible side effects that may be exhibited during the school day. When a child is on medication, it is helpful to the medical doctor to receive observational reports on the child's reaction to the medication during the school day. The side effects mentioned below do not include all the possible side effects of the medication. The more common ones that might be observed in the classroom will be noted. With this in mind, there are several common medications that are used for certain conditions.

Attention Deficit Hyperactive Disorder

Psychostimulants—These medications have been referred to as paradoxical because they act in the reverse. The main purpose of these medications is to increase wakefulness, attention to task, and alertness either by releasing the neurotransmitter norepinephrine in the case of Ritalin, Cylert, and Dexedrine, or by brain stimulation as in the case of Pondimin. These characteristics are usually not present in the behavior of ADHD children who appear to exhibit restlessness, impulsivity, distractibility, and inattention.

Ritalin

Generic Name: Methylphenidate

Ritalin is a mild stimulant that acts upon the central nervous system and is widely prescribed in cases of ADHD. This medication is usually part of a total treatment plan that may also include individual counseling, family counseling, educational intervention, and social behavior modification.

The more common possible side effects may include loss of appetite, nervousness, difficulty in sleeping, abdominal pain, and weight loss. Ritalin is usually taken 30 to 45 minutes before meals and also comes in the form of a sustained or time-release tablet.

Caution is noted in the prescription of this medication when there is a history of Tourette's syndrome in the family, when the individual is already experiencing a tic disorder, or when there may be a possibility of glaucoma.

Cylert

Generic Name: Pemoline

Cylert is a medication that is used to treat children with ADHD. It is usually taken once a day in the morning, and some common side effects may include drowsiness, dizziness, insomnia, headaches, irritability, tics, nausea, jaundice (yellowing of skin and eyes), and weight loss.

Children who are on Cylert for extended periods of time need to be monitored carefully because the drug can stunt growth and may affect the kidneys and liver.

Dexedrine

Generic Name: Dextroamphetamine

This medication is available in liquid as well as tablet form and sustained-release tablets. It is usually prescribed as part of the treatment plan for children with ADHD, in cases of narcolepsy, and obesity. Possible side effects may include irritability, excessive restlessness, difficulty in sleeping, agitation, and dry mouth, and it may aggravate any tendency that an individual may have toward tics.

This medication is usually taken in the morning because it may cause insomnia. The child should be closely monitored because of the possibility of the medication affecting the child's growth. Unlike Cylert, which is rarely prescribed under the age of six, Dexedrine is prescribed for children as young as three years of age.

Other psychostimulants include:

- Pondimin

Psychosis

Antipsychotic Medication—These medications work by blocking one of the chemical messengers of the central nervous system: dopamine. These drugs are sometimes referred to as neuroleptic drugs because they block the dopamine receptors in the brain and restore the imbalance of nerve transmissions associated with psychotic behaviors.

Neuroleptic drugs are very powerful and as a result pose potential risks. Careful monitoring is required, and withdrawal symptoms such as headaches, nausea, dizziness, and increased heart rate may occur if these drugs are stopped abruptly. Note that alcohol consumption during the time the individual is on these medications may enhance the effects of the drug and increase the risk of depression.

Haldol

Generic name: Haloperidol

Haldol is frequently prescribed to treat the psychotic behaviors associated with schizophrenia. It is also prescribed for children with oppositional or combative behavior patterns, hyperactivity, and tic disorders. This medication may also result in *tardive dyskinesia*, a condition marked by involuntary muscle spasms and twitches in the face and body.

Some common side effects that may be observed in the classroom include coughing, anxiety, blurred vision, chewing movements, dry mouth, dizziness, drowsiness, lack of muscular coordination, physical rigidity and stupor, and protruding tongue. Withdrawal symptoms may include muscle spasms and twitches.

Mellaril

Generic Name: Thioridazine

Mellaril is commonly used to treat psychotic disorders, depression, and anxiety in adults. It is also used to treat behavior problems in children and panic disorders in the elderly. As with Thorazine, tardive dyskinesia may be a side effect.

Some common side effects that may be observed in the classroom include hypokenesis (an abnormal lack of movement), muscle rigidity, blurred vision, chewing movements, dry mouth, eye spasms, fixed gaze, and swelling in the throat.

Navane

Generic Name: Thiothixene

Navane, like most neuroleptics, works by lowering levels of dopamine in the brain. Excessive levels of dopamine are associated with the severe sense of distorted reality typical of psychotic disorders.

Some common side effects that may be observed in the classroom are coughing, anxiety, blurred vision, chewing movements, dry mouth, dizziness, drowsiness, lightheadedness, puffing of cheeks, seizures, sensitivity to light, and restlessness.

Navane has been known to mask symptoms of brain tumors and intestinal obstructions. Consequently, close monitoring is important.

Prolixin

Generic Name: Fluphenazine

Prolixin is a neuroleptic medication that is used to reduce the symptoms associated with psychotic disorders such as schizophrenia. Prolixin may also cause tardive dyskinesia and should never be taken with alcohol.

Common side effects observed in the classroom may include muscle rigidity, blurred vision, chewing movements, complete loss of movement, dizziness, drowsiness, fixed gaze, muscle spasms, puckering of mouth, twitching, and jaundice (yellowing of the skin and the whites of the eyes).

Stelazine

Generic Name: Trifluoperazine

Stelazine is a medication that is used to reduce the symptoms associated with psychotic disorders such as schizophrenia. While not the medication of choice, Stelazine is sometimes used to treat anxiety that does not respond to ordinary tranquilizers. As with most neuroleptics, Stelazine may cause tardive dyskinesia and should not be taken with alcohol.

Some common side effects that may be observed in the classroom include coughing, anxiety, blurred vision, chewing movements, dry mouth, dizziness, drowsiness, lack of muscular coordination, physical rigidity and stupor, and protruding tongue.

Stelazine is usually not prescribed if the individual has liver problems, is already taking central nervous system depressants, or is suffering from blood conditions.

Thorazine

Generic Name: Chlorpromazine

Thorazine is a medication that is used to reduce the symptoms associated with psychotic disorders such as schizophrenia. During treatment with Thorazine, patients may experience a condition marked by involuntary muscle spasms and twitches in the face and body called tardive dyskinesia. This may be a chronic condition, but is usually more common with the elderly.

Some possible side effects of Thorazine may include chewing movements, difficulty breathing, drooling and difficulty swallowing, eye problems observed as a fixed gaze, and twitching in the body.

Trilafon

Generic Name: Perphenazine

Trilafon is used to reduce severe anxiety associated with psychotic disorders and to reduce the symptoms of hallucinations and delusions. Common side effects include drowsiness, tardive dyskinesia, and dry mouth.

Other antipsychotic medications may include the following:

- Serentil
- Moban
- Loxitane
- Compazine
- Orap
- Clozaril

Tourette's Syndrome

Tourette's syndrome is a disorder characterized by motor and vocal ticking that may be exhibited in the form of grunting, coughs, barks, touching, knee jerking, drastic head movements, head banging, squatting, and so forth. A variety of medications are used to reduce the symptoms, which can be so severe at times that they may be mistaken for seizures. With many Tourette's patients, one medication may be given for the ticking and one for the symptoms of OCD (obsessive compulsive disorder), while still other medications may be given to reduce the side effects of those already administered. The more common medications used to treat this disorder include the following.

Orap

Generic Name: Pimozide

Orap is an oral medication that is usually prescribed with Haldol, a primary choice medication. Orap reduces the intensity of physical and verbal tics, jerking motions, twitches, and verbally bizarre outbursts. This medication should only be used when the tics are so severe that it hampers the individual's ability to function.

Some side effects that may be observed in the classroom include increase in appetite, blurred vision, trembling of hands, drooling, dizziness, changes in handwriting, loss of movement, swelling around the eyes, and excessive thirst.

Catapres

Generic Name: Clonidine

Catapres is usually prescribed for high blood pressure, but has been used with Tourette's syndrome. The more common side effects include dry mouth, skin reactions, dizziness, and drowsiness.

Haldol

Generic Name: Haloperidol

Haldol is a widely prescribed medication used to suppress the symptoms associated with Tourette's syndrome. As previously mentioned, Haldol is also used to reduce the symptoms associated with psychotic behavior, as well as with children with severe behavior problems and hyperactivity.

Depression

Antidepressants—Sometimes referred to as tricyclic drugs, these drugs affect the symptoms associated with depression by adjusting the levels of neurotransmitters in the brain such as dopamine, serotonin, and epinephrine. These medications are usually prescribed when the treatment of the condition is considered long-term. Doctors do not usually like to use such powerful tricyclic antidepressants for short-term or transitory depression.

These medications tend to elevate the individual's mood, improve sleep patterns, increase energy levels and physical activity, and restore perception to a more positive level.

In the case of some antidepressants, once the doctor feels comfortable with the levels of medication attained, he or she may prescribe a single dose at night, a practice called *night-loading.*

Elavil

Generic Name: Amitriptyline hydrochloride

Other Brand Name: Endep

Elavil is a medication that is prescribed for the relief of severe mental depression. Some possible side effects that may be observed in the classroom include abnormal movements, speech difficulties, dry mouth, light-headedness, fatigue, fainting, hallucinations, insomnia, loss of coordination, tingling, and "pins and needles."

Tofranil

Generic Name: Imipramine

Other Brand Name: Janimine

Tofranil is a commonly used tricyclic antidepressant. It is also used to treat enuresis (bedwetting) on a short-term basis. It is a powerful medication that needs to be monitored closely. It is usually not prescribed for individuals who are already on MAO inhibitors such as Nardil and Parnate.

Some common side effects may include sensitivity to light, abdominal cramps, frequent urination, agitation, sore throat, fatigue, loss of appetite, nausea, insomnia, and inflammation of the mouth. It is not usually administered to children under the age of six.

Norpramin

Generic Name: Desipramine

Norpramin is a medication that is prescribed for the relief of symptoms associated with severe mental depression such as inability to fall asleep, inability to concentrate, loss of appetite, feelings of despondency, low energy levels, and feelings of helplessness.

Some common side effects may include black tongue; red, black, or blue spots on the tongue; sensitivity to light; abdominal cramps; frequent urination; agitation; sore throat; fatigue; loss of appetite; nausea; insomnia; and inflammation of the mouth.

Pamelor

Generic Name: Nortriptyline

Pamelor is prescribed to relieve the symptoms associated with severe mental depression. However, this medication seems to be more successful with *endogenous depression*, depression resulting from physical causes within the body.

This medication is never prescribed if the individual is already taking an MAO inhibitor such as Nardil, Parnate, or Marplan because high fevers, convulsions, and death have occurred with this combination of medications.

Some common side effects may include black tongue; red, black, or blue spots on the tongue; sensitivity to light; abdominal cramps; frequent urination; agitation; sore throat; fatigue; loss of appetite; perspiration; ringing in the ears; nausea; insomnia; and inflammation of the mouth.

Prozac

Generic Name: Fluoxetine

Prozac is a very popular medication that is prescribed for the treatment of long-term depression that has impaired the individual's ability to function on a daily basis. Prozac should never be taken with any MAO inhibitor because of serious complications.

Some possible side effects may include convulsions, dilation of pupils, dimness of vision, ear pain, eye pain, hostility, irrational ideas, and vague feelings of bodily discomfort.

Other tricyclic antidepressants include the following:

- Sinequan
- Adapin
- Desyrel
- Wellbutrin
- Parnate
- Vivactil
- Surmontil
- Asendin

- Ludiomil
- Marplan
- Eutonyl
- Elderyl
- Limbitrol

Anxiety or Panic Disorders

Antianxiety agents—These medications work by diminishing the activity of certain parts of the brain, called the limbic system. The symptoms associated with anxiety may include tension, agitation, irritability, panic attacks, and feelings of dying or going crazy. Physical symptoms include excessive sweating, heart palpitations, chills, fainting, racing pulse, and flushes. Anxiety may be a disorder by itself or a component of other psychiatric disorders.

Valium

Generic Name: Diazepam

Perhaps one of the more widely used antianxiety medications, Valium is used in the short-term treatment of the symptoms associated with anxiety. This medication is also prescribed in the treatment of acute alcohol withdrawal, as a muscle relaxant, and to treat certain convulsive disorders along with other medications. Valium belongs to a class of agents known as benzodiazepines.

Concerns about possible dependence need to be considered, and close monitoring is suggested. Serious withdrawal symptoms may occur if the medication is stopped abruptly.

Side effects may include loss of muscle coordination, light-headedness, and nausea.

Librium

Generic Name: Chlordiazepoxide

Other Brand Name: Libretabs

Librium is used in the short-term treatment of the symptoms associated with anxiety. This medication is also prescribed in the treatment of acute alcohol withdrawal and anxiety or apprehension before surgery. As with Valium, concerns about possible dependence need to be considered, and close monitoring is suggested. Serious withdrawal symptoms may occur if the medication is stopped abruptly.

Side effects may include confusion, drowsiness, and unsteadiness. Symptoms due to abrupt withdrawal may include convulsions, tremors, vomiting, muscle cramps, and sweating.

Xanax

Generic Name: Alprazolam

Xanax is a tranquilizer prescribed for the short-term treatment of symptoms associated with anxiety as well as panic disorders. This medication is also used to treat anxiety associated with depression. Xanax is considered a short-acting drug in that it acts quickly and, unlike Valium, leaves the body relatively quickly. Regardless of the nature and course of action, Xanax has a high dependency factor and should be closely monitored.

Some side effects may include dizziness, fainting, poor coordination, abnormal involuntary movement, agitation, confusion, dry mouth, and tremors.

Ativan

Generic Name: Lozazepam

Like Xanax, Ativan belongs to a group of drugs called benzodiazepines. It is considered short-acting and leaves and enters the body rapidly. It is usually prescribed for short-term treatment, about four months, and produces the fewest cumulative effects of all the medications in this group. It is commonly prescribed with other antidepressive or antipsychotic medications in the treatment of other psychiatric disorders.

When discontinuing use of the drug, taper it off slowly because rapid stoppage may result in irritability, insomnia, convulsions, depressed mood, and tremors.

Other antianxiety agents include the following:

- Buspar
- Catapres
- Inderal
- Tranxene
- Centrax
- Paxipam
- Serax

In conclusion, while medication can be a positive influence, monitoring by a trained professional is crucial. Parents should never administer an extra dosage or reduce the amount given to the child without consultation. If you have a child in your class who is on medication, you will need to inform the nurse so that he or she will have the information on file in case of an emergency or adverse reaction to the medication.

PART SIX

DEALING WITH PARENTS OF CHILDREN WITH DISABILITIES

Chapter 21

Helping Parents Help Their Children with Homework

Special education teachers spend a great deal of time and energy working with their students. However, a major factor in the success of these students in school is the support and involvement of their parents. Most parents need practical suggestions about how to interact with their children at home. The chapters in this part of the book provide you with some guidelines to offer your students' parents. We begin with homework.

Every night in millions of homes across the country you can imagine the same scenario playing out: parents are trying to get their children to do their homework. The scene may have different characters, but the script is usually the same.

Parents have always attempted to work with their children on homework. Their help ranges from a short occasional explanation to total completion of the task themselves. In an attempt to cope, parents will use trial and error, bribery, threats, reasoning, and anything else that they hope will work.

There seems to be little doubt that the parents' intentions are good. Who could find fault with their concern? However, it is not the intention that creates the anxiety and tension for both parents and children but the techniques they employ.

For some children, school can be a stressful place. With work demands, social pressures, concern over parental approval, fear of failure, and so much more, children may need the home as a haven to unwind. If they are stressed by their parents over homework, then where can they hang their hat? For adults, it is comparable to working all day at a job that has its share of stresses and then coming home to a tense environment. Think of how long you would be able to handle such a situation. And remember, adults have alternatives if the pressure gets to be too great. Children do not have the same options.

As a special education teacher, you can suggest the following techniques to parents to facilitate the process of homework and prevent frustration, anger, and disappointment.

Set Up a Homework Schedule

Many children benefit from a set homework schedule. For some children, such as children with learning disabilities, the responsibility of deciding when to sit down and do homework is too difficult. Children may decide to do their homework after school or after dinner; this is a personal choice and has to do with their learning style. However, once the time is determined, the schedule should be adhered to as much as possible. This will also relieve the problem of having to "hunt down" or "corral" children in order to get them to do their homework. After a while, this will become a natural part of their schedule. Of course, during this time no interruptions should be allowed. Phone calls, television, and so on can wait until the time is up.

Rank-Order Assignments

For some children, the decision about what to do first becomes a major chore. They may dwell over this issue for a long time. Some children use *horizontal perspective.* In other words, everything takes on the same level of importance and they can find no priority. Many children tend to use a *quantity orientation* (number of assignments left) rather than a *qualitative orientation* (difficulty of assignment). Suggest that parents rank-order—that is, choose which assignment to do first and so on. If the children have five tasks to do, have them do the four easy ones first. In their eyes, they will have only one assignment left even though it may be the more difficult task.

Do Not Sit Next to Child During Homework

This can be a big problem for some parents. Many will say that their children cannot work unless they are sitting next to them. But parents who employ this technique are not only setting themselves up for tremendous frustration and anger, but are also creating *learned helplessness.*

It is not that many children are unable to work, it is that they choose not to work. The work stoppage on their part occurs when the parent attempts to break away and no longer gives them undivided attention. This "dependency" is very unhealthy, because it is not imitated in the classroom. Consequently, such children may procrastinate about bringing unfinished work home. In this way they feel they can gain Mommy or Daddy's full attention. After a hard day's work, parents are tired and the thought of sitting down with children for up to three hours doing homework can only lead to problems.

If parents are already locked into this type of situation, suggest that they do not break away all at once. They should desensitize their child a little at a time. They may sit at the end of the table for a few days, then slowly increase the distance between themselves and the child until the child is working alone.

Check Correct Problems First

Parents sometimes zero in on the incorrect problems first. Explain to parents that when the child offers a paper to check, it is important to comment on how well the child did the correct problems, spelling words, and so on. Then, with the incorrect ones, they should say, "I bet if you go back and check these over you may get a different answer." Now the child will go back and redo the problems without animosity or feelings of inadequacy. If the parent were to zero in on the incorrect problems and become angry, there is a good chance that when the child returns to the work area he will spend more energy dealing with the loss of parental approval than finishing the task.

Never Let Homework Drag On All Night

Sometimes parents will allow their children to do their homework for several hours or until it is done. This is fine if the child's performance is consistent or the assignment realistically calls for such a commitment of time. However, if the child has gotten no further after one or two hours than ten minutes into the assignment, the homework should be stopped. The only thing accomplished by allowing a child to linger on hour after hour with little performance is increased feelings of inadequacy. Suggest that the parent end the work period after a reasonable amount of time, and then write you a note explaining the circumstances. Such concerns can be further worked out at a parent-teacher meeting.

There may be several reasons for such a behavior pattern. First, the child may not have understood the concept in class and therefore will not be able to finish the assignment at home. Second, the child may already have feelings of helplessness; consequently, waiting long periods of time may result in the completion of the assignment by the parents. Third, the child with serious learning difficulties may be overwhelmed by a series of assignments.

Discuss Homework Questions Before the Child Reads the Chapter

Most textbooks, except for the newer ones, have the chapter questions at the end. Thus, many children are not aware of what they should be looking for while reading. It is a good idea for parents to discuss and talk about the questions before their child begins reading. By using this strategy, children will know what important information to look for while they read.

Some children try to remember everything. Parents may want to give them a pencil and suggest that they lightly note a passage or word that sounds like something in one of the questions. This will help many when they have to skim back over the pages they have read.

Check Small Groups of Problems at a Time

Many children need immediate gratification. Suggest that parents have their child do five problems and then come back to them for a check. As already mentioned, parents should focus on the correct ones and then send the child back to do the next set of problems. In this way the child gets immediate feedback and approval and the necessary motivation for the next task. In addition, if the child is doing the assignment incorrectly, the error can be detected and explained, preventing the child from having to redo the entire assignment.

Put Textbook Chapters on Tape

Research indicates that the more sensory input children receive, the greater the chance they will retain information. Therefore, parents can tape-record science or social studies chapters so that children can listen while they read along. This allows both auditory and visual input of information. From time to time the parent may want to add a joke, a song, or a message to keep the child's interest. This recommendation would be especially useful for children with reading disabilities, language disabilities, and attentional problems.

Darken Page Lines for Children Learning How to Write

Sometimes, when children first learn to write, they experience problems with control. This may be a normal developmental problem. Parents can darken top and bottom lines so that the children have a reinforced boundary. This helps them maintain control and focus on letter formation. This technique can also be used with older children who have visual motor problems that are manifested in their handwriting.

Check Homework Assignments at the End of the Evening

Some children get very anxious about possibly bringing incorrect homework to school. Therefore, it is important for parents to take the time each night to check their homework. This gives the children a feeling of accomplishment, some positive attention, and a sense of security that the work is correct. This sense of academic security may carry over to the classroom and offer them a greater sense of confidence about their class work. However, if it becomes clear that the child did not understand a particular concept, tell the parent to let you know.

Be Aware of Negative Nonverbal Messages

Parents often say that they never get frustrated or yell while working with their children on homework. If all communication were verbal, these parents would have a good case. But nonverbal communication is a large part of overall communication. Many messages, especially negative ones, can be communicated easily without a person's awareness. Grimaces, body stiffness, sighs, raised eyebrows, and other body language are all nonverbal indicators. If children are sensitive, they will pick up on these messages and this can only add to the tension of the homework relationship. This is extremely important with younger children who cannot distinguish between loss of parental approval and loss of love. Such a state can only add stress to their ability to perform.

Avoid Finishing Assignments for the Child

As noted earlier, some parents will complete an entire assignment for their children. The result may be very destructive. Children tend to feel inadequate when parents finish their homework. First, they feel a sense of failure. Second, they feel a sense of inadequacy because they can never hope to do the assignment as well as Mommy or Daddy can. This can only foster increased dependency and feelings of helplessness on the part of children.

Explain that if the children cannot complete an assignment—and they have honestly tried to do so—the parent should write you a note explaining the circumstances. Explain that you will understand the situation.

Finally, before parents sit down to work with their children, they should make sure that they are not exhibiting symptoms that may reflect more serious concerns. When parents attempt to work with children who have severe learning problems or a high tension level they may feel tremendous frustration, anger, and disappointment. Following basic guidelines when helping with homework can result in a more rewarding situation for both parents and children.

Chapter 22

Helping Parents Use Effective Discipline at Home

Many parents find it difficult to use discipline and reward. What makes it difficult is parental confusion over what is either too strict or too lenient. The added pressure of confrontation adds to this discomfort. Certain techniques and attitudes are basic when it comes to this area of child rearing. It is very important that parents develop a healthy mental attitude about this area so they can be realistic, consistent, and supportive. You may wish to provide the parents with the following techniques to use as tools. Not all of these techniques work for all people, and some may take several tries before results are attained. Still, these strategies may help parents conserve energy and reduce the possibility of "parent burnout."

Limits and Guidelines Are Necessary for a Child's Emotional Development

Limits and guidelines represent a "safety net" within which children can behave. If limits are well defined, they know that any act of poor judgment will be brought to their attention. Consequently, they will be led back to the safety net. If children are not bound by well-defined limits, then there is no buffer between them and the outside world. The result may be a high level of tension and frequent inappropriate behavior.

All Behavior Must Have a Consequence

In other words, appropriate behavior should be rewarded and negative behavior punished. However, the consistency of such rewards and punishments from day to day is also crucial. Consistency of consequence, whether reward or punishment, aids children in developing a frame of reference.

Rewards Need Not Be Monetary

Although this is one possibility, rewards can also be in the form of verbal praise, written notes of thanks, extended playtime or bedtime, and so on. They should be natural and not mechanical. Variety is also nice when it comes to rewards.

Punishment Alone Is Not Effective in Changing Negative Behavior

Punishment tells children what not to do, but rewards tell children what behavior is acceptable. If long-term changes in behavior are desired, then reward must be included. Many parents shy away from rewards because they feel that doing what is expected should not be rewarded. However, all human beings need positive stroking regardless of whether or not the behavior is expected. Rewarding children for cleaning their room without having been told to do so reinforces the continuation of that behavior. This reward may be a positive comment of appreciation. Of course, not every behavior should be verbally rewarded. The key to any system is discrimination.

Limit Punishments to Something You Can Control

Quantity is not always important. For very young children with no concept of time, five minutes in a "time-out" chair (a controllable time limit) rather than fifty minutes (which is uncontrollable) is just as good. Similarly, delaying a teenager's departure for two hours on a Friday or Saturday night can be just as effective as and easier to carry out than grounding the child for a week. The most important thing for parents to remember about discipline is that they must begin it and end it. Maintaining both boundaries is crucial. Consequently, parents should avoid very harsh punishments at first. Harsh punishments will only confuse children and distort their frame of reference. Even worse, the parents will most likely be the ones punished if they choose long, unrealistic consequences.

Never Trade a Punishment for a Reward

If children do something inappropriate and then something appropriate, the two incidents should be treated separately. Parents may want to say that while they appreciate the appropriate behavior and feel good about that choice, the poor judgment shown with the other incident cannot be overlooked. If parents begin to trade off, children will learn to avoid punishment merely by doing something appropriate.

Project a United Front

If one parent should disagree with the other's tactics or reasoning, they should discuss it at a private moment. Open disagreement over a disciplinary action can confuse children and place them in the uncomfortable position of having to choose between parents.

Focus on Inappropriate Behavior, Not Personality

Children are not stupid; they know their inappropriate behavior is unacceptable. Parents may want to use phrases such as "poor judgment" or "inappropriate behavior" when confronting the act. Focusing on the act allows children to save face. It may also allow them to better understand and accept more appropriate options for the next time. Children who grow up in a home where personalities are attacked tend to model that behavior in their social relationships. They tend to be less tolerant and more critical of their peers.

Choose Battles Wisely

Parents should view energy like money. In this way they will decide whether an issue is worth a $2 or $200 investment. Overinvesting can only lead to parent burnout.

Parents should sit down with each other and discuss what they feel are the more important issues. As long as children are not verbally abusive or destructive, statements of frustration or healthy anger should be tolerated. However, if these statements become loudly vocalized to the point of screaming at the "top of their lungs," then limits must be set. They should then be taught more appropriate ways of venting feelings.

It is very destructive to allow children to use verbal abuse in any form. Parents are misguided if they feel that the child must be allowed to vent feelings. Verbal abuse is any verbal act directed at the parent: cursing, or making vulgar comments or attacks on the parent's personality—"jerk," "idiot," and so on. There are healthy ways to communicate anger; verbal abuse should not be an option.

Never Allow Temper Tantrums Before an Audience

Children sometimes choose the most inopportune place to throw a tantrum—at a supermarket, while visiting a relative's house, and so on. Regardless of the location, the parent should not allow them control of the situation. Removal from the audience is crucial. Removal to a room, a car, or some isolated area may be necessary.

Further, the more parents try to reason with children when they are in this state, the more control they relinquish. Parents should tell the child that they will be more than happy to discuss all concerns when the tantrum is over.

When the child is in a more rational state, the parent should teach the child other ways to discuss concerns and explain that if a tantrum is chosen rather than communication, there will be a consequence. The parent should also remember to reward any behavior that approaches verbal communication.

Do Not Conceal Problems from the Other Parent

Some parents choose this tactic to "protect" children. Yet they may actually increase a child's anxiety level with this approach. The message is that the other parent should be feared. If many issues are held back, children begin to worry about the other parent's reaction if they should be found out. This fantasy fear may increase internal tension and preoccupy them with unbiased fears.

In most cases, it is better for children to face reality rather than fantasize about what might happen. The only exception, of course, is if one parent is prone to violence and abuse. In this case such protection is a form of survival.

Do Not Relinquish Power to the Other Parent

Relinquishing power—that is, "Wait until Daddy gets home!"—sends a very negative message to children. It implies that the first parent cannot control the situation. What may be the real issue is that the parent has run out of techniques to use and is feeling frustrated. If this is the case, then the parent should delay dealing with the child. She can send the child to his room and tell him that she will deal with the issue later. She should regroup her own control rather than pass it off to the other parent. Further, relinquishing power tends to reduce feelings of self-esteem—both as a parent and as a person.

Use a Forced Choice Technique When Possible

The parent should choose two options that are both acceptable. Then, say to children, "You may do . . . or . . . . Which do you prefer?" This technique is more helpful than an open-ended "What would you like to do?" which may provoke no response or one that is not acceptable. Using a forced choice technique allows children to feel that they are making the decision even though either choice is acceptable. If children reply, "Neither," then the parent should remind them that "neither" is not an option. After a few minutes of testing, most children will make a choice.

Do Not Be Afraid to Delay a Consequence If You Are Very Angry

The use of delay allows for a different perspective. There is nothing wrong with saying, "I am so angry right now that I don't want to deal with this situation. Go to your room and I'll deal with you in fifteen minutes." The use of delay will also reduce impractical consequences.

In conclusion, parents should be made aware that parenting is not a popularity contest but a responsibility. The opportunity to select from a variety of tools when confronted with a positive or negative situation can only enhance the difficult but rewarding job of child rearing.

Chapter 23

Helping Parents Communicate Better with Their Children

Communication is one of the main factors in any good relationship, whether boyfriend and girlfriend, husband and wife, or parent and child. However, many parents are at a loss when it comes to communicating with their children. What may start out as communication may wind up as a lecture, argument, or worse.

Communication comes in many forms, and knowledge of certain techniques can greatly enhance a relationship. As a special education teacher, you can discuss the following guidelines with your children's parents to help them have positive interactions.

Communication Is a Two-Way Street

The technique of "I'll talk and you listen and then you talk and I'll listen" is a first step and should be taught to children as soon as possible. Many people think they are communicating but in a sense they never listen. The technique of active listening is a first step in the development of communication skills.

Do Not Attack When Communicating

Communication will deteriorate if either party feels he is being attacked. This feeling can come for many reasons but the most usual reason is when one speaker uses the word "you." This word more than any other creates a defensive structure and interrupts the flow of communication. When communicating feelings, parents should try using the words "I," "we," or "me" as often as possible. Even if the child has done something to hurt parents' feelings, they should focus on their feelings rather than on the behavior. They should inform the child how the behavior affected them.

Teach Children to Label Feelings Appropriately

Many times the only difference between communication and argument is choice of words. Many arguments could be avoided if either party used more appropriate labels. The ability to label one's feelings is an important factor in communication. Nowhere is that more evident than with children. Children may have a very hard time communicating because they lack experience in labeling their feelings. When they are unable to label an internal feeling correctly, it becomes trapped and the frustration may get manifested in behavior problems, physical symptoms, and so on. When such feelings are manifested in these forms, they are usually misunderstood or misinterpreted. Therefore, it is crucial for parents to assist their children in correctly labeling a feeling or emotion. They may want to say, for example, "Although the feeling you are expressing sounds like anger, it is really frustration, and frustration is . . . . " It is also helpful to have children develop an emotional vocabulary so that feelings and communication can flow more easily.

Use Connective Discussion Whenever Possible

Parents often use direct communication such as, "Tell me what is wrong," or "Tell me what you feel," or "Tell me why you did that." Yet this line of questioning has the least chance of obtaining a response from the child because most children do not possess the labels or experiences in communication necessary to provide such an answer. What parents may want to use instead is *connective discussion.* This technique assumes something and offers children reasonable labels for what they may be experiencing. For example, parents may say, "It seems to me that you are feeling upset over your new baby brother. I think you may be feeling somewhat jealous because you feel he gets more attention than you." Another example is this, "I get the feeling from your behavior that you are trying to say something. I think what you may be trying to say is . . . . " If the parent is close she may observe some nonverbal reaction, an intense denial, crying, or some other similar response. At this point children should have an easier time expressing themselves because they have a foundation from which to work.

All Behavior Has a Trigger

Sometimes the trigger is unconscious and not available for identification. However, in many cases, the trigger is conscious and the knowledge that an intense response will always follow some incident, feeling, and so on can be helpful. If parents can trace back children's responses to the source or trigger, they will have a very good chance of identifying the real problem. In fact, it may be good practice to have children do just that if they become upset or show inappropriate behavior. Ask them to think about what took place immediately prior to the behavior. If they cannot and the parent is aware, the parent can use connective discussion to make the bridge.

Be Aware of Nonverbal Misinterpretations

Children are very prone to nonverbal misinterpretations. They may, for instance, misread the look on a parent's face and personalize it into something negative. This is very typical of younger children.

If parents are upset, angry, or frustrated with something other than their children, they should let them know that fact in a verbal way. They do not have to go into detail but merely say, "I am very upset right now with something. But I want to tell you that it has nothing to do with you and after I think for a while we will get together."

This small piece of communication may prevent some very anxious moments for children.

Use Written Communication Whenever Possible

Another useful form of communication is writing. The use of writing to communicate feelings is an excellent tool in that it allows parents and children to phrase thoughts as desired for the best results. Notes thanking a child for some positive behavior are great.

Notes telling children to have a nice day or that the parents love them very much or that they appreciated their cooperation are all examples of written communication.

Notes can also be used to register a complaint without nose-to-nose confrontation. This is nice to use when the issue at hand is not a major one.

Spontaneity is also a very nice message. Notes in a lunchbox or a notebook or slipped into a textbook are excellent. Of course, as mentioned earlier, discrimination with any technique is suggested.

Use Direct Love Whenever Possible

Many clients in therapy talk about the way their parents expressed love to them. The need to feel loved and cared for is a primary need for any individual at any age. Many of these clients as well as other adults talk about their parents' indirectness when it came to communicating feelings of love and caring.

For instance, when asked the question "How did you know your father or mother loved you?" some clients respond by saying, "Because they used to take care of me when I was sick." Other responses include bringing home presents when they were good, being kept neat and clean, giving help with homework, and so on. All these messages are fine, but they all represent *indirect love.*

If indirect love is the only "game in town," then the individuals receiving it from parents must make interpretations and assumptions. These individuals assume that because there is "A," then "B" must be true. Such a need for assumption when dealing with indirect messages of love can be dangerous. The same assumption can be made and is often made that such love is conditional. The individual assumes that illness, injury, and other situations are the conditions for love and caring.

Parents should be aware of this and provide as many direct messages of love as they can. Direct messages of love require no interpretation or assumption by children. Even teenagers, who on some verbal level will reject such expressions of love, need to hear it anyway. Direct messages include verbal statements like "I am a very lucky parent to have a son (or daughter) like you." Or "You mean a great deal to me." Or "There may be times when I am angry with you, but I want you to know I always love you." It is important not to assume that the children know that parents feel this way. Parents must communicate to their children directly.

Another very necessary and important example of direct love is through physical demonstration of feelings. When dealing with children, parents should demonstrate love by hugging, kissing, cuddling, holding, allowing the child to sit on their lap, and other physical expressions. These should be an everyday part of communication. Although not every adult has learned the ability to use such direct messages, the absence of this form of communication in a parent-child relationship may have adverse effects on the child in later life.

The higher the *approachability factor* on the part of parents, the easier it is for children to express and show direct love to them. In later life, these children may have an easier time employing direct forms of love in their own relationships. The lower the approachability factor, the more difficult it is for children to communicate love to their parents. In later life, these individuals may have unproductive relationships.

Examples of Alternative Responses

Avoid	*Try*
Use of the word "you."	Use of the words" I," "me," or "we."
"Tell me what you feel."	"I get the feeling that . . . . "
	"It seems to me that . . . . "
	"I get the feeling from your behavior that you are trying to say . . . . "
"You listen to me!"	"I'll talk and you listen and then you can talk and I'll listen."
"What would you like?"	"You can choose between . . . and . . . . Which do you prefer?"
"Speak with me later."	"Let's get together in ten minutes."
"Clean your room."	"Please clean your room, and by clean I mean the following . . . . "
"Be home early."	"Please be home between . . . and . . . . "
"I don't trust you."	"Trust is not the issue. It's your sense of judgment that concerns me."
"You are grounded forever."	"I am so angry. I'll deal with you later."

In conclusion, the ability to communicate using proper labels will relieve both children's and parents' emotional turmoil and benefit the relationship in the long run.

Chapter 24

Helping Parents Improve Their Children's Self-Esteem

Self-esteem is feeling good about yourself. Because it is a feeling, self-esteem is expressed in the way that people behave. However, success is important for the growth of positive feelings about oneself. High self-esteem will allow children to keep failure situations in proper perspective. Whether a failure situation is perceived as a learning experience or as a self-punishment depends on one's level of self-esteem.

Both children and adults vary in the type of self-esteem they exhibit. We all feel more confident on some days than on others. Feeling low self-esteem from time to time is not a problem. However, if a pattern of low self-esteem is observed, there should be concern. Parents can easily observe children's self-esteem by seeing what they do and how they accomplish it.

A child with high self-esteem will:

- Feel capable of influencing other's opinions or behaviors in a positive way.
- Be able to communicate feelings and emotions in a variety of situations.
- Behave independently.
- Approach new situations in a positive manner.
- Exhibit a high level of frustration tolerance.
- Take on and assume responsibility.
- Keep situations in proper perspective.
- Communicate positive feelings about themselves.
- Be willing to try a new situation without major resistance.

Such children possess an internal locus of control. Consequently, they feel whatever happens to them is a direct result of their own behavior or actions. These children therefore feel a sense of power over their environment.

Children with low self-esteem will:

- Communicate self-derogatory statements.
- Exhibit a low frustration tolerance.
- Become easily defensive.
- Listen to the judgment of others rather than make their own decisions.
- Be resistant to new situations and experiences.
- Constantly blame others for their failures and problems.

- Have very little feeling of power and control.
- Lose perspective easily (blow things out of proportion).
- Avoid any situation that creates tension.
- Be unwilling to reason.

Such children possess an external locus of control. They feel that whatever happens to them is the result of fate, luck, or chance.

In order to understand self-esteem fully, we must consider the factors involved. Self-esteem occurs when children experience the positive feelings of satisfaction associated with feeling:

- *Connected.* A child feels good relating to people, places, and things that are important to her, and these relationships are approved and respected by others.
- *Unique.* A child acknowledges and respects the personal characteristics that make him special and different, and receives approval and respect from others for those characteristics.
- *Powerful.* A child uses the skills, resources, and opportunities that she has in order to influence the circumstances of her own life in important ways.

As a special education teacher, you can make the following suggestions to parents to enhance their children's positive feelings about themselves. These recommendations require consistency, genuineness, and discrimination on the part of parents. No one suggestion by itself will have long-lasting effects. A combination of techniques will have greater impact. Parents should always keep in mind that many other factors not in their control—peer group, school success or failure, perception, and so on—will also contribute to a child's self-esteem. But the role of the parents is a crucial one and can offset difficulties in other areas.

Be Solution-Oriented

An important step in building children's self-esteem is to teach solutions rather than blame. Some families are very "blame-oriented." When something goes wrong, everyone is quick to "point the finger" at each other. Children who grow up in this type of environment not only become easily frustrated but never learn how to handle obstacles. Teaching children solutions begins with simple statements like "Who's at fault is not important. The more important question is what we can do so that it doesn't happen again." Being solution-oriented allows children a sense of control and resiliency when confronted with situations that could be ego-deflating.

Allow Children the Right to Make Decisions

Although the statement "No one promised them a democracy" may hold true in some parental situations, allowing children the right to make decisions that affect their daily life can only enhance their self-esteem. Decisions about clothing, room arrangement, friends to invite to a party, menu for dinner, and so on can allow children to feel some sense of control in what happens to them. Coupled with a solution orientation, mistakes can be used as a positive learning experience.

Offer Alternative Ways When Handling a Situation

Some people know only one or two alternatives to handle situations. After these fail, they become frustrated. Conditioning children to see many alternative ways of handling a situation or obstacle can also enhance their self-esteem. Asking children what they have tried and offering them options to other possible solutions increases their "toolbox." The more "tools" we have at our disposal, the easier life becomes. Individuals with limited "tools" tend to use avoidance and flight.

Teach Children the Proper Labels When Communicating Feelings

The ability to label one's feelings correctly is a factor in self-esteem. Children have a difficult time communicating because they lack the proper labels for their feelings. When children are unable to label an internal feeling, it becomes trapped and the frustration may become manifested in behavior problems, physical symptoms, and so on. When such feelings are manifested in other forms, they are usually misunderstood or misinterpreted. As we discussed earlier, parents can offer children the correct labels. Building an emotional vocabulary allows communication to flow more easily and reduces a child's unwillingness to deal with situations.

Allow Children the Opportunity to Repeat Successful Experiences

Whenever possible, allow children the chance to handle any job or responsibility in which they have proven success. A foundation of positive experiences is necessary for self-esteem. Because the child has mastered skills required for the job, any opportunity to repeat success can only be ego-inflating. Jobs such as cooking dinner, cutting the lawn, fixing something around the house, and making the shopping list are examples of repetitive experiences.

Allow Avenues for Disagreement

Children with higher self-esteem always feel they have an avenue to communicate their concerns. Even though the result may not be in their favor, the knowledge that a situation or disagreement can be discussed allows children to feel some involvement in their destiny. In contrast, many children with low self-esteem feel a loss of power in effecting change.

Help the Child Set Realistic Goals

This is a crucial issue in helping children improve their self-esteem. Some children set unrealistic goals, fall short, and feel like failures. When this is repeated over a period of time, children begin to feel a sense of urgency leading to more unrealistic goals. This circular behavior sometimes results in children becoming unwilling to venture out or take chances. The more limited children become in their experiences, the less their chances for success. Avoidance, passivity, and rejection of an idea or experience will only reinforce feelings of inadequacy.

Parents should help children by defining their objective. They may want to ask them what they want to accomplish. After this, they should try to help them define the steps necessary to accomplish the task. Each step becomes a goal in itself. Children should not see one final goal, but a series of smaller goals leading to a final point. In this way they will feel accomplishment at every step.

Use a Reward System to Shape Positive Behavior

Punishment tells a child what not to do, while rewards inform them of what to do. Rewarding positive behavior increases self-esteem. Children enjoy winning the approval of parents, especially when it comes to a job or task. Parents may want to use rewards such as notes indicating how proud they feel about what the child has accomplished. Rewards can also be special trips, special dinners with one parent, extra time before bed, a hug and a kiss. Monetary rewards can also be given every so often.

Do Not Pave All Your Children's Roads

Some parents make the mistake of reducing frustration for children to the point where the child is given a distorted view of the world. Children with high self-esteem get frustrated. However, they tend to be more resilient because they have previously handled frustrating situations and worked out the solutions themselves. When parents rush to the aid of their children, or change the environment to prevent them from becoming frustrated, they are unwittingly reinforcing the children's low self-esteem. After a while, children become dependent on their parents to "bail them out" when they are confronted with frustration. The need to master the environment and find solutions to challenges is crucial to positive self-esteem. The old saying "Catch me a fish and I'll eat today, teach me to fish and I'll eat forever" seems to apply.

In conclusion, parents need to evaluate their own feelings of self-esteem. If they are experiencing feelings of inadequacy, changing children's feelings about themselves will be more difficult. Improving children's self-esteem is a process that needs to be viewed in a positive way. When feelings of low self-esteem are reduced, the child has a more positive future.

Chapter 25

What Parents Need to Know About Retention

Retention of a student's grade placement is a very difficult decision for both parents and educators. In some cases the decision is based on a single factor such as classroom performance. In other cases several factors are considered. Whatever the input, it is a decision that should not be taken lightly. The implications for the student and the family can be long-lasting.

When parents are first presented with this suggestion by the school, they may become very overwhelmed and confused. Instead of looking into the possible reasons, some parents get angry and exert more pressure on the child. They may see this action as a social stigma, rather than an educational recommendation. In other cases parents agree to the school's recommendation without question. If you are going to present parents with this option, then take great care in examining all the variables.

We have all heard stories from friends, neighbors, teachers, and family on the results of grade retention. Some adults say that the decision was a positive step and gave them the opportunity to "catch up." Others express negative feelings about the ridicule, family pressure, loss of self-esteem, social problems, and continued difficulties in school even after retention.

Present research seems somewhat divided about the use of this educational alternative. Some studies have shown that such action has the greatest chance for success in kindergarten and first grade. The chances for success dramatically decrease as children get older. Other studies seem to indicate that if retention is exercised as an option in kindergarten and first grade, boys seem to benefit more. This result seems to support the developmental pattern of a more advanced social and academic maturity in girls. Some parents even choose to wait an extra year before enrolling their sons in school. Because most referrals to psychologists, resource rooms, and special education classes in elementary school are for boys, this "waiting period" should be further explored. However, the emphasis in today's education is to begin earlier, around age four, not later. Consequently, further research is needed.

Because parents should be involved in the decision of retention, it is important that they become educated in this area. The following factors should be taken into consideration prior to the final action.

Present Grade Placement

As previously mentioned, the greatest chance for retention to work is in kindergarten and first grade. By the time children are in fourth or fifth grade, the chances for success decrease dramatically.

Immature Behavior Patterns

The level of interpersonal relations exhibited by children is also a factor to consider. If they tend to play with children much younger than themselves, retention will have fewer consequences. However, if they choose peers who are equal or older in age, retention may have more negative results.

Age

Children who are younger than their classmates will experience fewer problems with retention. But children who are one or two years above their classmates may have more serious adjustments to this action.

Brothers and Sisters

Children without siblings seem to make a better adjustment when repeating a grade. Others with brothers or sisters in the same grade or one year below find retention much more difficult. Children in this category find the experience ego-deflating and feel a loss of familial status.

Attendance

The more time a child is out of school, the greater the reason for retention. Children who are ill and miss over twenty-five days of school are prime candidates. This is especially important in the early grades, when the foundations of reading and basic skills are learned. Some children with excellent attendance are less suitable candidates.

Intellectual Ability

Children with average intelligence have the better chance of success with retention. However, those with below average (lower by 2 to 10 percent) or superior ability (upper by 2 to 10 percent) tend to have more difficulty. Children who fall into these categories may be having difficulties in school for other reasons. These other issues—emotional problems, retardation—may not be addressed by retention alone and may require a more global intervention program such as special education.

Physical Size

Children who are smaller in stature are better candidates for retention. Those who are physically larger than their present classmates will have more problems when retained.

Gender

As previously mentioned, boys in kindergarten and first grade tend to make the better candidates. After fourth grade, both boys and girls will have little chance of success if they are retained.

Present Classroom Performance

Students who are performing one year behind in most academic subjects may find retention a help. Those who are more than two years behind may need an alternate type of program, such as special education class or resource room. Children who are functioning on grade level or above should be reviewed carefully.

Present Emotional State

Children who do not exhibit any signs of serious emotional difficulties—impulsivity, nervous habits, distractibility, unwillingness to reason, and tantrums—have a better chance when retained. Children who exhibit serious emotional concerns should not be considered for retention. However, other educational options should be explored such as individual and family counseling.

Parents' Attitude

This factor is crucial. Children will have the best chance of adjusting to retention when their parents see it as a positive step. Frustrated, angry, and disappointed parents will negate any chance of success.

Student's Attitude

Children who see retention as an opportunity to "catch up" will have a better chance of success. Children who become very upset, exhibit denial about poor performance, or show indifference may have greater difficulty.

Number of Schools Attended

Children who have attended several schools during their first two years of school will have less success with retention.

Evidence of Learning Disabilities

Children with intact learning skills and processes have a greater chance for success when they are retained. Children who have been diagnosed with learning disabilities should receive alternative educational support. In such cases, retention should not be considered an option, but instead the present special education intervention program should be reviewed. There may be a need for a more restrictive program or changes to the IEP concerning test modifications or assistive technology.

These factors are offered as a general guide for parents to follow. Other factors should be considered as well. Regardless, parental input into this decision is crucial.

Chapter 26

Helping Parents Improve Their Children's Study Skills

Many children have difficulty in school because they have weak study skills. Here are various strategies for you to present to parents that promote efficient study habits and thereby enhance a child's chance for academic success.

When you have decided which strategies might be beneficial, introduce them to the parent one at a time as a helpful hint or in a game format. Parents should try these activities on a trial and error basis. They should be flexible in following each strategy. If it works, that's great! If not, they should abandon it.

It is important to keep in mind that not every strategy will work with every child. Success will depend on the child's individual learning style and needs, motivation, and willingness to accept parental guidance. At all times, the parental relationship is of primary importance. It should be relaxed and stress-free. Parents should offer praise and encouragement frequently. If implementation of any of these strategies creates anxiety or resentment (on the part of either parent or child), it is advisable to discontinue it.

Although many of the following suggestions may be applicable, they are not intended as a solution for children who have severe learning problems.

Keep Your Place When Reading

If the child loses his place, skips lines, or mixes up words in successive lines, parents should suggest he use a place marker. If a pencil or fingertip does not do the trick, the child could try using a blank unlined index card as a marker. The index card can also be used effectively on a page of questions to expose one question at a time. In this way, the child can focus on each question without becoming confused or overwhelmed by all the writing on the page.

Use a Bookstand

Using a bookstand is helpful to many children when reading or copying from a textbook. The diagonal position the bookstand provides makes it easier to read the material because the viewing angle is better. Positioning the bookstand directly above the paper also makes for easier copying. Because children can raise and lower their eyes without moving their head sideways, it becomes simpler to shift from the book to the writing paper and back again.

A Special Way to Read Textbooks

Think of all the information we get from watching a movie or television preview. Similarly, a student can gather much information by previewing and surveying textbook material. It is advisable to do this in order to know when to cue into important content as one goes along.

Parents should not have the student start at the beginning and read through to the end of the chapter. First, the child should survey the chapter by looking at the title and paragraph headings in bold print. The parent should suggest that the student think of these as "road signs" to help find the way through the chapter. The student also should look at graphic material (pictures, charts, maps) and read captions.

Next, the student should read the summary and the questions at the end of the chapter. That's the preview. By now, the student should have some idea of what the chapter will be about and what information she should look for.

Restate the Main Idea

This strategy is particularly effective when reading content area material, such as social studies, science, and so on. After the child has read a paragraph, the parent should ask her to think about what she read and explain the most important idea or facts in her own words. It may be necessary for the child to reread the paragraph. If difficulty persists, the parent may have to discuss several paragraphs and provide appropriate responses for each of them until the child is able to do so independently.

The parent should be sure to stress that the overall main idea must be followed from paragraph to paragraph. In the upper grades, the student may wish to write down the main ideas or tape them. This will provide an excellent review format for tests.

Corroborate Answers

If a child works quickly or carelessly and makes errors when answering comprehension questions, parents should try this strategy. Encourage the child to "prove" his answers by locating supporting information in the text. When demonstrating, point out that the words in dark print will help find the section that is most likely to contain the information. (Again, the words in dark print may be thought of as road signs to help the reader find the way.)

This strategy discourages "guessing" and promotes accuracy in locating information. The next time a similar assignment is given, the parent should remind her youngster that she expects him to be able to "prove" the answers.

Develop Memory Using Word Strategies

Mnemonic strategies (memory aids) can be effectively used to help children recall information. Letters and words can be arranged in a variety of ways to enhance memory.

- *The first letter of each item to be remembered forms a word.* For example, to recall the names of the Great Lakes, think of the word HOMES: *H*uron, *O*ntario, *M*ichigan, *E*rie, *S*uperior.

- *Group items by first letters.* For example, of the seven continents, six begin with the letter A and one begins with the letter E (Asia, Australia, Antarctica, Africa, N. America, S. America, and Europe).
- *Words used in a sentence.* For example, "Spring forward and fall back" (to recall time changes).

Remembering the key word or clue will help organize the material to be retrieved. Gradually, parents should encourage children to make up their own clues.

Use Games to Enhance Learning

When a child has to learn new vocabulary and factual information, a game format can take the chore out of study and actually make it fun. The games are easy to make and to individualize for specific tasks.

For example, write new vocabulary words on a set of three-inch-by-five-inch index cards and the corresponding definitions on another set of cards. Your child can help create the games.

- *Matching.* Mix up each set of cards. Place both sets of cards on the table (writing side up). See if the child can match the words to the correct definitions. Then review any words the child is unsure of. When the child can match all the pairs correctly, she is ready to proceed to the next game.
- *Concentration.* Turn about six or seven pairs of cards face down on the table. (The number of cards used can be adjusted to suit the child's capabilities.) Player 1 turns over any two cards, reading them aloud. If they match, he or she keeps the pair and takes another turn. If not, the cards are replaced, face down, in the same position and Player 2 takes a turn. The game proceeds until all the cards have been matched. The player with more pairs wins.
- *Password.* Place the set of vocabulary words face down. Player 1 picks the top card, reads the word to himself, and then gives clues to the other player. Player 2 must guess the word from the clue. (Both players must be familiar with the definitions in order to play.) An advanced form of this game involves selecting a card and writing the definition with points awarded for correct answers and bonus points for correct spelling.

The games are not limited to vocabulary. They can be used to study different kinds of information: explorers and places of exploration, famous men and women and their discoveries, states and capitals, and so on. The game formats and rules can be varied to meet each child's functional and motivational needs.

How to Do Research

If research is assigned on a topic that is totally unfamiliar to the child, or if reading skills are weak, the parents should ask the school librarian to suggest simple books that deal with the topic. Then they should explain to the child that if they, as adults, were taking a first course in something they had never studied before (such as chemistry, physics, and so on), a good place to start might be in a middle school or high school book, just to get some really basic information in simpler language, in order to build a foundation for understanding the harder material.

Repeat Information Out Loud

For many children, simply reading material is an ineffective method of study. Verbalizing or repeating information aloud is an important aid to retention. Parents should encourage the child to read a small segment, verbalizing softly. Then they should cover the material and quietly repeat aloud what the child wishes to remember. This kind of "verbal rehearsal" is a beneficial strategy for many youngsters.

PART SEVEN

A LAW PRIMER FOR SPECIAL EDUCATORS

Chapter 27

Basic Educational Law

There is little doubt that special education teachers need to have a good working knowledge of the laws that govern disabled children. These laws are always changing, and it is crucial to keep as up to date as possible. As a special education teacher, you will come into contact with parents, administrators, and sometimes even students who are very knowledgeable about the law and their rights. Without a thorough understanding, you may find yourself in an uncomfortable position or give advice that is contrary to the rights of the students.

Every state's interpretation of the rights of disabled children varies somewhat. But although regulations from the commissioner of education of each state may be complex, covering numerous pages of "legalese," only the sections of the state law that pertain specifically to special education and the education of disabled students need to be learned. It is not necessary to become a lawyer. However, there are basic concepts that should be common among all interpretations.

The areas that are most relevant for special education teachers are parents' rights, due process, and the responsibilities of the special education teacher in the special education process. The review presented here in no way covers all the legal requirements or aspects of each state's laws, so it would be to your advantage to request a copy of all the laws on special education from your state department of education, which is usually located in the state capital. The state department of education can provide you with many materials on all special education requirements, both state and federal.

A working knowledge of basic special educational law starts with common terminology. Appendix C at the end of the book presents a list of common legal terminology. You will need to know these terms in order to communicate with other special educators, parents, students, and administrators.

Next, you will need to know about the eligibility committee. As we have seen in earlier chapters, at some point you may be asked to present information to this committee concerning a child you have evaluated, observed, or taught.

Chapter 28

Understanding Eligibility Committees

According to federal law PL 94–142, every public school district is required to have an eligibility committee. In some states this is known by a different name: the IEP committee or the committee on special education, for example. If the population of special education students reaches a certain level, then more than one eligibility committee may be formed. Eligibility committees are responsible for identifying disabled children in the district and recommending appropriate education at public expense for students identified as having a disability.

This committee is usually made up of mandated members and assigned members whom the board of education deems necessary. Most states require that certain professionals and individuals be core members. These usually include an administrator or director of pupil personnel services or director of special education, a school psychologist, a medical doctor (this person does not need to be in attendance at every meeting but should be present when medical issues are involved, such as health-related classifications, medication, and so on), a special education teacher, and one of the parents of a disabled child residing in the district. Other professionals may be appointed as well, including a guidance counselor, social worker, school nurse, and so on. The child's teacher is usually required to attend the meeting, but at the secondary level, when a child may have numerous teachers, the guidance counselor usually represents all the teachers' views and comments after consultation with the child's teachers.

Responsibilities of Eligibility Committees

Some of the responsibilities of these committees are as follows:

- Follow appropriate procedures and take appropriate action on any child referred as having a suspected disability.
- Determine the suitable classification for a child with a suspected disability. (The classifications from which the committee chooses are defined in Chapter Two.)
- Review, at least annually, the status of each disabled child residing in the district.
- Evaluate the adequacy of programs, services, and facilities for the disabled children in the district.
- Review and evaluate all relevant information that appears on each disabled student.

- Maintain ongoing communication in writing to parents in regard to planning, modifying, changing, reviewing, placing, or evaluating the program, classification, or educational plan for their disabled child.
- Advise the board of education on the status and recommendations for all disabled children in the district.
- Determine the least restrictive educational setting for any child having been classified as having a disability.

Most eligibility committees try to keep the tone as informal as possible to reduce the anxiety of the situation. This is a crucial issue, because a parent may enter the room containing numerous professionals and feel overwhelmed or intimidated. The parent member usually serves as a liaison and advocate for other parents, establishing contact prior to the meeting to reduce anxiety and alleviate any concerns that the parents may have. School personnel should also be in contact with the parents prior to the meeting to go over the process and what may take place at the meeting. At no time should anyone in contact with the parents prior to the meeting give them false hope, make promises, or second-guess the eligibility committee. What needs to be communicated are procedural issues and options and the understanding that the eligibility committee as a whole will make the recommendation for the child, not one individual. Further, the parents must be made aware of their rights.

The process of identifying and finding an appropriate educational placement for a disabled child should be a joint process between the district and the family. When both work in the best interests of the child, the process can be very positive and rewarding. However, at times the district and the family disagree. When this occurs, both the parents and the school have the right to due process. This procedure protects the rights of both the school and the family and allows another avenue for resolution. Making sure parents understand their rights before the meeting may reduce the possibility of conflict.

Chapter 29

The Concept of Procedural Due Process

The procedure of due process as it applies to special education describes the legal procedures and requirements developed to protect the rights of children, parents, and school districts. In the case of children suspected of having a disability, due process guarantees a free and appropriate public education in the least restrictive educational setting. For parents, due process protects their rights to have input into the educational program and placement of their child, and to be given options in cases of disagreement with the recommendations of the school district. For school districts, due process offers recourse in cases of parent resistance with a request for evaluation, challenges to an independent evaluation sought by parents at public expense, or unwillingness of parents to consent to the eligibility committee recommendation.

Due process includes procedural safeguards such as these:

- *Appropriate written notice.* Notice to parents is required in the following situations: actions are proposed by the eligibility committee to evaluate the existence of a suspected disability; there will be meetings of the eligibility committee to discuss the results of the evaluation to determine a suspected disability; there will be meetings to discuss the development of an Individualized Education Program (IEP); there are proposed actions to review an IEP; there are proposed actions to reevaluate a child's classification or placement; the child is aging out—that is, the disabled child is no longer eligible for tuition-free educational services.
- *Written consent from parents.* Written consent is required in four specific situations: an initial evaluation on a child not previously classified as having a disability; enforcement of the provisions recommended by the eligibility committee in regard to classification and special education placement; prior to providing services for the first time for a disabled child in a twelve-month program; prior to the disabled child's aging out of public education.
- *Confidentiality of records.* A parent's confidentiality of records is protected under due process. Confidentiality ensures that only educational institutions or agencies that have a legitimate interest in the child's education will be permitted to see the records. However, written consent from parents is required for the release of any information on their child other than for the following two reasons: review by staff members or school officials in the school district in which the child is a resident who have a legitimate interest in the child's education, and release of information to other school districts in which the disabled child may

enroll. In this case, the parents are notified of the transfer of information, may request copies of the information sent, and may contest through a hearing the content of the transferred information.

- *Surrogate parents.* In most cases the parents at eligibility committee meetings represent the child with a suspected disability. However, if the parents are unknown, unavailable, or the child is a ward of the state, the eligibility committee must determine if there is a need for the assignment of a surrogate parent to represent the child. When this happens, the board of education chooses a surrogate from a list of eligible individuals.
- *Impartial hearings.* An impartial hearing is a procedure used to resolve disagreements between parents and the school district. This due process procedure can be employed when a parent disagrees with an eligibility committee recommendation; a parent disagrees with a board of education determination; the eligibility committee fails to evaluate and recommend a program within thirty days of the signed consent by the parents; the eligibility committee fails to implement its recommendations within the thirty-day requirement period; there is failure on the part of the school district to administer a triennial evaluation; there is failure on the part of the school district to hold an annual review on a child with a disability; the parents are unwilling to give consent for an evaluation; the parents are unwilling to consent to the recommendations of the eligibility committee concerning the classification or special education placement of the disabled child.
- *Appeals to the commissioner of education.* This option provides another level of resolution for parents and school districts when an impartial hearing cannot resolve the disagreement. This is a legal process and the procedures are usually outlined in state manuals on the commissioner's regulations.

Chapter 30

The Concept of Least Restrictive Environment

The concept of *least restrictive environment* (LRE) refers to the placement of disabled students in the most advantageous educational placement suitable for their needs. Contrary to the belief of many teachers and parents, LRE does not mean every disabled student should be placed in a regular classroom. As a special education teacher, you should understand this concept fully so you can relieve the anxiety of other teachers, parents, and students when it comes to appropriate educational placement.

The placement of disabled students is the responsibility of the eligibility committee with the input of staff and the consent of parents. The eligibility committee must analyze all the available information and determine the best "starting placement" for the child to ensure success and provide the child with the highest level of stimulation and experience for his specific disability and profile of strengths and weaknesses.

In order to accomplish this task, the committee has a variety of placements from which to choose. They range in level of restriction, including class size, student-teacher ratio, length of program, and degree of mainstreaming.

In the normal course of events it is hoped that children only be placed in a more restrictive environment if it is to their educational advantage. Furthermore, they should be moved to a less restrictive setting as soon as they are capable of being educated in that environment.

The following placements are listed in order of least restrictive to most restrictive.

Regular Class Placement

Regular class placement is the least restrictive placement for all children. This placement alone, without some type of special education supportive services, is not suitable for a child with a disability and is usually considered unsuitable by the eligibility committee.

Inclusion Classroom

Placement in an inclusion classroom involves the maintenance of the child in a regular mainstreamed classroom assisted by the presence of a second teacher who is certified in special education.

Regular Class Placement with Consulting Teacher Assistance

A consultant teacher model is used when supportive special education services are required, but the eligibility committee feels that the child will be better served while remaining in the classroom rather than being pulled out for services. Because the child remains in the class, even though he or she is receiving services, this placement is considered the next LRE setting.

Regular Class Placement with Some Supportive Services

Regular class placement with supportive services may be used for students with mild disabilities who require supportive services but can remain in the regular class for most of the day. The services that may be applied to this level include adaptive physical education, speech and language therapy, in-school individual or group counseling, physical therapy, and occupational therapy.

Regular Class Placement with Itinerant Specialist Assistance

Itinerant services are services subcontracted by the district and provided by outside agencies. These services are usually provided for students when the district wishes to maintain them in the district but there is an insufficient number of students with that disability to warrant hiring a special teacher. For example, a hard-of-hearing child may be maintained in a regular class placement as long as supportive itinerant services by a teacher specializing in hearing impairments are provided.

Regular Class Placement with Resource Room Assistance

A resource room program is usually provided for students who need supportive services but can successfully remain in the regular classroom for the majority of the day. This is a "pullout" program, and the services are usually provided in a separate room. The student-teacher ratio is usually five to one, and the amount of time spent in the resource room cannot exceed 50 percent of the child's day.

Special Class Placement with Part Time in Regular Class

Part-time placement is for students who need a more restrictive setting for learning, behavioral, or intellectual reasons; cannot be successful in a full-time regular class or with a pullout supportive service; but can be successfully mainstreamed (participation in a regular classroom setting) for a part of the school day. The special education teacher determines the nature of the mainstream experience.

Full-Time Special Class in a Regular School

A full-time special class in a regular school placement is viewed as the LRE setting for students whose disability does not permit successful participation in any type of regular class setting, even for part of the day. The students in a special class usually require a very structured, closely monitored program on a daily basis but not so restrictive as to warrant an out-of-district placement. These students can handle the rules and structure of a regular school building but not the freedom or style of a less restrictive setting in the school.

Special Day School Outside the School District

A special day school is a desirable placement for students whose disability is so severe that they may require a more therapeutic environment and closer monitoring by specially trained special education teachers or staff members. The child is transported by district expense to the placement, and many state policies try to limit travel time on the bus to no more than one hour.

These types of programs may have student-teacher-aide ratios of 6:1:1, 6:1:2, 9:1:1, 9:1:2, 12:1:1, or 15:1:1, depending on the severity of the child's disability. The more severe the disability, the lower the student-teacher ratio. These programs can run ten or twelve months per year, again depending on the severity of the disability and the individual needs of the child.

Residential School

Residential school placements are considered the next most restrictive placement. The student with a disability not only receives his education in this setting but also usually resides there for the school term. The nature and length of home visits depend on several factors that are usually determined by the residential school staff after evaluation and observation. For some students, home visits may not take place at all, whereas others may go home every weekend.

Some students are put in residential placements by the court. In this case, the child's local school district is only responsible to provide the costs of the educational portion, including related services if needed.

Hospital or Institution

One of the most restrictive settings is a hospital or institution. Although this is a very restrictive setting, it may be the LRE for certain students, such as when an adolescent has attempted suicide, when there is pervasive clinical depression, or when the child is severely or profoundly retarded.

Homebound Instruction

Homebound instruction is a very restrictive setting that is usually reserved for students who are in the process of transition between programs and have yet to be placed. It should never be used as a long-term placement because of the social restriction and limitations.

This option is also used when a child is restricted to his or her house because of an illness, injury, and so on, and this option remains the only realistic educational service until the child recovers. Homebound instruction requires an adult at home when the teacher arrives. Or this instruction can be given at a community center, library, or some other site deemed appropriate by the eligibility committee.

Chapter 31

Parents' Rights in the Special Education Process

Special educators need to be aware of the rights of all those involved in the special education process. Knowing your own rights and responsibilities is very important. However, equally important are the rights of your students and their parents in the special education process. In this way, you can assist students and parents in this complicated and sometimes overwhelming process.

Parents have specific rights when involved in the special education process. These rights must be and usually are transmitted to parents in a variety of ways. Districts may provide preprinted parents' rights brochures or materials. The state may provide books on a child's right to special education that contain everything parents need to know about this process. However, the special education teacher needs to make sure both that parents have received some form of this information and that they fully understand it. You should assist parents in understanding this information or be able to point them to someone who can answer their questions. It is a good idea to find out who this person might be in your district.

Generally, parents have the following rights in the special education process:

- The child is entitled to a free, appropriate public education that meets the unique educational needs of the child at no cost to the parents.
- Parents will be notified whenever the school wishes to evaluate their child, wants to change their child's educational placement, or refuses the parents' request for an evaluation or a change in placement.
- The parents may request an evaluation if they think their child needs special education or related services.
- The parents should be asked by their school to provide "parent consent," meaning that they understand and agree in writing to the evaluation and initial special education placement for their child. Their consent is voluntary and may be withdrawn at any time.
- Parents may obtain an independent low-cost evaluation if they disagree with the outcome of the school's evaluation. The school district will supply the parents with the names of such agencies.
- Parents may request a reevaluation if they suspect their child's current educational placement is no longer appropriate. The school must reevaluate the child at least every three years, but the child's educational program must be reviewed at least once during each calendar year.

- Parents may have their child tested in the language the child knows best. For example, if the child's primary language is Spanish, he must be tested in Spanish. Students who are hearing impaired also have the right to an interpreter during the testing.
- The school must communicate with the parents in their primary language. The school is required to take whatever action is necessary to ensure that the parents understand any oral and written communication, including arranging for an interpreter if the parents are hearing impaired or if their primary language is not English.
- Parents may review all of their child's records and obtain copies of these records, but the school may charge them a reasonable fee for making copies. Only parents and those persons directly involved in the education of the child will be given access to personal records. If parents feel that any of the information in their child's records is inaccurate, misleading, or violates the privacy or other rights of the child, they may request that the information be changed. If the school refuses this request, the parents then have the right to request a hearing to challenge the questionable information in the child's records.
- Parents must be fully informed by the school of all the rights provided to them and to their child under the law. Parents may participate in the development of their child's Individualized Education Program (IEP), or in the case of a child under school age, the development of an Individualized Family Service Plan (IFSP). The IEP and IFSP are written statements of the educational program designed to meet their child's unique needs. The school must make every possible effort to notify them of the IEP or IFSP meeting and arrange it at a time and place agreeable to the parents. As important members of the team, the parents may attend the IEP or IFSP meeting and share their ideas about the child's special needs, the type of program appropriate to meeting those needs, and the related services the school will provide to help the child benefit from his or her educational program.
- Parents may have their child educated in the least restrictive school setting possible. Every effort should be made to develop an educational program that will provide the greatest amount of contact with children who are not disabled.
- Parents may request a due process hearing to resolve differences with the school that cannot be resolved informally.

Chapter 32

Mandated Reporting of Abuse and Neglect

Definition of Abuse and Neglect

According to the National Clearinghouse on Child Abuse and Neglect, in 2000 three million referrals concerning the welfare of approximately five million children were made to Child Protective Services (CPS) agencies throughout the United States. Of these, approximately two-thirds (62 percent) were screened in, and one-third (38 percent) were screened out. Screened-in referrals alleging that a child was being abused or neglected received investigations or assessments to determine whether the allegations of maltreatment could be substantiated. Some of the screened-out reports were referred to the attention of other service agencies. Professionals, including teachers, law enforcement officers, social services workers, and physicians, made more than half (56 percent) of the screened-in reports. Others, including family members, neighbors, and other members of the community, made the remaining 44 percent of screened-in referrals.

Almost one-third of investigations or assessments (32 percent) resulted in a finding that the child was maltreated or at risk of maltreatment. The remaining investigations resulted in a finding that the maltreatment did not occur, the child was not at risk of maltreatment, or there was insufficient information to make a determination.

Several terms are used in laws governing child abuse and neglect. They include the following.

Abused Child

An abused child is usually defined in the law as someone under the age of eighteen whose parent, legal guardian, or person legally responsible for the child's care *inflicts or allows to be inflicted upon the child:* physical injury by other than accidental means; a substantial risk of physical harm or injury that is created or allowed to be created that could result in serious injury or death, disfigurement, prolonged impairment of emotional or physical health; *or commits or allows to be committed* sex offenses against the child including incest, prostitution, or obscene sexual conduct, allowing the child to engage in sexual performance.

Maltreated or Neglected Child

A maltreated or neglected child is usually defined in the law as someone under the age of eighteen who has had serious physical injury inflicted upon him or her or has been impaired physically, mentally, or emotionally or is in imminent danger of becoming impaired as a result of the failure of his or her parent or other person legally responsible for his or her care to exercise a minimum degree of care in supplying the child with adequate food, adequate clothing, adequate shelter, adequate and required educational opportunities and exposure, adequate medical care when required, adequate dental care when required, adequate optometric care when required, adequate surgical care when required.

These conditions apply when the parents or guardians are financially able or are offered assistance to seek help from professionals.

Further indications of maltreatment or neglect are present when the parents or guardians:

- Do not provide the child with proper supervision or guardianship.
- Unreasonably inflict or allow harm to be inflicted or a substantial risk, including the infliction of excessive corporal punishment.
- Misuse drugs or alcohol.
- Misuse alcoholic beverages to the extent that they lose control over their actions.
- Have abandoned the child.

You may want to keep in mind that the terms *maltreated* and *neglected* are often interchangeable, although some interpretations of the laws list them separately.

Mandated Reporters

All states have specific laws governing the identification and reporting of suspected child abuse. Most states now mandate teachers and other education and health professionals to take a course on child abuse and neglect in order to receive or renew their licenses. As a special education teacher, you will be considered a mandated reporter. A mandated reporter is anyone coming in contact with children on a professional basis who may suspect possible abuse or neglect and is therefore required by law to report the case. Other mandated reporters include psychologists, psychiatrists, nurses, doctors, teachers, and principals. Possible abuse or neglect need only be suspected prior to making a report. Any person required to report a case of suspected abuse or neglect who willfully fails to do so may be guilty of a misdemeanor and possible civil penalties.

Procedures to Follow If You Suspect Abuse or Neglect

Remember, you only need to suspect abuse or neglect to report the case. If you suspect possible abuse or neglect, take the following steps:

Gather all the information you can about the suspected incident or incidents and write it up in *factual and behavioral terminology*—this means no opinions, interpretations, assumptions, or guesses, just factual observations or information. For example: "The child said . . . ." "I directly observed . . . ." "There were black-and-blue marks on her legs."

Notify your direct administrator (usually a building principal) of the information you have that caused you to suspect abuse or neglect. Here again verbalize only facts. At this point the administrator will usually call the child abuse hot line or assign someone to call. If you are assigned to call, keep the following in mind:

- Make sure you call the mandated reporters' hot line. Many states have two lines, one for the public to report cases and one for mandated reporters. The numbers can be found in the phone book or by calling (800) 555-1212 and asking for the State Child Abuse and Neglect Hot Line for Mandated Reporters, because most of these hot lines are 800 numbers.
- Once you have a counselor on the phone, immediately ask for his or her name and note the time and date of your call.
- Inform the counselor that you believe you have a suspected case of abuse or neglect. He (or she) will ask you some basic questions for their records and then ask you what evidence you have to suspect that something has taken place.
- Again, report only facts and direct observations. At this point the counselor may indicate that it is either a reportable or not a reportable case.
- If the case is reportable, the counselor will ask you more questions so be prepared with the following information: the child's full name, the address of the child, the child's birth date, the parent's or guardian's first and last names (if different), the child's telephone number, the parent's or guardian's work number if known, other siblings in the house and their ages, the grade of the child, the school and school district of the child, and the number and nature of any previous reports.

  After this individual gathers all the information, he may assign a case number, so be prepared to jot this down. He will inform you that he will be passing the case on to a local case worker who will be in touch with the school.

  Ask the counselor if he feels that the child can go home or if the school should retain her until the case worker appears. The school has this right if the child's health or safety will be compromised in any way by returning home after school. Many times the case worker will come immediately if it is deemed a serious case and will speak with the child before the end of the school day. A home visit is usually made within twenty-four hours or less if the case is considered serious.

  The school nurse under the direction of the building administrator may photograph any obvious marks or contusions for evidence.

  Once the case is reported, you will probably receive a Report of Suspected Child Abuse or Maltreatment form from the Department of Social Services. The school must fill this out and return it within twenty-four hours. Here again, the person who made the original contact with the state counselor may be the one who fills out the form. An example of this type of form appears at the end of this chapter. Keep in mind that this is a legal requirement.
- In some instances, the counselor may indicate that a case does not sound reportable as abuse or neglect. He may indicate that it does represent poor judgment on the part of parents but does not constitute abuse or neglect. At this point you can ask why and ask advice for the next step. However, if it is not reportable,

write your administrator a letter indicating the time, date, and the name of the counselor to whom you spoke, and the reasons why the case was not accepted as reportable. Your legal responsibilities are now covered. However, your moral responsibilities have just begun.

If the administrator listens to the facts and does not see it as a reportable case, ask why and suggest that the case be presented to the state's child abuse hot line for input. However, if the administrator continues to indicate that he does not feel it needs to go any further, inform him that as a mandated reporter you feel a responsibility to call the child abuse hot line and ask the counselor on call if he feels it is a reportable case. If an administrator does not want to report a case and you go along, and it is later determined that abuse or neglect was taking place, you may find yourself in very serious trouble. The excuse "I told my administrator" is not acceptable. Remember, you are a mandated reporter and as such are directly responsible for actions taken or not taken.

Clinical and Behavioral Clues to Possible Abuse

Because special education teachers are mandated reporters, you should be aware of clinical and behavioral clues to possible abuse.

Physical Abuse

Behavioral signs of physical abuse include fear or resistance to going home; past history of self-injurious behavior; extreme neurotic conditions (obsessions, compulsions, phobias); clothing that is inappropriate for the season (long pants, skirts, sleeves in the summertime; this may be to cover up bruises); extreme mood changes and periods of aggressive behavior; apprehensiveness or fear of adults; flinching or defensive reactions to adult gestures or behavior that is not considered dangerous. These children may also say that they are constantly falling or hitting into things as an excuse for their bruises.

Some physical signs of physical abuse are unexplained marks, welts, bites, or bruises on the body; unexplained burns or burn marks; and unexplained injuries to the head area.

Sexual Abuse

Some behavioral signs of sexual abuse are as follows: The child acts in an infantile manner and exhibits frequent withdrawal and fantasy. The child has difficulties maintaining peer relationships. The child engages in sexual activities with other children. The child is frequently late or absent from school. The child resists physical examinations. The child has a history of running away. The child may have a history of self-injurious behavior. The child expresses sophisticated, bizarre, or unusual knowledge of sexual acts or behavior and expresses these to other children or adults.

Some physical signs of sexual abuse include these: expresses the presence or exhibits bruises in genital areas; has difficulty walking or sitting for long periods of time because of pain; exhibits bruises to the mouth area; exhibits extreme pain, itching, or discomfort in the genital area; has a history of urinary tract infections; has developed sexually transmitted diseases especially in the preadolescent period.

Neglect or Maltreatment

Some behavioral signs of neglect include these: is frequently caught taking food from other children; arrives at school much earlier than the other children; seems to hesitate going home at the end of the day and is seen wandering the halls; exhibits constant fatigue; frequently falls asleep in class; develops habit disorders such as tics and other signs of tension; exhibits symptoms typical of conduct disorder, such antisocial behavior; frequently uses drugs or alcohol; develops clinging behavior patterns toward other adults.

Some physical signs of neglect include the following: seems to have medical or physical conditions that go untreated; has severe lags in physical development as a result of malnutrition; expresses constant hunger; comes to school exhibiting poor hygiene; comes to school inappropriately dressed for the particular weather conditions; mentions that he or she is left home alone a great deal; exhibits chronic absences from school; has a history of lateness to school.

Of course, you should use common sense and proper judgment before reporting suspected abuse. Such reports are a serious matter. On the other hand, never hesitate if you suspect abuse, believing that "such a family could never do such things." As a mandated reporter you are really an advocate for children in cases of suspected abuse or neglect. Never assume that something is so obvious that someone else must have called it in already. It is always better to be safe than sorry.

EXAMPLE REPORT FORM: SUSPECTED CHILD ABUSE OR MALTREATMENT

Subjects of Report

List all children in household, adults responsible for household, and alleged perpetrators:

	Last name:	First name:	Middle initial:	Aliases:	Sex (M/F):	Birth date or age:	Ethnic code:	Suspect or relationship code:	Check if alleged perpetrator:
1.									
2.									
3.									
4.									
5.									
6.									
7.									

If known, list addresses and telephone numbers:

Basis of Suspicions

Alleged consequences or evidence of abuse or maltreatment. Place the line numbers from the previous section next to the appropriate area below. If all children, write "ALL."

_____Sexual abuse
_____Emotional neglect
_____Abandonment
_____Lack of supervision
_____DOA/Fatality
_____Fractures
_____Lacerations, bruises, welts
_____Excessive corporal punishment
_____Drug withdrawal
_____Child's drug/alcohol
_____Lack of medical care
_____Malnutrition
_____Failure to thrive
_____Educational neglect
_____Lack of food, clothing, shelter
_____Internal injuries
_____Other (specify)____

State reason for suspicion. If possible, include type and extent of the child's injury, abuse or maltreatment to the child or any siblings. Also list suspicions of any behavior on the part of the parents that may contribute to the problem.

Time___________A.M.____P.M.____

If known, give time and date of alleged incident:

Sources for the Report

Person making this report:

Name ______________________________

Telephone ______________________________

Address ______________________________

Agency/institution ______________________________

Source of this report if different:

Name ______________________________

Telephone ______________________________

Address ______________________________

Agency/institution ______________________________

Relationship (mark X for reporter and * for source)

___Medical examiner/coroner ___Physician ___Hospital staff ___Law enforcement

___Neighbor ___Relative ___Social services ___Public health

___Mental health ___School staff ___Other (specify)____________________

This Section for Physicians Only

Medical diagnosis on child: ______________________________

Signature of physician who examined or treated child: ______________________________

Telephone number: ______________

Hospitalization required:

___None ___Under 1 week ___1–2 weeks ___Over 2 weeks

Actions Taken or About to Be Taken:

___Medical examination ___Hospitalization ___Notified D.A. ___Notified medical examiner

___Notified coroner ___Returned home ___Removal/keeping ___X-ray ___Photographs

Signature of person making this report: ______________________________

Title: ______________________________

Date submitted: ______________

PART EIGHT

APPENDIXES

Appendix A

Sample Psychoeducational Reports

The following is an example of a psychoeducational report for an elementary school-aged child referred by his teacher for a suspected learning disability.

Identifying Data

Name: John Carson

Address: 15 Williams Street, Newton, N.Y. 11687

Phone: 546-9864

School: Benton Ave.

Teacher: Mrs. Grissom

Grade: 4

Date of birth: August 10, 1984

Chronological age: 9 years 10 months

Date of testing: June 7, 1993

Date of report: June 18, 1993

Referred by: Teacher

Parents' names: Jane/Robert

Reason for Referral

John was referred for a psychoeducational evaluation as a result of a suspected learning disability.

Background History

John is a ten-year-old boy presently living in an intact household with his mother, a teacher; his father, an engineer; an older brother age fifteen; and a younger sister age seven. At the present time no other relatives reside in the home.

According to parent intake, John was the result of a full-term pregnancy and normal delivery. According to the mother, John was operated on for a hernia but there were no complications. Developmental milestones seem to have been within normal limits except for talking, which the parent indicated was later than expected. Early history indicates normal childhood illnesses, no traumatic experiences, and no long hospital stays. However, John had frequent middle ear infections during the first three years. The mother indicated that he has not had his eyesight or hearing checked since last year.

Academic history indicates that John seems to have been experiencing difficulties since the early grades. Concerns have been expressed by several teachers indicating weaknesses in the language arts areas. According to his present and past teachers John's overall performance in the classroom was and is poor, despite above-average potential intelligence.

His past and present teachers have reported that he does not participate in class, is verbally resistant, has problems remembering and following through on directions, has a short attention span, procrastinates handing in written assignments and has difficulty working independently. His present teacher reports that his organizational skills seem weak, and he needs step-by-step instructions from the teacher. She also reported that John is having social difficulties and is being isolated by his peers.

Socially, his parents reported that John does not seem to have many friends and the ones he does have are much younger. He enjoys collecting stamps and baseball cards and is very involved with the computer.

Behavioral Observations

John, a thin, frail-looking ten-year-old, entered the testing situation in a relatively guarded manner. He wore a baseball cap pulled down over his forehead and made very little eye contact with the examiner. John did not initiate conversation, but remained cooperative throughout the sessions. His pattern of performance seemed labored on written tasks and he frequently asked to have the questions repeated.

John did briefly comment that he did not like school and wished he didn't have to come. He indicated that he had "a lot of friends" and kept asking how long the testing would take.

John is right-handed and holds his pencil with an awkward grasp. He seemed resistant to changing the grip and kept his head fairly close to the paper when writing, slightly tilting his head to the right.

Tests Administered

Wide Range Achievement Test-Revised

Beery Test of Visual Motor Integration

Woodcock-Johnson Achievement and Cognitive Battery-Revised

Test Results

On the Wide Range Achievement Test-Revised John achieved grade score equivalents of 2B in spelling, placing him at the 8th percentile; 4E in math (computation), placing him at the 35th percentile; and 2B in reading (decoding), placing him at the 12th percentile.

Analysis of the spelling subtest indicated below grade level performance. In looking at the spelling results, one sees adequate spacing and size relationships but very poor letter formation, characterized by difficulty with sequencing and closure–i.e., spla for spell. Further analysis indicated letter omissions–i.e., liht for light–erratic use of capitals, and low frustration tolerance as the words became more difficult.

Analysis of the math section indicated more than adequate skills.

Analysis of the reading section indicated good sight word vocabulary but when it came to multisyllabic words, John did not decode by a sequential blending of isolated sounds, but rather by maneuvering all or some of the sounds until he got a recognizable word. However, in many cases the wrong word was pronounced. He seemed to take a great deal of time decoding, which will affect his reading rate in class.

John's performance on the Woodcock-Johnson Battery-Revised placed him in the average range with respect to cognitive ability. Strength areas were noted in the areas of processing speed, which involved the rapid performance of relatively trivial cognitive tasks; visual processing, the capability to perceive and think with visual patterns; and comprehension-knowledge, a measurement of the breadth and depth of knowledge and its effective application. John's scores on tasks measuring short-term memory were within the average range. However, his effectiveness in storing and retrieving information over extended periods of time was in the low average range.

The area of greatest concern seemed to center around comprehension and synthesis of auditory patterns involved in auditory processing (4th percentile). The skills of auditory closure and sound blending which comprise this cluster would directly affect John's word attack skills, which were measured at the 31st percentile on this battery.

John's performance in reading on this battery indicated an achievement score that exceeded his estimated aptitude. However, upon closer analysis John's word attack skills were at the 2.6 grade level and were considerably lower than his reading vocabulary grade score of 4.3 and reading comprehension of 4.6.

In the area of written language, John's achievement was significantly below his measured aptitude, resulting in a grade score of 2.4. This places him within the 12th percentile when compared to his peers and would affect his willingness and ability to complete written assignments, especially those with time constraints. His most notable difficulties involved capitalization, punctuation, and spelling. His encoding problems were consistent with the decoding deficits indicated throughout the testing.

Conclusions

John is a ten-year-old boy presently functioning in the average range of intellectual ability.

Results of testing seem to indicate that John presently exhibits adequate skills in areas involving mathematics, reading comprehension, and reading vocabulary. However, his most significant weakness appears to be in the area of auditory processing, which has significantly affected his decoding skills in reading and his ability to spell.

Visual motor integration skills also appear to be of concern and were evident in John's written work.

Other factors may also be contributing to John's overall lack of performance in school. His overall high level of distractibility, avoidance, procrastination, low self-esteem, and resistance may be symptomatic of secondary tension arising from school frustration.

Overall analysis of the test results seem to indicate that John's difficulties should be considered moderate in nature and his overall pattern is similar to students with learning disabilities.

Recommendations

Results of testing, observation, and intake suggest the following recommendations:

To the school:

1. Considering the profile of scores, John's test behavior, and dates since last exam, a new vision and hearing test are suggested to rule out any possibility of these factors contributing to his present situation.
2. In view of the nature and severity of John's school-related difficulties, a review by the Committee on Special Education is recommended. The CSE may want to explore the possibility of resource room assistance.
3. The school may want to consider placing John in remedial reading to increase his ability in decoding.

To the teacher:

1. John's spelling difficulties may result in resistance to written assignments. The teacher may want to allow John the use of a word processor with a spell-checker for written tasks.
2. Further, oral spelling tests or spelling tests that require John to identify each correctly spelled word from a list of four words may be beneficial. In this way John may gain some confidence in this area.
3. John will need assistance in the classroom with identifying long vowel sounds, words with the silent "e" spelling pattern, vowel digraphs, and common endings–i.e., ble, dle, tle, ary, ery, cry, and so on.
4. The teacher may want to seat John closer to her desk to increase attention and focus.
5. Further recommendations will be addressed at a meeting with the teacher.

To the parents:

1. Mr. and Mrs. Carson may want to set a homework schedule for John. In this way he will have a structured time when homework needs to be addressed. Further, they may want to check his work at the end of the night to make sure it's complete and correct. In this way John can feel more comfortable when he comes to school.
2. Unison reading at home is also suggested. Unison reading means that both the parent and the child have the same book and read aloud together, thereby reinforcing the correct pronunciation.
3. Further recommendations will be addressed at the meeting with the parent.

The following is an example of a psychoeducational report on a secondary school-aged child referred by her teacher for a suspected disability.

Identifying Data

Name: Mary Wilson

Address: 110 Arnold Street, Munsey, PA 11687

Phone: 947-9964

School: Wilshire Middle School

Counselor: Mr. Kirby

Grade: 8

Date of birth: Sept. 29, 1980

Chronological age: 13 years 3 months

Date of testing: Sept. 30, 1993

Date of report: Oct. 12, 1993

Referred by: Pupil Personnel Team

Parents' names: Mildred/Art

Reason for Referral

Mary was referred for an educational evaluation by the Pupil Personnel Team due to behavioral and academic difficulties.

Background History

See psychological report dated Oct. 7, 1993 for a complete history profile.

Behavioral Observations

Mary remained attentive and cooperative throughout the testing sessions. She demonstrated good attention to task and her speech and verbal abilities seemed age-appropriate. Mary was very engaging with the examiner, frequently initiating conversation, and was very responsive in answering questions by the examiner. At the end of the sessions Mary indicated that she had enjoyed the testing and would like to come back.

Mary is right-handed and did not wear glasses.

Tests Administered

Woodcock-Johnson Psycho-Educational Battery; Stanford Achievement Test-Advanced II

Test Results

Mary's performance on the Woodcock-Johnson Broad Cognitive Ability Full Scale cluster, which measures a broad set of verbal and nonverbal cognitive abilities, resulted in a score at the 58th percentile for her grade, with a confidence interval of 50–66. This performance should be considered average for her grade.

Among her cognitive abilities, strengths were indicated in verbal ability (80th percentile, 12.8 G.E.), a measure of receptive and expressive vocabulary, and memory ability (74th percentile, 12.9 G.E.), a measure of auditory and symbol recognition. Mary obtained scores within the average range in the area of reasoning ability (39th percentile, 7.5 G.E.), a measure of nonverbal abstract reasoning and problem solving. Her lowest scores fell in the low average range in perceptual speed (22nd percentile, 6.6 G.E.), a measure of visual perceptual ability. Based on these cognitive measures, Mary should be expected to achieve academically at the following levels:

Achievement Cluster	***Percentile***	***Grade Equivalent***
Reading	75	11.4
Knowledge	56	9.4
Written expression	39	8.2
Mathematics	38	8.1

On the Woodcock-Johnson Achievement Clusters, Mary's performance indicated high average scores for her grade on the knowledge achievement cluster (82nd percentile, 12.2 G.E.), and in the average range for her grade on the written expression (59th percentile, 9.5 G.E.), mathematics (50th percentile, 8.6 G.E.), and reading (44th percentile, 8.2 G.E.) achievement clusters.

When Mary's academic achievement in knowledge is compared with her scholastic aptitude in knowledge, her present functioning level is in the high average range. When her academic achievement in mathematics and written language is compared to her scholastic aptitude in both of these areas, her present functioning level is within the average range. However, when her academic achievement in reading is compared with her scholastic aptitude in reading, her present functioning is in the low average range.

Mary's test results on the Stanford Achievement Test were as follows:

Achievement Cluster	***Percentile***	***Grade Equivalent***
Reading comprehension	45	8.4
Reading vocabulary	66	11.4
Mathematical applications	19	6.4
Total mathematics	22	6.7

Mary's performance on the reading comprehension and reading vocabulary subtests of the Stanford are consistent with her average reading achievement on the Woodcock-Johnson.

In contrast, Mary's total mathematics score on the Stanford was not consistent with her average achievement score on the Woodcock-Johnson. An analysis of her math achievement on the Stanford indicates below average achievement in mathematical applications, a test that measures the student's ability to apply mathematical skills to the solution of problems. This subtest contributed to the overall low total math score on the Stanford. However, since applied problems (a subtest that assesses skill in solving practical arithmetic problems) on the Woodcock-Johnson was found to be above average, the difficulty that Mary experienced on the Stanford mathematics applications may have been the result of working under timed, group-administered conditions.

Mary's writing sample provided a logical sequence of ideas and she maintained coherence throughout the story. The content was found to be both age-appropriate and well focused. A definite theme was evident and mature vocabulary was employed. In addition to the fine content, Mary demonstrated good command of the mechanics of written expression. The only exception was several run-on sentences and minor spelling errors.

Conclusions

Mary's test profile reveals strength in verbal ability and a relative strength in memory. Mary also obtained scores that reflected average performance on nonverbal abstract reasoning and problem-solving tasks. Overall, there was very little variation among her cognitive abilities.

Results of achievement measures indicated that Mary possesses average to above average skills in knowledge, written expression, mathematics, and reading. When Mary's academic achievement is compared with her scholastic aptitude, her present level of achievement is in the average range.

Recommendations

To the school:

1. On the basis of these test results and the most recent individual IQ score indicating average ability, no significant discrepancies seem to exist in Mary's cognitive and achievement areas. However, other factors may be contributing to her behavior and low class performance. As a result, a full psychological evaluation is suggested.

To the teacher:

1. Additional time may assist Mary in the completion of assignments.
2. Mary may benefit from exercises involving proofreading for run-on sentences and minor spelling errors.
3. Setting very clear and consistent boundaries is very important with Mary. The teacher may want to preempt Mary's behavior pattern by speaking with her alone before class and explaining what is acceptable and not acceptable when she enters the room. Clear consequences and rewards need to be expressed by the teacher.

To the parents:

1. Set up a homework schedule with Mary so that she has a routine every night.
2. Rank-order Mary's homework assignments so that she knows what to do first, second, third, etc.
3. Make sure Mary's homework is complete every night so that Mary has the confidence of going to school the next day with all her assignments completed.

Appendix B

Acronyms Used in Special Education

Acronym	*Meaning*
ABA	Applied Behavior Analysis
ACLC	Assessment of Children's Language Comprehension
ADD	Attention Deficit Disorder
ADHD	Attention Deficit Hyperactive Disorder
AE	Age Equivalent
AUD.DIS.	Auditory Discrimination
BINET	Stanford Binet Intelligence Test
BVMGT	Bender Visual Motor Gestalt Test
CA	Chronological Age
C.A.T.	Children's Apperception Test
CEC	Council for Exceptional Children
C.P.	Cerebral Palsy
CSE	Committee on Special Education
CST	Child Study Team
DAP	Draw a Person Test
Db	Decibel—Hearing Measurement
DDST	Denver Developmental Screening Test
DQ	Developmental Quotient
DTLA-4	Detroit Tests of Learning Aptitude-4
ED/BD	Emotional Disturbances and Behavioral Disorders
EC	Eligibility Committee
E.D.	Emotionally Disturbed
EMR	Educable Mentally Retarded
FAPE	Free Appropriate Public Education
fq	Frequency Range—Hearing Measurement
GE	Grade Equivalent
GFW	Goldman-Fristoe-Woodcock Test of Auditory Discrimination
H.H.	Hard of Hearing
HTP	House-Tree-Person Test
Hz	Hertz—Hearing Measurement
IEP	Individualized Education Program
IEU	Intermediate Educational Unit

Acronym	*Meaning*
IHE	Institutions of Higher Education
IQ	Intelligence Quotient
ITPA	Illinois Tests of Psycholinguistic Abilities
LA	Learning Aptitude
L.D.	Learning Disabled
LEA	Local Education Agency
LPR	Local Percentile Rank
MA	Mental Age
M.B.D.	Minimal Brain Dysfunction
M.H.	Multiply Handicapped
MMPI	Minnesota Multiphasic Personality Inventory
MR	Mentally Retarded
MVPT	Motor-Free Visual Perception Test
NPR	National Percentile Rank
PBS	Positive Behavioral Support
PDD	Pervasive Developmental Disorder
PIAT-R	Peabody Individual Achievement Test-Revised
PINS	Person in Need of Supervision
PLA	Psycholinguistic Age
PQ	Perceptual Quotient
PPT	Pupil Personnel Team
PPVT	Peabody Picture Vocabulary Test
PR	Percentile Rank
P.S.	Partially Sighted
PSEN	Pupils with Special Educational Needs
P.T.A.	Pure Tone Average—Hearing Measurement
SAI	School Abilities Index
SCSIT	Southern California Sensory Integration Tests
SEA	State Education Agency
SIT	Slosson Intelligence Test
S.R.T.	Speech Reception Threshhold—Hearing Measurement
TACL	Test for Auditory Comprehension of Language
T.A.T.	Thematic Apperception Test
TBI	Traumatic Brain Injury
TMR	Trainable Mentally Retarded
TOWL	Test of Written Language
VAKT	Visual/Auditory/Kinesthetic/Tactile
VIS.DIS.	Visual Discrimination
VMI	Beery-Buktenica Developmental Test of Visual Motor Integration
WAIS-III	Wechsler Adult Intelligence Scale-3rd edition
WISC-IV	Wechsler Intelligence Scale for Children-4th edition
WPPSI-III	Wechsler Preschool and Primary Scale of Intelligence-3rd edition
WRAT-3	Wide Range Achievement Test-3

Appendix C

Basic Legal Terminology

Adaptive physical education—specially designed physical education program for disabled children who cannot, as a result of their disability, benefit from the normal school program. This program is an individually designed program of games, sports, and developmental activities that are individually suited to the needs, interests, capabilities, and limitations of each disabled child.

Aging out—the date upon which the disabled child will no longer be eligible for tuition-free educational services.

Annual review—an annual review of a disabled child's classification and educational program by the CSE. The purpose of this review meeting, which includes the parent and sometimes the student, is to recommend the continuation, modification, or termination of classification, placement, or IEP needs and related services for the upcoming year.

Approved private school—a private school that has met state and federal guidelines for providing appropriate services to disabled children and as a result appears on a state-approved list from which public schools may enter into contract for services.

Change in placement (with reference to a disabled child)—refers to any change of educational setting from or to a public school, local special school, or state-approved school.

Change in program (with reference to a disabled child)—refers to any change in any component of a child's IEP.

Committee on Preschool Special Education (CPSE)—the multidisciplinary team that oversees the identification, monitoring, review, and status of disabled preschool children under the age of five.

Eligibility committee (also called committee on special education [CSE] or IEP committee)—the multidisciplinary district team that oversees the identification, monitoring, review, and status of all disabled children residing in the school district.

Impartial hearing officer—an independent individual assigned by the district's board of education or commissioner of education to hear an appeal and render a decision. These individuals can in no way be connected to the school district, may have to be certified (depending on state regulations), are trained, and usually must update their skills.

Independent evaluation—a full and comprehensive individual evaluation conducted by an outside professional or agency not involved in the education of the child.

Individual psychological evaluation—a full and comprehensive evaluation by a state-certified school psychologist (if the child is evaluated in the school district) or a licensed psychologist for the purpose of educational planning.

Occupational therapy—the evaluation and provision of services for disabled children in order to develop or maintain adaptive skills designed to achieve maximal physical and mental functioning of these individuals in their daily life tasks.

Physical therapy—treatment by a specialist under the supervision of a physician to students with motor disabilities.

Preschool program—a special education program for disabled children who are not of public school age.

Pupil with a disability—any school-aged child (any child who has not attained the age of twenty-one prior to September 1) who, because of mental, physical, or emotional reasons, has been identified as having a disability and is entitled to special education services.

Related services—auxiliary services provided to disabled children, including speech pathology, audiology, psychological services, physical therapy, occupational therapy, counseling services, and art therapy.

Resource room program—part-time supplementary instruction on an individual or small group basis outside the regular classroom for disabled children.

Special class—a class consisting of children with the same disability or different disabilities who have been grouped together as a result of similar educational needs and levels for the purpose of being provided with special educational services.

Surrogate parent—any person appointed to act on the parent's or guardian's behalf when a child's parents are not known, unavailable, or the child is a ward of the state.

Transitional support services—temporary special education services, according to a child's IEP, provided to students who are no longer classified as disabled and may be transferring to a regular program, or to disabled children who may be moving to a program or service in a less restrictive environment.

Triennial review—a full and comprehensive reexamination of a disabled child held every three years. This reexamination may include educational, psychological, medical, and any other evaluation deemed necessary by the CSE in order to determine the child's continuing eligibility for special education.

Appendix D

Educational Terminology Associated with Special Education

Ability grouping—the grouping of children based on their achievement in an area of study.

Accelerated learning—an educational process that allows students to progress through the curriculum at an increased pace.

Achievement—the level of a child's accomplishment on a test of knowledge or skill.

Adaptive behavior—an individual's social competence and ability to cope with the demands of the environment.

Adaptive physical education—a modified program of instruction implemented to meet the needs of special students.

Advocate—an individual, either a parent or a professional, who attempts to establish or improve services for exceptional children.

Age norms—standards based on the average performance of individuals in different age groups.

Agnosia—the child's inability to recognize objects and their meaning, usually resulting from damage to the brain.

Amplification device—any device that increases the volume of sound.

Anecdotal record—a procedure for recording and analyzing observations of a child's behavior; an objective, narrative description.

Annual goals—yearly activities or achievements to be completed or attained by the disabled child that are documented on the Individualized Education Program (IEP).

Aphasia—the inability to acquire meaningful spoken language by the age of three, usually resulting from damage or disease to the brain.

Articulation—the production of distinct language sounds by the vocal chords.

At risk—usually refers to infants or children with a high potential for experiencing future medical or learning problems.

Attention deficit hyperactive disorder (ADHD)—a psychiatric classification used to describe individuals who exhibit poor attention, distractibility, impulsivity, and hyperactivity.

Baseline measure—the level or frequency of behavior prior to the implementation of an instructional procedure that will later be evaluated.

Behavior modification—the techniques used to change behavior by applying principles of reinforcement learning.

Bilingual—the ability to speak two languages.

Career education—instruction that focuses on the application of skills and content area information necessary to cope with the problems of daily life, independent living, and vocational areas of interest.

Categorical resource room—an auxiliary pullout program that offers supportive services to exceptional children with the same disability.

Cognition—the understanding of information.

Consultant teacher—a supportive service for disabled children in which the services are provided by a specialist in the classroom.

Criterion referenced tests—tests in which the child is evaluated on his or her own performance to a set of criterion and not in comparison to others.

Declassification—the process by which a disabled child is no longer considered in need of special education services. This requires a meeting of the CSE and can be requested by the parent, school, or child if over the age of eighteen.

Deficit—a level of performance that is less than expected for a child.

Desensitization—a technique used in reinforcement theory in which there is a weakening of a response, usually an emotional response.

Diagnosis—refers to the specific disorder(s) identified as a result of some evaluation.

Distractibility—difficulty in maintaining attention.

Due process—the legal steps and processes outlined in educational law that protect the rights of disabled children.

Dyscalculia—a serious learning disability in which the child has an inability to calculate, apply, solve, or identify mathematical functions.

Dysfluency—difficulty in the production of fluent speech, as in the example of stuttering.

Dysgraphia—a serious learning disability in which the child has an inability or loss of ability to write.

Dyslexia—a severe type of learning disability in which a child's ability to read is greatly impaired.

Dysorthographia—a serious learning disability that affects a child's ability to spell.

Enrichment—providing a child with extra and more sophisticated learning experiences than those normally presented in the curriculum.

Etiology—the cause of a problem.

Exceptional children—children whose school performance shows significant discrepancy between ability and achievement and as a result require special instruction, assistance, or equipment.

Free Appropriate Public Education (FAPE)—used in PL 94–142 to mean special education and related services that are provided at public expense and conform to the state requirements and to the child's IEP.

Group home—a residential living arrangement for handicapped adults, especially the mentally retarded, along with several nondisabled supervisors.

Habilitation—an educational approach used with exceptional children that is directed toward the development of the necessary skills required for successful adulthood.

Homebound instruction—a special education service in which teaching is provided by a specially trained instructor to students unable to attend school. A parent or guardian must always be present at the time of instruction. In some cases, the instruction may take place at a neutral site and not in the home or school.

Hyperactivity—behavior that is characterized by excessive motor activity or restlessness.

Impulsivity—non-goal-oriented activity that is exhibited by individuals who lack careful thought and reflection prior to a behavior.

Inclusion—returning disabled children to their home school so that they may be educated with nonhandicapped children in the same classroom.

Individualized Education Program (IEP)—a written educational program that outlines a disabled child's current levels of performance, related services, educational goals, and modifications. This plan is developed by a team, including the child's parent(s), teacher(s), and support staff.

Interdisciplinary team—the collective efforts of individuals from a variety of disciplines in assessing the needs of a child.

Intervention—preventive, remedial, compensatory, or survival services made on behalf of a disabled individual.

Itinerant teacher—a teacher hired by a school district to help in the education of a disabled child. The teacher is employed by an outside agency and may be responsible for several children in several districts.

Learning disability—a disability in which children with average or above average potential intelligence experience a severe discrepancy between their ability and achievement.

Least restrictive environment—applies to the educational setting of exceptional children and the education of handicapped children with nonhandicapped children whenever realistic and possible. It is the least restrictive setting in which the disabled child can function without difficulty.

Mainstreaming—the practice of educating exceptional children in the regular classroom.

Mental age—the level of intellectual functioning based on the average for children of the same chronological age. When dealing with severely disabled children, the mental age may be more reflective of levels of ability than the chronological age.

Mental retardation—a disability in which the individual's intellectual level is measured in the subaverage range and there are marked impairments in social competence.

Native language—the primary language used by an individual.

Noncategorical resource room—a resource room in a regular school that provides services to children with all types of classified disabilities. The children with these disabilities are able to be maintained in a regular mainstream classroom.

Norm referenced tests—tests used to compare a child's performance to the performance of others on the same measure.

Occupational therapist—a professional who programs or delivers instructional activities and materials to help disabled children and adults participate in useful daily activities.

Paraprofessional—a trained assistant or parent who works with a classroom teacher in the education process.

Physical therapist—a professional trained to assist and help disabled individuals maintain and develop muscular and orthopedic capability and to make correct and useful movements.

Positive behavioral support (PBS)—involves the assessment and reengineering of environments so that people with problem behaviors experience redirections in their behaviors and increase their social, personal, and academic life.

Positive reinforcement—any stimulus or event that occurs after a behavior has been exhibited that affects the possibility of that behavior recurring in the future.

Pupil personnel team—a group of professionals from the same school who meet on a regular basis to discuss children's problems and offer suggestions or a direction for resolution.

Pupils with Special Educational Needs (PSEN)—students defined as having math and reading achievement lower than the 23rd percentile and requiring remediation. These students are not considered disabled but are entitled to assistance to elevate their academic levels.

Related services—services provided to disabled children to assist in their ability to learn and function in the least restrictive environment. Such services may include in-school counseling, speech and language services, and so on.

Remediation—an educational program designed to teach children to overcome some deficit or disability through education and training.

Resource room—an auxiliary service provided to disabled children for part of the school day. It is intended to service children's special needs so that they can be maintained in the least restrictive educational setting.

Screening—the process of examining groups of children in hopes of identifying potential high-risk children.

Section 504—refers to Section 504 of the Rehabilitation Act of 1973, in which guarantees are provided for the civil rights of disabled children and adults. It also applies to the provision of services for children whose disability is not severe enough to warrant classification, but could benefit from supportive services and classroom modifications.

Self-contained class—a special classroom for exceptional children usually located in a regular school building.

Sheltered workshop—a transitional or long-term work environment for disabled individuals who cannot currently work or who are preparing for work in a regular setting. In this setting the individual can learn to perform meaningful, productive tasks and receive payment.

Token economy—a system of reinforcing various behaviors through the delivery of tokens. These tokens can be in the form of stars, points, candy, chips, and so on.

Total communication—the approach to the education of deaf students that combines oral speech, sign language, and finger spelling.

Underachiever—a term generally used in reference to a child's lack of academic achievement in school. However, it is important that the school identify the underlying causes of such underachievement because it may be a symptom of a more serious problem.

Vocational rehabilitation—a program designed to help disabled adults obtain and hold a job.

Appendix E

Psychological Terminology Associated with Special Education

Affective reactions—psychotic reactions marked by extreme mood swings.

Anxiety—a general uneasiness of the mind characterized by irrational fears, panic, tension, and physical symptoms, including palpitations, excessive sweating, and increased pulse rate.

Assessment—the process of gathering information about children in order to make educational decisions.

Baseline data—an objective measure used to compare and evaluate the results obtained during some implementation of an instructional procedure.

Compulsion—a persistent, repetitive act that the individual cannot consciously control.

Confabulation—the act of replacing memory loss by fantasy or by some reality that is not true for the occasion.

Defense mechanisms—the unconscious means by which individuals protect themselves against impulses or emotions that are too uncomfortable or threatening. (See *Denial*, *Displacement*, *Intellectualization*, *Projection*, *Rationalization*, *Reaction formation*, *Repression*, and *Suppression*.)

Delusion—a groundless, irrational belief or thought, usually of grandeur or of persecution. It is usually a characteristic of paranoia.

Denial—a defense mechanism in which the individual refuses to admit the reality of some unpleasant event, situation, or emotion.

Depersonalization—a nonspecific syndrome in which the individual senses that he has lost his personal identity, that he is different, strange, or not real.

Displacement—a defense mechanism; the disguising of the goal or intention of a motive by substituting another in its place.

Echolalia—the repetition of what other people say, as if echoing them.

Etiology—the cause(s) of something.

Hallucination—an imaginary visual image that is regarded as a real sensory experience by the person.

Intellectualization—a defense mechanism in which the individual exhibits anxious or moody deliberation, usually about abstract matters.

Magical thinking—primitive and prelogical thinking in which the person creates an outcome to meet his or her fantasy rather than the reality.

Neologisms—made-up words that only have meaning to the child or adult.

Obsession—a repetitive and persistent idea that intrudes into a person's thoughts.

Panic attack—a serious episode of anxiety in which the individual experiences a variety of symptoms including palpitations, dizziness, nausea, chest pains, trembling, fear of dying, and fear of losing control. These symptoms are not the result of any medical cause.

Paranoia—a personality disorder in which the individual exhibits extreme suspiciousness of the motives of others.

Phobia—an intense irrational fear, usually acquired through conditioning to an unpleasant object or event.

Projection—a defense mechanism; the disguising of a source of conflict by displacing one's own motives onto someone else.

Projective tests—methods used by psychologists and psychiatrists to study personality dynamics through a series of structured or ambiguous stimuli.

Psychosis—a serious mental disorder in which the individual has difficulty differentiating between fantasy and reality.

Rationalization—a defense mechanism; the interpretation of one's own behavior so as to conceal the motive it expresses by assigning the behavior to another motive.

Reaction formation—a defense mechanism; complete disguise of a motive that is expressed in a form directly opposite to its original intent.

Repression—a defense mechanism; refers to the psychological process involved in not permitting memories and motives to enter consciousness although they are operating at an unconscious level.

Rorschach test—an unstructured psychological test in which the individual is asked to project responses to a series of ten inkblots.

School phobia—a form of separation anxiety in which the child's concerns and anxieties are centered around school issues and as a result he or she has an extreme fear of going to school.

Suppression—a defense mechanism; the act of consciously inhibiting an impulse, affect, or idea, as in the deliberate act of forgetting something so as not to have to think about it.

Symptom—any sign, physical or mental, that stands for something else. Symptoms are usually generated from the tension of conflicts. The more serious the problem or conflict, the more frequent and intense the symptom.

Syndrome—a group of symptoms.

Thematic Apperception Test—a structured psychological test in which the individual is asked to project his or her feelings onto a series of drawings or photos.

Wechsler Scales of Intelligence—a series of individual intelligence tests measuring global intelligence through a variety of subtests.

Appendix F

Medical Terminology Associated with Special Education

Albinism—a congenital condition marked by severe deficiency in or total lack of pigmentation.

Amblyopia—a dimness of sight without any indication of change in the eye's structure.

Amniocentesis—a medical procedure done during the early stages of pregnancy for the purpose of identifying certain genetic disorders in the fetus.

Anomaly—some irregularity in development or a deviation from the standard.

Anoxia—a lack of oxygen.

Aphasia—the inability to acquire meaningful spoken language by the age of three as a result of brain damage.

Apraxia—pertains to problems with voluntary or purposeful muscular movement with no evidence of motor impairment.

Astigmatism—a visual defect resulting in blurred vision caused by uneven curvature of the cornea or lens. The condition is usually corrected by lenses.

Ataxia—a form of cerebral palsy in which the individual suffers from a loss of muscle coordination, especially those movements relating to balance and position.

Athetosis—a form of cerebral palsy characterized by involuntary, jerky, purposeless, and repetitive movements of the extremities, head, and tongue.

Atrophy—the degeneration of tissue.

Audiogram—a graphic representation of the results of a hearing test.

Audiologist—a specialist trained in the evaluation and remediation of auditory disorders.

Binocular vision—vision using both eyes working together to perceive a single image.

Blind, legally—visual acuity measured at 20/200 in the better eye with best correction of glasses or contact lenses. Vision measured at 20/200 means the individual must be twenty feet from something to be able to see what the normal eye can see at two hundred feet.

Cataract—a condition of the eye in which the crystalline lens becomes cloudy or opaque. As a result, a reduction or loss of vision occurs.

Catheter—a tube inserted into the body to allow for injections or withdrawal of fluids or to maintain an opening in a passageway.

Cerebral palsy—an abnormal succession of human movement or motor functioning resulting from a defect, insult, or disease of the central nervous system.

Conductive hearing loss—a hearing loss resulting from obstructions in the outer or middle ear or some malformations that interfere in the conduction of sound waves to the inner ear. This condition may be corrected medically or surgically.

Congenital—a condition present at birth.

Cretinism—a congenital condition associated with a thyroid deficiency that can result in stunted physical growth and mental retardation.

Cyanosis—a lack of oxygen in the blood characterized by a blue discoloration of the skin.

Cystic fibrosis—an inherited disorder affecting pancreas, salivary, mucous, and sweat glands that causes severe, long-term respiratory difficulties.

Diplegia—paralysis of the same body part on both sides of the body or of two similar parts on opposite sides of the body.

Down's syndrome—a medical abnormality caused by a chromosomal anomaly that often results in moderate to severe mental retardation. The child with Down's syndrome will exhibit certain physical characteristics such as a large tongue, heart problems, poor muscle tone, and a broad, flat bridge of the nose.

Electroencephalogram (EEG)—a graphic representation of the electrical output of the brain.

Encopresis—a lack of bowel control that may also have psychological causes.

Endogenous—originating from within.

Enuresis—a lack of bladder control that may also have psychological causes.

Exogenous—originating from external causes.

Fetal alcohol syndrome (FAS)—a condition usually found in the infants of alcoholic mothers. As a result low birth weight; severe retardation; and cardiac, limb, and other physical defects may be present.

Field of vision—the area of space visible with both eyes while looking straight ahead; measured in degrees.

Glaucoma—an eye disease characterized by excessively high pressure inside the eyeball. If untreated, the condition can result in total blindness.

Grand mal seizure—the most serious and severe form of an epileptic seizure in which the individual exhibits violent convulsions, loses consciousness, and becomes rigid.

Hemiplegia—paralysis involving the extremities on the same side of the body.

Hemophilia—an inherited deficiency in the blood-clotting factor that can result in serious internal bleeding.

Hertz—a unit of sound frequency used to measure pitch.

Hydrocephalus—a condition present at birth or developing soon afterwards from excess cerebrospinal fluid in the brain and results in an enlargement of the head and mental retardation. This condition is sometimes prevented by the surgical placement of a shunt, which allows for the proper drainage of the built-up fluids.

Hyperactivity—excessive physical and muscular activity characterized by extreme inattention, excessive restlessness, and mobility. The condition is usually associated with attention deficit disorder or learning disabilities.

Hyperopia—farsightedness; a condition causing difficulty with seeing near objects.

Hypertonicity—a heightened state of excessive tension.

Hypotonicity—an inability in maintaining muscle tone or an inability in maintaining muscle tension or resistance to stretch.

Insulin—a protein hormone produced by the pancreas that regulates carbohydrate metabolism.

Iris—the opaque, colored portion of the eye.

Juvenile diabetes—a children's disease characterized by an inadequate secretion or use of insulin, resulting in excessive sugar in the blood and urine. This condition is usually controlled by diet and medication. However, in certain cases, control may be difficult and if untreated, serious complications may arise, such as visual impairments, limb amputation, coma, and death.

Meningitis—an inflammation of the membranes covering the brain and spinal cord. If untreated, can result in serious complications.

Meningocele—a type of spina bifida in which there is protrusion of the covering of the spinal cord through an opening in the vertebrae.

Microcephaly—a disorder involving the cranial cavity characterized by the development of a small head. Retardation usually occurs from the lack of space for brain development.

Monoplegia—paralysis of a single limb.

Multiple sclerosis—a progressive deterioration of the protective sheath surrounding the nerves, leading to a degeneration and failure of the body's central nervous system.

Muscular dystrophy—a group of diseases that eventually weakens and destroys muscle tissue, leading to a progressive deterioration of the body.

Myopia—nearsightedness; a condition that results in blurred vision for distance objects.

Neonatal—the time usually associated with the period between the onset of labor and six weeks following birth.

Neurologically impaired—individuals who exhibit problems associated with the functioning of the central nervous system.

Nystagmus—a rapid, rhythmic, and involuntary movement of the eyes. This condition may result in difficulty reading or fixating on objects.

Ocular mobility—the eye's ability to move.

Ophthalmologist—a medical doctor trained to deal with diseases and conditions of the eye.

Optic nerve—the nerve in the eye that carries impulses to the brain.

Optician—a specialist trained to grind lenses according to a prescription.

Optometrist—a professional trained to examine eyes for defects and prescribe corrective lenses.

Organic—factors usually associated with the central nervous system that cause a handicapping condition.

Ossicles—the three small bones of the ear that transmit sound waves to the eardrum. They consist of the malleus, incus, and stapes.

Osteogenesis imperfecta—also known as "brittle bone disease," this hereditary condition affects the growth of bones and causes them to break easily.

Otitis media—middle ear infection.

Otolaryngologist—a medical doctor specializing in diseases of the ear and throat.

Otologist—a medical doctor specializing in the diseases of the ear.

Otosclerosis—a bony growth in the middle ear that develops around the base of the stapes, impeding its movement and causing hearing loss.

Paralysis—an impairment to or a loss of voluntary movement or sensation.

Paraplegia—a paralysis usually involving the lower half of the body, including both legs, as a result of injury or disease of the spinal cord.

Perinatal—occurring at or immediately following birth.

Petit mal seizure—a mild form of epilepsy characterized by dizziness and momentary lapse of consciousness.

Phenylketonuria—referred to as PKU, this inherited metabolic disease usually results in severe retardation. However, if detected at birth, a special diet can reduce the serious complications associated with the condition.

Photophobia—an extreme sensitivity of the eyes to light. This condition is common in albino children.

Postnatal—occurring after birth.

Prenatal—occurring before birth.

Prosthesis—an artificial device used to replace a missing body part.

Psychomotor seizure—an epileptic seizure in which the individual exhibits many automatic seizure activities of which he or she is not aware.

Pupil—the opening in the middle of the iris, which expands and contracts to let in light.

Quadriplegia—paralysis involving all four limbs.

Retina—the back portion of the eye, containing nerve fibers that connect to the optic nerve on which the image is focused.

Retinitis pigmentosa—a degenerative eye disease in which the retina gradually atrophies, causing a narrowing of the field of vision.

Retrolental fibroplasia—an eye disorder resulting from excessive oxygen in incubators of premature babies.

Rh incompatibility—a blood condition in which the fetus has Rh positive blood and the mother has Rh negative blood, leading to a buildup of antibodies that attack the fetus. If untreated, can result in birth defects.

Rheumatic fever—a disease characterized by acute inflammation of the joints, fever, skin rash, nosebleeds, and abdominal pain. This disease often damages the heart by scarring its tissues and valves.

Rigidity cerebral palsy—a type of cerebral palsy characterized by minimal muscle elasticity, and little or no stretch reflex, which creates stiffness.

Rubella—referred to as German measles, this communicable disease is usually only of concern when developed by women during the early stages of pregnancy. If contracted at that time, there is a high probability of severe handicaps in the offspring.

Sclera—the tough white outer layer of the eyeball, which protects as well as holds contents in place.

Scoliosis—a weakness of the muscles that results in a serious abnormal curvature of the spine. This condition may be corrected with surgery or a brace.

Semicircular canals—the three canals in the middle ear that are responsible for maintaining balance.

Sensorineural hearing loss—a hearing disorder resulting from damage or dysfunction of the cochlea.

Shunt—a tube inserted into the body to drain fluid from one part to another. This procedure is common in cases of hydrocephalus to remove excessive cerebrospinal fluid from the head and redirect it to the heart or intestines.

Spasticity—a type of cerebral palsy characterized by tense, contracted muscles, resulting in muscular incoordination.

Spina bifida occulta—a type of spina bifida characterized by a protrusion of the spinal cord and membranes. This form of the condition does not always cause serious disability.

Strabismus—crossed eyes.

Triplegia—paralysis of three of the body's limbs.

Usher's syndrome—an inherited combination of visual and hearing impairments.

Visual acuity—sharpness or clearness of vision.

Vitreous humor—the jelly-like fluid that fills most of the interior of the eyeball.

Appendix G

Occupational Therapy Terminology

As a special educator, you should be familiar with some terminology used by occupational therapists because there is a good possibility they will be working with at least some of your students.

Abduction—movement of limb outwards away from body.

Active movement—movement a child does without help.

Adaptive equipment—devices used to position or to teach special skills.

Associated reaction—increase of stiffness in spastic arms and legs resulting from effort.

Asymmetrical—one side of the body is different from the other; unequal or dissimilar.

Ataxic—no balance, jerky.

Athetoid—child with uncontrolled and continuously unwanted movements.

Atrophy—wasting of the muscles.

Automatic movement—necessary movement done without thought or effort.

Balance—not falling over; ability to keep a steady position.

Bilateral motor—refers to skill and performance in purposeful movement that requires interaction between both sides of the body in a smooth manner.

Circumduction—to swing the limb away from the body to clear the foot.

Clonus—shaky movements of spastic muscle.

Compensory movement—a form of movement that is atypical in relation to normal patterns of movement.

Congenital—from birth.

Contracture—permanently tight muscle or joint.

Coordination—combination of muscle in movement.

Crossing the midline—refers to skill and performance in crossing the vertical midline of the body.

Deformity—body or limb fixed in abnormal position.

Diplegia—legs mostly affected.

Distractible—not able to concentrate.

Equilibrium—balance.

Equilibrium reaction—automatic pattern of body movements that enable restoration and maintenance of balance against gravity.

Equinus—toe walks.

Extension—straightening of the trunk and limbs.

Eye-hand coordination—eye is used as a tool for directing the hand to perform efficiently.

Facilitation—making it possible for the person to move.

Figure-ground perception—to be able to see foreground against the background.

Fine motor—small muscle movements; use of hands and fingers.

Flexion—bending of elbows, hips, knees, and so on.

Fluctuating tone—changing from one degree of tension to another—for example, from low to high tone.

Form constancy—ability to perceive an object as possessing invariant properties such as shape, size, color, and brightness.

Gait pattern—description of walking pattern, including *swing to gait* (walking with crutches or walker by moving crutches forward and swinging body up to crutches); *swing through* (walking with crutches by moving crutches forward and swinging body in front of the crutches).

Genu valgus—knock-kneed.

Genu varum—bowlegged.

Gross motor—coordinated movements of all parts of the body for performance.

Guarded supervision—when an individual is close to the disabled individual to provide physical support if balance is lost while sitting, standing, or walking.

Guarding techniques—techniques used to help maintain balance, including *contact guarding* (when a person requires hands-on contact to maintain balance).

Head control—ability to control the position of the head.

Hemiplegia—one side of the body is affected.

Hypertonicity—increased muscle tone.

Hypotonicity—decreased muscle tone.

Inhibition—positions and movements that stop muscle tightness.

Involuntary movement—unintended movement.

Kyphosis—increased rounding of the upper back.

Lordosis—swayback or increased curve in the back.

Manual muscle test—test of isolated muscle strength: normal—100 percent; good—80 percent; fair—50 percent; poor—20 percent; zero—0.

Mobility—movement of a body muscle or body part or movement of the whole body from one place to another.

Motivation—making the person want to move or perform.

Motor patterns—ways in which the body and limbs work together to make movement; also known as *praxis*.

Nystagmus—series of automatic back-and-forth eye movements.

Organization—a person's ability to organize him- or herself in approach to and performance of activities.

Orthosis—brace.

Paraplegic—an individual whose paralysis involves the lower half of the body including both legs.

Passive—anything that is done to the person without his or her help or cooperation.

Pathological—due to or involving abnormality.

Perception—the organization of sensation for useful functioning.

Perservation—unnecessary repetition of speech or movement.

Position in space—person's ability to understand the relationship of an object to him- or herself.

Positioning—ways of placing an individual that will help normalize postural tone and facilitate normal patterns of movement and that may involve the use of adaptive equipment.

Postural balance—skill and performance in developing and maintaining body posture while sitting, standing, or engaging in an activity.

Praxis—ability to think through a new task that requires movement; also known as motor planning.

Pronation—turning of the hand with palm down.

Prone—lying on the stomach.

Quadriplegic—an individual whose paralysis involves all four limbs.

Range of motion—joint motion.

Reflex—stereotypic posture and movement that occurs in relation to specific eliciting stimuli and outside of conscious control.

Righting reaction—ability to put head and body right when position is abnormal or uncomfortable.

Right/left discrimination—skill and performance in differentiating right from left and vice versa.

Rigidity—very stiff movements and postures.

Rotation—movement of the trunk; the shoulders move opposite to the hips.

Sensation—feeling.

Sensory-motor experience—the feeling of one's own movements.

Sequencing—the ordering of visual patterns in time and space.

Scoliosis—*C* or *S* curvature of the spine.

Spasm—sudden tightness of muscles.

Spasticity—increased muscle tone.

Spatial relation—the ability to perceive the position of two or more objects in relation to each other and to oneself.

Stair climbing—methods of climbing include *mark stepping* (ascending or descending stairs one step at a time) and *alternating steps* (step over step).

Stereognosis—the identification of form and nature of objects through the sense of touch.

Subluxation—a partial dislocation where joint surfaces remain in contact with one another.

Supination—turning of the hand with palm up.

Symmetrical—both sides equal.

Tactile—pertaining to the sense of touch of the skin.

Tandem walking—moving in a forward progression placing heel to toe.

Tone—firmness of muscles.

Vestibular system—a sensory system that responds to the position of the head in relation to gravity and accelerated and decelerated movements.

Visual memory—ability to recall visual stimuli, in terms of form, detail, position, and other significant features, on both short- and long-term bases.

Visual-motor integration—ability to combine visual input with purposeful, voluntary movement of other body parts involved in the activity.

Voluntary movement—movement done with attention and with concentration.

Appendix H

Organizations Associated with Special Education

Alliance of Genetic Support Groups
4301 Connecticut Avenue NW, Suite 404
Washington, DC 20008
(800) 338-GENE; (202) 966-5557
E-mail: info@geneticalliance.org
Web site: http://www.geneticalliance.org
Resource useful to: Parents, professionals, others interested in genetic issues

The Alliance for Genetic Support Groups is a nonprofit coalition of consumers and professionals dedicated to promoting the common interests of children, adults, and families with genetic disorders. The alliance serves as a major resource center for information, education, and referral to consumer and professional communities and to people interested in genetic issues. Supported by a resource database and numerous publications, the alliance connects families and individuals to national support groups, genetic counselors, peer support, genetic services, and a variety of supportive community resources. It also pursues innovative educational projects and promotes a partnership of consumers and professionals to address health care and information problems, and legal, social, and ethical issues.

ARCH National Resource Center for Respite and Crisis Care Services
Chapel Hill Training-Outreach Project
800 Eastowne Drive, Suite 105
Chapel Hill, NC 27514
(800) 473-1727 (Voice); (800) 773-5433 (National Respite Locator Service); (919) 490-5577 (Voice)
E-mail: HN4735@connectinc.com
Web site: http://chtop.com/archbroc.htm
Resource useful to: Crisis care and respite care providers, parents, advocates, caregivers

The mission of the Access to Respite Care and Help (ARCH) National Resource Center is to provide support to service providers through training, technical assistance, evaluation, and research. The center provides a central contact point for the identification and dissemination of materials relevant to crisis and respite care programs. Numerous fact sheets and general resource sheets about respite care and crisis care (including state contact sheets) are available. ARCH also operates the National Respite Locator Service, which gives parents contact information for the respite care provider nearest them.

Center for Children with Chronic Illness and Disability
Division of General Pediatrics and Adolescent Health
University of Minnesota, Box 721-UMHC
420 Delaware Street, SE
Minneapolis, MN 55455–0374
(612) 626–4032 (Voice); (612) 624–3939 (TTY)
E-mail: c3id@gold.tc.umn.edu
Resource useful to: Families; health, education, and social services professionals; advocates

The Center for Children with Chronic Illness and Disability is dedicated to the study and promotion of the psychological and social well-being of children with chronic illness and disabilities and their families. The center: (a) conducts research to better understand resilience and social competence across the childhood life span; (b) provides training for health, education, and social service professionals on resiliency and competency in children with disabilities, legal and policy issues, financing and insurance concerns for children and their families, and the special needs of children of color and their families; and (c) disseminates accessible translations of the most current research available.

The center has one publication, *Children's and Youth's Health Issues*, which details the most current thinking on resilience of caregiving to children at risk in our society. The center also produces monographs and other published materials that define the environment, raise questions, identify strategies, or provide clarification of issues critical to providing care for children and their families.

Center for Human disAbilities
George Mason University
4400 University Drive, Mail Stop IF2
Fairfax, VA 22030-4444
(800) 333-7958 (Voice/TTY); (703) 993-3670 (Voice/TTY)
Web site: http://GSE.GMU.EDU/DEPART/CHD/CHD.HTM
Resource useful to: Special educators, related services providers, special education administrators, parents, policymakers

The Center for Human disAbilities, a part of the Graduate School of Education of George Mason University, is an interdisciplinary, campus-based organization that focuses on externally funded activities related to improving the lives and productivity of persons with disabilities. The center engages in technology-related and other projects, including policy analysis for local, state, and national needs; research and development; and technical assistance to professionals and parents. Major areas of emphasis include assistive and instructional technology, early childhood education, and severe disabilities.

Communication and Information Services
Office of Special Education and Rehabilitative Services
Room 3132, Switzer Building
330 C Street, SW
Washington, DC 20202-2524
(202) 205-8241 (Voice/TTY)
Resource useful to: Individuals with disabilities, families, agencies, information providers, others

Communication and Information Services (formerly the Clearinghouse on Disability Information) responds to inquiries on a wide range of topics, particularly in the areas of federal funding for programs serving people with disabilities, federal legislation affecting the disability community, and federal programs benefiting people with disabilities. The information center refers callers to appropriate sources of information. The center also distributes publications such as the *Pocket Guide to Federal Help for Individuals with Disabilities* and the *Summary of Existing Legislation Affecting Persons with Disabilities.* All services are provided free of charge.

Council for Exceptional Children (CEC)
1920 Association Drive
Reston, VA 20191-1589
(703) 620-3660 (Voice); (703) 264-9446 (TTY); (800) 845-6232 (membership and renewal information)
E-mail: cec@cec.sped.org
Web site: http://www.cec.sped.org/home.htm
Resource useful to: Teachers, administrators, students, parents, related services personnel, others working with individuals with disabilities and those who are gifted

The Council for Exceptional Children (CEC) is the largest international professional organization committed to improving educational outcomes for individuals with exceptionalities. To this end, CEC shares new knowledge and skills through an annual convention, topical conferences, symposia, and workshops. CEC's seventeen divisions provide focus on a wide variety of aspects of special education. Each division develops professional programs and publications geared to respond to areas of particular need and specialization.

As a major publisher of special education literature, CEC also makes a comprehensive publications catalogue available semiannually. Membership journals such as *TEACHING Exceptional Children* and *Exceptional Children* provide a wealth of information on the latest teaching strategies, research, resources, and special education news.

Council on Quality and Leadership in Supports for People with Disabilities
100 West Road, Suite 406
Towson, MD 21204
(410) 583–0060 (Voice)
E-mail: council@accredcouncil.org
Web site: http://www.accredcouncil.org
Resource useful to: Agencies serving individuals with disabilities

The Council on Quality and Leadership in Supports for People with Disabilities is a diversified, quality enhancement organization with an international focus in the field of human services, dedicated to ensuring that people with disabilities have full and abundant lives.

Formerly known as the Accreditation Council, the council conducts international quality enhancement work through the development of standards and other measures of quality; the development and dissemination of materials; the provision of training, consultation, and technical assistance; and the operation of an accreditation program. The council produces a variety of resource materials, including *Outcome-Based Performance Measures*, *Outcome Measures for Early Childhood Intervention Services*, and other manuals.

Disability Statistics Rehabilitation, Research and Training Center
Institute for Health and Aging
Box 0646, Laurel Heights
San Francisco, CA 94143-0646
(415) 502-5210 (Voice); (415) 502-5217 (TTY)
E-mail: Information_Specialist@quickmail.ucsf.edu
Web site: http://dsc.ucsf.edu
Resource useful to: Families, students, researchers

The Disability Statistics Rehabilitation, Research and Training Center provides statistical information on a wide variety of topics concerning disability in the United States. The center has the most recent published sources of statistical data on disability, including such products as *Disability Statistics Reports* and *Disability Statistics Abstracts*. Data cover demography; epidemiology; health services use, costs, and coverage; employment and earnings; and social services and benefits. Data are also available on the following national programs: vocational rehabilitation; Medicaid and Medicare; veterans programs; Social Security (SSDI and SSI); and special education.

Easter Seals, National Office
230 West Monroe Street, Suite 1800
Chicago, IL 60606
(800) 221-6827 (Voice); (312) 726-6200 (Voice); (312) 726-4258 (TTY)

E-mail: nessinfo@seals.com

Web site: http://www.easter-seals.org

Resource useful to: Organizations, Easter Seal affiliates, individuals

The National Easter Seal Society provides services including comprehensive medical or vocational rehabilitation, technological assistance, recreation, equipment loans, public education, advocacy, and programs for the prevention and treatment of disabilities. The society, acting as headquarters for the federation of 125 local and state organizations, conducts national public awareness campaigns, disseminates information, and advocates on behalf of people with disabilities. To find out about Easter Seals programs and services, you can either consult your local telephone directory for the location of an Easter Seals affiliate near you or call the national headquarters, which will refer you to your local affiliate.

ERIC Clearinghouse on Disabilities and Gifted Education (ERIC EC)

Council for Exceptional Children (CEC)

1920 Association Drive

Reston, VA 20191

(800) 328-0272 (Voice/TTY); (703) 264-9474 (Voice)

E-mail: ericec@cec.sped.org

Web site: http://www.cec.sped.org/ericec.htm

Resource useful to: Teachers, administrators, policymakers, parents, researchers, students, related service personnel, others working with individuals with disabilities and those who are gifted

Housed at the Council for Exceptional Children (CEC), the ERIC Clearinghouse on Disabilities and Gifted Education gathers and disseminates educational information on all disabilities and on giftedness across all age levels. As part of the ERIC network, the clearinghouse acquires, selects, abstracts, and indexes the professional literature on disabilities and giftedness for the ERIC database. The clearinghouse responds to hundreds of requests for information on disability and giftedness each month. It also develops publications, including digests, research syntheses, and bibliographies; provides information users with references and referrals; and runs custom computer searches of the ERIC and Exceptional Child Education Resources (ECER) databases.

National Council on Disability (NCD)

1331 F Street, NW, Suite 1050

Washington, DC 20004-1107

(202) 272-2004 (Voice); (202) 272-2074 (TTY)

E-mail: mquigley@ncd.gov

Web site: http://www.ncd.gov

Resource useful to: Policymakers, individuals with disabilities

The National Council on Disability is an independent federal agency led by fifteen members who are appointed by the president and confirmed by the U.S. Senate. The overall purpose of NCD is to promote policies, programs, practices, and procedures that guarantee equal opportunity to all individuals with disabilities, regardless of the nature or severity of the disability, and to empower individuals with disabilities to achieve economic self-sufficiency, independent living, and inclusion and integration into all aspects of society.

National Information Center for Children and Youth with Disabilities (NICHCY)
P.O. Box 1492
Washington, DC 20013-1492
(800) 695-0285 (Voice/TTY); (202) 884-8200 (Voice/TTY)
E-mail: nichcy@aed.org
Web site: http://www.nichcy.org
Resource useful to: Parents, educators, service providers, individuals with disabilities

NICHCY provides parents, professionals, and others with information on issues of concern to children and youth with disabilities and their families, and referrals to other organizations and sources of assistance. This includes information on specific disabilities, early intervention, special education, related services, transition planning, and a host of other disability issues. Numerous publications are available, including disability fact sheets, state resource sheets (useful for identifying resources within each state), *Transition Summary* and *News Digest* issue briefs, and *Parent Guides.* NICHCY also has many publications available in Spanish. A publications catalogue is available upon request.

National Institute on Disability and Rehabilitation Research (NIDRR)
330 C Street, SW
Washington, DC 20202-2524
(202) 205-8134 (Voice); (202) 205-9136 (TTY)
Web site: http://www.ed.gov/offices/OSERS/NIDRR/
Resource useful to: Professionals, administrators, rehabilitation specialists

Part of the U.S. Department of Education in the Office of Special Education and Rehabilitative Services, NIDRR provides leadership and support for a national and international program of comprehensive and coordinated research on the rehabilitation of individuals with disabilities. NIDRR's mission also encompasses the dissemination of information concerning developments in rehabilitation procedures, including methods and devices that can improve the lives of people of all ages with physical and mental disabilities, especially those with severe disabilities.

One of the most important aspects of research supported by NIDRR is that it helps to ensure the integration of persons with disabilities into independent and semi-independent community life. NIDRR funds the National Rehabilitation Information Center (NARIC) and ABLEDATA (a database on assistive devices).

National Maternal and Child Health Clearinghouse
2070 Chain Bridge Road, Suite 450
Vienna, VA 22182
(703) 821-8955, ext. 254
E-mail: nmchc@circsol.com
Resource useful to: Professionals, educators, policymakers, legislators, families

The National Maternal and Child Health Clearinghouse distributes current publications on maternal and child health and human genetics issues. Publications cover such topics as pregnancy, nutrition, special health needs, chronic illness, and disabilities. A publications catalogue is available from the clearinghouse. Many items are free; for others, there is a charge. This information is specified in the catalogue. Although most of the publications are written for a professional audience, the clearinghouse welcomes calls from the general public and can provide referrals to other organizations and sources of assistance.

National Organization on Rare Disorders (NORD)
100 Route 37
P.O. Box 8923
New Fairfield, CT 06812-8923
(800) 999-6673 (Voice); (203) 746-6518 (Voice); (203) 746-6927 (TTY)
E-mail: orphan@nord-rdb.com
Web site: http://www.nord-rdb.com/~orphan
Resource useful to: Parents, professionals

NORD acts as a clearinghouse, providing callers with information about thousands of rare disorders and bringing families with similar disorders together for mutual support. NORD also promotes research, accumulates and disseminates information about orphan drugs and devices, provides technical assistance to newly organized support groups, and educates the general public and medical professions about diagnosis and treatment of rare disorders. NORD's Rare Disease Database is accessible on its Web page. Single written copies of disease information are available through a literature order form.

National Technical Assistance Center for Children's Mental Health
Georgetown University Child Development Center
3307 M Street, NW, Suite 401
Washington, DC 20007
(202) 687-5000 (Voice)
E-mail: gucdc@medlib.georgetown.edu
Resource useful to: Policymakers, administrators, mental health service providers, families

The National Technical Assistance Center for Children's Mental Health (formerly called the CASSP) emphasizes the development of systems of care for children and their families, community-based service approaches, cultural competence, services for special populations of high-risk youth, and strategies for financing services. Policymakers, administrators, service providers, and families interested in finding out about services in their state for children and adolescents who have serious emotional disturbances can contact the center. They will be put in touch with a state child mental health staff member or with someone who can inform them about state or local services for children and adolescents with a serious emotional disturbance.

Research and Training Center on Family Support and Children's Mental Health

Portland State University

P.O. Box 751

Portland, OR 97207-0751

(800) 628-1696 (Voice); (503) 725-4040; (503) 725-4165 (TTY)

E-mail: stepheb@rri.pdx.edu

Web site: http://www-adm.pdx.edu/user/rri/rtc

Resource useful to: Professionals, families whose children have behavioral or emotional disorders

This research and training center clearinghouse provides information and referrals to parents, professionals, and policymakers. The main focus of the clearinghouse is on addressing children's mental, emotional, and behavioral disorders. Available resources include a series of free fact sheets and state resource files. Numerous publications are available as well, including the *National Directory of Organizations Serving Children and Youth with Emotional and Behavioral Disorders.* A publication list is available upon request.

Appendix I

Organizations on Transition and Vocational Skills

Americans with Disabilities Act (ADA)
Disability and Business Technical Assistance Centers (DBTACs)
(800) 949-4232 (Voice/TTY; for information, materials, or technical assistance)
Resource useful to: Employers, persons with disabilities, others

The Americans with Disabilities Act (ADA), signed into law in 1990, is an important piece of federal legislation prohibiting discrimination against persons with disabilities. It also requires most public and private accommodations, buildings, and transportation systems to be accessible to persons with disabilities. Callers are automatically routed to the DBTAC in their region. The DBTACs provide information, referral, technical assistance, and training on the ADA to businesses, state and local governments, and persons with disabilities to facilitate employment for these individuals and accessibility in public accommodations and government services. The DBTACs also conduct training and promote public awareness on the ADA.

Association on Higher Education and Disability (AHEAD)
P.O. Box 21192
Columbus, OH 43221
(614) 488-4972 (Voice/TTY)
E-mail: ahead@postbox.acs.ohiostate.edu
Web site: http://www.ahead.org
Resource useful to: Professional disability support personnel, college-bound students with disabilities

AHEAD provides a vehicle to strengthen the professionalism, expertise, and competence of personnel working with postsecondary students who have disabilities. The association's membership is international, representing residential and nonresidential campuses, and two-year and four-year institutions. AHEAD sponsors an annual conference and offers a number of publications, including a newsletter called *ALERT*, a quarterly bulletin *(Journal of Postsecondary Education and Disability)*, an annotated bibliography of information sources, proceedings of its national conferences, and guides such as *Reflections Through the Looking Glass* (on giving quality support to students with disabilities in higher education), *Testing Accommodations for Students with Disabilities* (written for service providers), *Peer Mentoring* (how to create support groups for college students with disabilities), and *How to Choose a College* (for students with disabilities). An employment exchange in the field of disability support services is also available.

HEATH Resource Center
American Council on Education
One Dupont Circle, Suite 800
Washington, DC 20036-1193
(800) 544-3284 (Voice/TTY, toll-free outside DC); (202) 939-9320 (Voice/TTY)
E-mail: heath@ace.nche.edu
Web site: http://www.acenet.edu/about/programs/access&equity/heath/home.html
Resource useful to: Individuals with disabilities, parents, professionals

The HEATH Resource Center serves as the national clearinghouse on postsecondary education for individuals with disabilities. The center collects and disseminates information so that people with disabilities can develop their full potential through education and training after high school. HEATH publishes the newsletter *Information from HEATH*, several topical directories, and a number of resource papers that focus on specific aspects of education after high school for individuals with disabilities. Topics include accessibility, career development, classroom and laboratory accommodations, counseling, financial aid, functional limitations (vision, hearing, mobility, information processing), and vocational rehabilitation. Subscription to the newsletter and single copies of each publication are free by request. HEATH publications are also available by request in alternate format (cassette or computer disk) for those unable to read conventional print. In addition, HEATH staff are available to respond to inquiries by mail and telephone.

Job Accommodation Network (JAN)
West Virginia University
P.O. Box 6080
Morgantown, WV 26506-6080
(800) 526-7234 (Voice/TTY, toll-free in United States); (800) 526-2262 (Voice/TTY, toll-free in Canada); (304) 293-7186 (Voice/TTY, local)
E-mail: jan@jan.icdi.wvu.edu
Web site: http://janweb.icdi.wvu.edu
Resource useful to: Employers, professionals, individuals with disabilities, families

The Job Accommodation Network (JAN), a service of the President's Committee on Employment of People with Disabilities, brings together information from many sources about practical steps employers can take to make accommodations for the functional limitations of employees and applicants with disabilities. JAN has a database containing specific information about how individual tasks can be performed by persons with disabilities. JAN consultants provide technical details and assistance with accommodations and the implementation of products and procedures in the workplace. Information about the Americans with Disabilities Act, as it pertains to employment, is also available from JAN. Information is available in English, French, and Spanish, as well as in Braille and large print, and on tape and disk. There is no charge for JAN services.

National Center for Youth with Disabilities (NCYD)
University of Minnesota
General Pediatrics and Adolescent Health
Box 721
420 Delaware Street, SE
Minneapolis, MN 55455-0392
(612) 626-2825 (Voice); (612) 624-3939 (TTY)
E-mail: ncyd@gold.tc.umn.edu
Resource useful to: Parents, professionals, health care providers, educators, social workers, social service providers, advocates

NCYD was established as an information and resource center focusing on adolescents with chronic illness and disabilities and the issues surrounding their transition to adult life. NCYD's mission is to raise awareness of the needs of youth with disabilities and to foster coordination and collaboration among agencies, professionals, and youth in planning and providing services. Information specialists can conduct searches of the NCYD's National Resource Library database and provide information about research literature, programs, training-education, and technical assistance. NCYD publishes a newsletter, *CYDLINE Reviews* (a series of topical annotated bibliographies), and *FYI Bulletins* (a series of fact sheets that provide statistical data). NCYD also publishes special reports on issues unique to adolescents and young adults with chronic illness or disability.

National Rehabilitation Information Center (NARIC)/ABLEDATA
8455 Colesville Road, Suite 935
Silver Spring, MD 20910
(800) 346-2742 (Voice); (301) 588-9284 (Voice); (301) 495-5626 (TTY)
Web site: http://www.naric.com/naric
Resource useful to: Professionals, service providers, researchers, individuals with disabilities, families

The National Rehabilitation Information Center (NARIC) is a library and information center on disability and rehabilitation. NARIC collects and disseminates the results of federally funded research projects. The collection also includes commercially published books, journal articles, and audiovisual materials. The NARIC bibliographic database, REHABDATA, covers all aspects of the rehabilitation field and includes citations and abstracts of the materials in the center's collection. NARIC performs customized searches of REHABDATA for a nominal charge. The NARIC database is also available publicly through the NARIC home page. Copies of documents cited in the database may be obtained for a photocopying fee. In addition to providing bibliographic searches and document delivery, NARIC's information specialists provide quick reference and referral services, helping inquirers locate names, addresses, statistics, and other factual information. NARIC publishes several free publications, including brochures and resource guides. The center also publishes the NIDRR program directory and a companion compendium of products, the *NARIC Guide to Disability and Rehabilitation Periodicals*, *Directory of National Information Sources on Disabilities*, and the *REHABDATA Thesaurus*.

National Transition Alliance for Youth with Disabilities (NTA)
113 Children's Research Center
51 Gerty Drive
Champaign, IL 61820
(217) 333-2325 (Voice/TTY)
E-mail: nta@aed.org
Web site: http://www.dssc.org/nta
Resource useful to: Transition specialists, model transition project directors, school-to-work specialists, professionals, special educators, administrators, families

The National Transition Alliance for Youth with Disabilities works to ensure that all youth, especially those with disabilities, acquire skills and knowledge, gain experience, and receive services and supports necessary to achieve successful results in post-secondary education, community living, work, and independent living.

Office of Student Services
National Center for Research in Vocational Education
University of Illinois
345 Education Building
1310 South 6th Street
Champaign, IL 61820
(217) 333-0807 (Voice)
E-mail: l-iliff@uiuc.edu
Web site: http://ncrve-oss.ed.uiuc.edu
Resource useful to: Vocational and special educators, administrators

The Office of Student Services works nationally to increase vocational program accessibility, quality, and availability for youth and adults from special populations. The office conducts the following services and activities: (a) publication and production of papers and monographs, and presentations at conferences; (b) resource and referral service; (c) initiation and support of networks and professionals; (d) promotion of exemplary programs and adoption of model practices; and (e) collaborative activities with state and national organizations. These activities target all special populations in vocational education, including individuals with disabilities. A list of publications is available upon request.

President's Committee on Employment of People with Disabilities (PCEPD)
1331 F Street, NW, Suite 300
Washington, DC 20004

(202) 376-6200 (Voice); (202) 376-6205 (TTY)

E-mail: info@pcepd.gov

Web site: http://www.pcepd.gov

Resource useful to: Business leaders, organized labor, rehabilitation and service providers, advocacy organizations, families, individuals with disabilities

The President's Committee is an independent federal agency. The committee's mission is to facilitate the communication, coordination, and promotion of public and private efforts to empower Americans with disabilities through employment. The committee provides information, training, and technical assistance to the audience listed above. Its information programs include publications dealing with the Americans with Disabilities Act (ADA), employment issues, job accommodation, and data relating to people with disabilities. In addition to conducting a national conference on issues related to employment and empowerment of people with disabilities, the committee sponsors the Job Accommodation Network (JAN), a free service that provides information and consulting on accommodating people with disabilities in the workplace (see earlier description of JAN).

Project ACTION

700 13th Street, NW, Suite 200

Washington, DC 20005

(800) 659-6428 (Voice/TTY)

E-mail: projaction@aol.com

Web site: http://www.projectaction.org

Resource useful to: People with disabilities, transportation providers

Project ACTION (Accessible Community Transportation in Our Nation) is a national program that supports innovation and cooperation in solving transit accessibility problems. Project ACTION works with both the disability community and the transit industry to provide assistance in the implementation of the transportation provisions of the Americans with Disabilities Act (ADA). Project ACTION provides various direct forms of technical assistance and training, and maintains a library of information and materials addressing accessible transportation for people with disabilities. Project ACTION disseminates its newsletter *Project ACTION Update*, training curricula, surveys, technical materials, and reports.

Transition Research Institute at Illinois

113 Children's Research Center

51 Gerty Drive

Champaign, IL 61820

(217) 333-2325 (Voice/TTY)

Web site: http://www.ed.uiuc.edu/coe/sped/tri/institute.html

Resource useful to: Transition specialists, model transition project directors, school-to-work specialists, professionals, special educators, administrators, families, individuals with disabilities

The ongoing mission of the Transition Research Institute is to define effective practices that will promote the successful transition of youths with disabilities from school to adult life. The institute is designed to address the theoretical and practical problems of transition, and to organize and conduct a complementary set of activities, including research, evaluation, and technical assistance. Many publications focusing on transition are available. The Transition Research Institute is a lead partner of the five-year National Transition Alliance contract (see earlier description).

Vocational Rehabilitation (VR)

Consult your local telephone directory for the office in your vicinity.

Resource useful to: Youth and adults with disabilities

Vocational Rehabilitation is a nationwide federal-state program for assisting eligible people with disabilities to define a suitable employment goal and become employed. The state office provides callers with the address of the nearest rehabilitation office where persons with a disability can discuss issues of eligibility and services with a counselor. VR provides medical, therapeutic, counseling, education, training, and other services needed to prepare people with disabilities for work. VR is an excellent place for a youth or adult with a disability to begin exploring available training and support service options.

Appendix J

Special Education Web Sites

ADDA Kids Area—This site helps kids live with Attention Deficit Disorder (ADD); http://www.add.org/content/kids1.htm

American Association of Mental Retardation (AAMR)—http://www.aamr.org/index.ns4.7.shtml

American Sign Language Dictionary—http://www.masterstech-home.com/ASLDict.html

The Arc—Huge volunteer organization dedicated to the welfare of all people with mental retardation; http://TheArc.org

Autism-PDD Resources—http://www.autism-pdd.net

Autism Resources—http://www.autism-info.com

Autism Resources—http://www.vaporia.com/autism/

Autism Society of America—http://www.autism-society.org

Children and Adults with Attention Deficit and Hyperactivity Disorder—A resource for parents; http://www.adhdsupportcompany.com/about_adhd.html

Council for Exceptional Children—http://www.cec.sped.org/

Disabilities Links—http://www.irsc.org/disability.htm

Disability Net—http://www.disabilitynet.co.uk/

Disability Resources on the Internet—http://www.makoa.org/

Disability Resources on the Internet—http://www.valleyweb.com/

Down's Syndrome-Understanding the gift of life—http://www.nas.com/downsyn/

ERIC Clearinghouse on Disabilities and Gifted Education—http://ericec.org/

IDEA 1997—Copies of the reauthorized IDEA in its entirety are located on the Internet; www.ed.gov/offices/OSERS/IDEA. This is the Department of Education's Office of Special Education and Rehabilitation Services (OSERS); click on "The Law."

Inclusion—http://www.uni.edu/coe/inclusion/

Inclusion Network—http://www.inclusion.org/

Individuals with Disabilities Education Act (IDEA) Practices—http://www.ideapractices.org

InfiNet Kids—http://www.hclinfinet.com/kids/

Internet Resources for Special Children (IRSC)—http://www.irsc.org/

Internet Special Education Resources (ISER)—http://www.iser.com

LD Association of America—http://www.ldanatl.org0

LD Online—Lots of things to learn and do; a special KidZone has games and activities for kids with LD; http://www.ldonline.org

LD Resources—http://www.ldresources.com

Learning Disabilities Research and Resource Site—http://www.hopkins.k12.mn.us/pages/north/ld_research

National Center for Learning Disabilities—http://www.ncld.org

National Information Center for Children and Youth with Disabilities (NICHCY)—http://www.nichcy.org

National Information Clearinghouse on Children Who Are Deaf-Blind (DB-LINK)—http://www.tr.wou.edu/dblink.cfm

National Institute of Child Health and Human Development (NICHD) Clearinghouse—http://www.hih.gov/nichd/publications/publications.html

National Parent Information Network (NPIN)—http://www.npin.org

National Rehabilitation Information Center—http://www.naric.com/

Office of Special Education and Rehabilitative Services (OSERS), U.S. Department of Education—http://www.ed.gov/offices/OSERS/

PeopleNet DisAbility DateNet—http://members.aol.com/bobezwriter/pnet.htm

Selective Mutism Group-Childhood Anxiety Network (SMG-CAN)—http://selectivemutism.org/

Special EDges—An excellent site that gets you to great sites on all special education topics; http://www.blue.net/~goose

Special Education Resources on the Internet (SERI)—http://www.seriweb.com/

Special Education Site—Great links and "topic of the week"; http://www.pacificnet.net/~mandel/SpecialEducation.html

Appendix K

Sample IEP

Section 1: Background Information

School District/Agency: Barlow School District

Name and Address: Edison Township, VA

Individualized Education Program

Date of Eligibility Committee/CPSE Meeting: June 12, 2004 **Purpose of Meeting:** Initial

Student Name: Julien Danna

Date of Birth: 2/5/90 **Age:** 14

Street: 13 Benson Ave.

City: Edison **Zip:** 19876

Telephone: 675-8976 **County of Residence:** Edison Township

Male __X__ **Female** ____ **Student ID#:** 3467H **Current Grade:** 9

Dominant Language of Student: English **Interpreter Needed:** Yes ____ No __X__

Racial/Ethnic Group of Student:

(optional information)

American Indian or Alaskan Native: __NA__

Black (not of Hispanic origin): __X__

White (not of Hispanic origin): __NA__

Asian or Pacific Islander: __NA__

Hispanic: __NA__

Date of Initiation of Services: 9/1/2004 **Projected Date of Review:** 5/2005

Date of Eligibility: 5/2000 **Date for Reevaluation:** 4/2007

Medical Alerts: ADHD

Mother's Name/Guardian's Name: Leona Smith

Street Address: same

City: same

Zip: same

Telephone: same

County of Residence: same

Dominant Language of Parent/Guardian: English

Interpreter Needed: Yes _____ No__X__

Father's Name/Guardian's Name: Malcolm

Street Address: same

City: same

Zip: same

Telephone: same

County of Residence: same

Dominant Language of Parent/Guardian: English

Interpreter Needed: Yes _____ No __X__

Section 2: Present Levels of Performance and Individual Needs

1. *Academic/Educational Achievement and Learning Characteristics:* Address current levels of knowledge and development in subject and skill areas, including activities of daily living, level of intellectual functioning, adaptive behavior, expected rate of progress in acquiring skills and information, and learning style.

Present Levels: **Academic development**

Julien is currently functioning below his chronological age in the area of academic development.

Present Levels: **Cognitive ability**

Julien is currently functioning at his chronological age in the area of cognitive ability.

Present Levels: **Language ability**

Julien is currently functioning below his chronological age in the area of language development.

Julien is currently functioning below his chronological age in the area of receptive development.

Julien is currently functioning below his chronological age in the area of pragmatic/social speech development.

Abilities: Julien understands multistep directions.

Needs: None

Present Levels: **Learning style**

Julien has a multisensory learning style.

Present Level: **General**

Given Julien's functional level, Julien's disability affects his involvement and progress in the general education program.

Julien models math/goal skills only with teacher support.

Julien is able to independently perform language arts goals/skills with minimal support.

Present Level: **Rate of Progress**

Julien's Rate of Progress is below average.

Julien reads on or above grade level.

Julien's computational skills impact his ability to perform general education at his grade level.

Abilities: Julien is able to read and follow written directions.

Needs: Julien requires an individualized and/or small group for instruction in math.

Julien needs to develop self-monitoring skills as a means of avoiding carelessness and focusing attention on detail (e.g., copying homework, completing class work).

2. *Social Development:* Describe the quality of the student's relationships with peers and adults, feelings about self, social adjustment to school and community environment, and behaviors that may impede learning.

Present Levels: **Social Interaction with Peers**

Julien is presently functioning below his chronological age in the area of social development.

Abilities: Julien has developed some friendships.

Needs: Julien needs to relate appropriately to peers in the classroom.

Julien needs to relate appropriately to adults in the classroom.

Julien needs to relate appropriately to adults outside the classroom.

Julien needs to learn how to communicate effectively in social situations.

Present Levels: **Feelings About Self**

Julien is currently functioning below his chronological age level in regard to feelings about self.

Abilities: Julien identifies himself as an individual.

Needs: Julien needs to develop a positive self-concept.

Present Levels: **School/Community**

Julien is currently functioning below his chronological age level in regard to school and community.

Abilities: Julien initiates social interactions with adults.

Needs: Julien needs to respond to adult intervention.

Julien needs to respond to adult praise.

Present Levels: **Adjustment to School/Community**

Julien does not display appropriate social adjustment to school, family, and/or community environment skills.

Abilities: Julien can adapt to changes in routine.

Needs: Julien needs guidance to participate in small groups.

Julien needs to take initiative in social situations.

3. *Physical Development:* Describe the student's motor and sensory development, health, vitality, and physical skills or limitations that pertain to the learning process.

Present Levels: Julien has an ADHD medical diagnosis, which impacts learning—see health file.

Abilities: Julien may participate in all school activities.

Needs: Julien needs to develop the skills required to sit independently.

Julien needs to improve attending skills when visual distractions are present.

4. *Management Needs:* Describe the nature and degree to which environmental modifications and human or material resources are required to address academic, social, and physical needs.

A functional behavior assessment should be completed for any student who demonstrates behaviors that impede learning. A functional behavioral assessment becomes the basis for positive behavioral interventions, strategies, and supports for the student.

Present Levels: Julien has moderate management needs to address academic goals.

Julien has moderate needs to address social goals.

Julien has no management needs to address physical goals.

Abilities: Julien is able to perform effectively/complete tasks in the classroom environment with additional personnel.

Needs: Julien needs full-time general education placement with moderate support through special education.

Section 3: Long-Term Adult Outcomes Statement

Long-Term Adult Outcomes: **Beginning at age 14, or younger if appropriate, state long-term adult outcomes reflecting the student's needs, preferences, and interests in the following:**

Postsecondary Education/Training:

Julien anticipates receiving the following post-secondary education/training:

Julien will attend college.

The transition service needs of Julien to meet long-term adult outcomes are:

Julien will receive guidance/career counseling.

Julien will take college entrance courses.

Julien will take regents courses.

Employment: NA

Community Living: NA

Section 4: Measurable Annual Goals and Short-Term Instructional Objectives

Annual Goal: Julien will maintain and improve study skill levels.

Short-term instructional objective	Evaluation procedures	Evaluation schedule
1. Improve work habits and study skills. 2. Organize material including class work, major assignments, and homework.	Classroom teacher contact	Quarterly

Annual Goal: Successfully complete academic course requirements.

Short-term instructional objective	Evaluation procedures	Evaluation schedule
1. Incorporate writing process strategies. 2. Improve math computation.	Quizzes, tests	Quarterly

Annual Goal: Increase attentiveness and concentration skills.

Short-term instructional objective	Evaluation procedures	Evaluation schedule
1. Develop necessary behaviors, attitudes, and expectations that will lead to self growth. 2. Learn to express feelings both positive and negative.	Observation, teacher contact	Quarterly

Section 5: Special Education Programs and Related Services/Program Modifications

A. Special Education Programs/Related Services	Initiation Date	Frequency	Duration
In-school counseling	September 2004	1X per week	45 min.

B. Extended school year services: Yes _____ No __X__

***Specify group/class size if appropriate**

C. Supplementary aids and modifications or supports for the student	Initiation Date	Frequency	Duration
Modification of curriculum	Sept 2004		
Extra time between classes	Sept 2004		
Calculator	Sept 2004		

D. Describe any assistive technology devices or services needed:

Given Julien's functional level, Julien does not need assistive technology services and devices in order to have an equal opportunity to succeed academically.

E. Describe the program modifications or supports for school personnel that will be provided on behalf of the students to address the annual goals and participation in general education curriculum and activities.

School staff will be provided with information on a specific disability and implications for instruction for Julien.

F. 1. Individual Testing Modification(s):

Julien requires time and a half to complete standardized tests.

Julien requires double time to complete classroom tests.

Julien requires tests to be administered in a small group in a separate location.

Julien will have tests administered in a location with minimal distractions.

2. State why the student will not participate in a state or districtwide assessment: NA

3. Explain how the student will be assessed: Districtwide standardized tests

Section 6: Participation in General Education Classes, Nonacademic and Extracurricular Activities

Explain the extent of participation in general education programs and extracurricular and other nonacademic activities, including physical education or adaptive (adapted) physical education and occupational education (if appropriate). Explain the extent, if any, to which the student will not participate with nondisabled students in the regular class and in other activities.

Julien will participate in all general education classes with support personnel.

If the student is exempt from the second language requirement, explain why.

Julien will be exempt from foreign language requirements due to the following reasons:

Julien exhibits a significant discrepancy between verbal and performance areas on IQ testing, where profile suggests significant verbal difficulties; this exempts Julien from participation in a required second language course.

Section 7: Participating Agencies for Students Who Require Transition Services

Participating agencies that have agreed to provide transition services/supports (before the student leaves the secondary school program):

Agency Name: __NA__ **Telephone Number:** __________ **Service:** __________

Implementation date if different from IEP implementation date: __________

Agency Name: __________ **Telephone Number:** __________ **Service:** __________

Implementation date if different from IEP implementation date: __________

Agency Name: __________ **Telephone Number:** __________ **Service:** __________

Implementation date if different from IEP implementation date: __________

Agency Name: __________ **Telephone Number:** __________ **Service:** __________

Implementation date if different from IEP implementation date: __________

Section 8: Coordinated Set of Activities Leading to Long-Term Adult Outcomes

If any of the following areas are not addressed, explain why:

1. **Instruction:** NA
2. **Related services:** NA
3. **Employment/postsecondary education:** NA
4. **Community experience:** NA
5. **Activities of daily living:** NA
6. **Functional vocational assessment:** NA

Section 9: Graduation Information for Secondary Students

Credential/diploma sought: Local diploma

Expected date of high school completion: June 2008

Section 10: Summary of Selected Recommendations

Classification of the Disability: Other Health Impaired

Recommended Placement Sept.–June: Inclusion

Extended School Year (ESL) Services? Yes _____ No __X__

Recommended Placement July and August: None

Transportation Needs: None

Section 11: Reporting Progress to Parents

State manner and frequency in which progress will be reported. Parents/guardians or student over 18 will be informed of the student's progress toward meeting the academic goals and objectives with the same frequency as nondisabled students using the following criteria:

Textbook tests, quizzes, and standardized tests

Review of report card grades

Contact with classroom teachers on an ongoing basis

Appendix L

References and Suggested Reading

Algozzine, B., Christensen, S., and Ysseldyke, J. (1982). Probabilities associated with the referral-to-placement process. *Teacher Education and Special Education, 5*, 19–23.

Allinder, R. (1994). Use of time by teachers in various types of special education programs. *Special Services in the Schools, 9*(1), 125–136.

American Association on Mental Retardation. (1992). *Mental definition, classification, and systems of support* (9th ed.). Washington, DC: Author.

American Psychiatric Association. (1994). *DSM-IV®-TR*. 4th edition. Arlington, VA: American Psychiatric Publishing.

American Psychological Association. (1985). *Standards for educational and psychological testing*. Washington, DC: Author.

American Psychological Association. (1990). *Guidelines for providers of psychological services to ethnic, linguistic, and culturally diverse populations*. Washington, DC: Author.

Anastasi, A. (1998). *Psychological testing*. New York: Macmillan.

Anderson, W., Chitwood, S., and Hayden, D. (1990). *Negotiating the special education maze: A guide for parents and teachers* (2nd ed.). Rockville, MD: Woodbine House.

Archibald, D. A. (1991). Authentic assessment: Principles, practices, and issues. *School Psychology Quarterly, 6*, 279–293.

Artiles, A. J., and Trent, S. C. (1994). Overrepresentation of minority students in special education: A continuing debate. *Journal of Special Education, 27*, 410–437.

Baca, L., and Cervantes, H. T. (1984). *The bilingual special education interface*. Columbus, OH: Merrill.

Baca, L., Escamilla, K., and Carjuzaa, J. (1994). Language minority students: Literacy and educational reform (pp. 61–76). In N. J. Ellsworth, C. N. Hedley, and A. N. Baratta (eds.), *Literacy: A redefinition*. Hillsdale, NJ: Lawrence Erlbaum Associates, Inc.

Bailey, D. B., and Wolery, M. (1989). *Assessing infants and preschoolers with handicaps*. Columbus, OH: Merrill.

Bailey, D. B., Wolery, M., and McLean, M. (1996). *Assessing infants and preschoolers with special needs* (2nd ed.). Upper Saddle River, NJ: Prentice Hall.

Baker, B., and Brightman, A. (with Blacher, J., Heifetz, L., Hinshaw, S., and Murphy, D.). (1997). *Steps to independence: Teaching everyday skills to children with special needs* (3rd ed.). Baltimore, MD: Paul H. Brookes.

Batzle, J. (1992). *Portfolio assessment and evaluation: Developing and using portfolios in the classroom*. Cypress, CA: Creative Teaching Press.

Bayley, N. (1993). *Bayley Scales of Infant Development-2nd ed. (BSID-II)*. San Antonio, TX: Psychological Corporation.

Beaumont, C., and Langdon, H. W. (1992). Speech-language services for Hispanics with communication disorders: A framework (pp. 1–19). In H. W. Langdon, and L. L. Cheng (eds.), *Hispanic children and adults with communication disorders*. Gaithersburg, MD: Aspen.

Beery, K. E. (1997). *Developmental Test of Visual Motor Integration-Fourth ed. (VMI-4)*. Austin, TX: PRO-ED.

Bellak, L., and Bellak, S. (1974). *Children's Apperception Test*. Larchmont, NY: C.P.S.

Bender, L. (1938). *Bender Visual Motor Gestalt Test (BVMGT)*. New York: American Orthopsychiatric Association.

Berdine, W. H., and Meyer, S. A. (1987). *Assessment in special education*. Boston: Little, Brown. [Distrib. by HarperCollins.]

Bernstein, D. K. (1989). Assessing children with limited English proficiency: Current perspectives. *Topics in Language Disorders, 9,* 15–20.

Bigge, J., and Stump, C. (1999). *Curriculum, assessment, and instruction for students with disabilities.* Belmont, CA: Wadsworth.

Bigge, J. L. (1990). *Teaching individuals with physical and multiple disabilities* (3rd ed.). Columbus, OH: Merrill.

Billingsley, B. S. (1993). Teacher retention and attrition in special and general education: A critical review of the literature. *Journal of Special Education, 27,* 137–174.

Black, J., and Ford, A. (1989). Planning and implementing activity-based lessons (pp. 295–311). In A. Ford, R. Schnorr, L. Meyer, L. Davern, J. Black, and P. Dempsey (eds.), *The Syracuse community-reference curriculum guide for students with moderate and severe disabilities.* Baltimore, MD: Paul H. Brookes.

Bloom, L., and Lahey, M. (1978). *Language development and language disorders.* New York: Wiley.

Boehm, A. E. (1986). *Boehm Test of Basic Concepts-Revised (BTBC-R).* San Antonio, TX: Psychological Corporation.

Bogdan, R., and Knoll, J. (1988). The sociology of disability (pp. 449–477). In E. L. Meyen and T. M. Skrtic (eds.), *Exceptional children and youth* (3rd ed.). Denver: Love Publishing.

Bogdan, R., and Kugelmass, J. (1984). Case studies of mainstreaming: A symbolic interactionist approach to special schooling (pp. 173–191). In L. Barton and S. Tomlinson (eds.), *Special education and social interests.* New York: Nichols.

Boyce, D., and Ohm, C. A. Day in the life of co-teachers: Inclusion class. *Who's teaching our children with disabilities? NICHCY News Digest, 27,* 1997.

Bracken, B. A. (1984). *Bracken Basic Concept Scale (BBCS).* San Antonio, TX: Psychological Corporation.

Brigance, A. H. (1991). *Brigance Diagnostic Inventory of Basic Skills.* Billerica, MA: Curriculum Associates.

Brown, V., Hammill, D., Larson, S., and Wiederholt, J. L. (1994). *Test of Adolescent and Adult Language-3rd ed. (TOAL-3).* Austin, TX: PRO-ED.

Brown, V. L., Cronin, M. E., and McEntire, E. (1994). *Test of Mathematical Abilities-2nd ed.* Austin, TX: PRO-ED.

Brown, V. L., Hammill, D. D., and Wiederholt, J. L. (1995). *Test of Reading Comprehension-3rd ed.* Austin, TX: PRO-ED.

Bullis, M., and Gaylord-Ross, R. (1991). *Moving on: Transitions for youth with behavioral disorders.* Reston, VA: Council for Exceptional Children.

Burgemeister, B. B., Blum, L. H., and Lorge, I. (1972). *Columbia Mental Maturity Scale (CMMS).* San Antonio, TX: Psychological Corporation.

Campione, J. C., and Brown, A. L. (1987). Linking dynamic assessment with school achievement (pp. 82–115). In C. S. Lidz (ed.), *Dynamic assessment: An interactional approach to evaluating learning potential.* New York: Guilford.

Carlson, J. S., and Wiedl, K. H. (1978). Use of testing-the-limits procedures in the assessment of intellectual capabilities of children with learning difficulties. *American Journal of Mental Deficiency, 82,* 559–564.

Carlson, J. S., and Wiedl, K. H. (1979). Toward a differential testing approach: Testing-the-limits employing the Raven Matrices. *Intelligence, 3,* 323–344.

Center for Applied Research in Education. (1995). *Classroom strategies for children with Tourette's.* West Nyack, NY: Author. [http://www.angelfire.com/ok/onedayatatime/class.html]

Chalfant, J. C. (1989). Learning disabilities: Policy issues and promising approaches. *American Psychologist, 44*(2), 392–398.

Clark, C. (1994, August). *Exito: A dynamic team assessment approach for culturally diverse students.* Presentation at the BUENO Bilingual Special Education Institute, Boulder, Colorado.

Code of Federal Regulations (CFR). *Title 34; Education; Parts 1 to 499, July 1986.* Washington, DC: U.S. Government Printing Office.

Code of Federal Regulations (CFR). *Title 34; Parts 300 to 399, July 1, 1993.* Washington, DC: U.S. Government Printing Office.

Colarusso, R., and Hammill, D. D. (1996). *Motor-Free Visual Perceptual Test-Revised (MVPT-R).* Novato, CA: Academic Therapy Publications.

Collier, C. (1994). *Multicultural assessment: Implications for regular and special education* (3rd ed.). Boulder, CO: BUENO Center for Multicultural Education.

Conners, K. C. (1997). *Conners' Parent and Teacher Rating Scales.* North Tonawanda, NY: Multi-Health Systems.

Connolly, A., Nachtman, W., and Pritchett, M. (1997). *Key Math Diagnostic Arithmetic Tests-Revised.* Circle Pines, MN: American Guidance Service.

Conoley, J. C., and Kramer, J. J. (eds.). (1992). *Eleventh mental measurement yearbook.* Lincoln: University of Nebraska Press.

Copenhaver, J. (1995). *Section 504: An educator's primer: What teachers and administrators need to know about implementing accommodations for eligible individuals with disabilities.* Logan, UT: Mountain Plains Regional Resource Center.

Cortâs, C. E. (1986). The education of language minority students: A contextual interaction model (pp. 3–33). In California State Department of Education, Bilingual Education Office, *Beyond language: Social and cultural factors in schooling language minority students.* Los Angeles: California State University.

Cox, L. S. (1975). Diagnosing and remediating systematic errors in addition and subtraction computations. *Arithmetic Teacher, 22,* 151–157.

Cummins, J. (1986). Empowering minority students: A framework for intervention. *Harvard Educational Review, 56*(1), 18–36.

Cummins, J. (1989). A theoretical framework for bilingual special education. *Exceptional Children, 56*(2), 111–119.

Cutler, B. C. (1993). *You, your child, and "special" education: A guide to making the system work.* Baltimore, MD: Paul H. Brookes.

DeStefano, L., and Wermuth, T. R. (1992). IDEA (P.L. 101–476): Defining a second generation of transition services (pp. 537–549). In F. R. Rusch, L. DeStefano, J. Chadsey-Rusch, L. A. Phelps, and E. Szymanshi (eds.), *Transition from school to adult life: Models, linkages, and policy.* Sycamore, IL: Sycamore Publishing.

Duffy, J. B., Salvia, J., Tucker, J., and Ysseldyke, J. (1981). Nonbiased assessment: A need for operationalism. *Exceptional Children, 7,* 427–434.

Dunn, L. M., and Williams, K. T. (1997). *Peabody Picture Vocabulary Test-3 (PPVT-III).* Circle Pines, MN: American Guidance Service.

Durrell, D. O., and Catterson, J. H. (1980). *Durrell Analysis of Reading Difficulty.* San Antonio, TX: Psychological Corporation.

Elksnin, L., and Elksnin, N. (1990). Using collaborative consultation with parents to promote effective vocational programming. *Career Development for Exceptional Individuals, 13*(2), 135–142.

Elliott, R. (1987). *Litigating intelligence: IQ tests, special education, and social science in the courtroom.* Dover, MA: Auburn House.

Falvey, M. (ed.). (1989). *Community-based curriculum: Instructional strategies for students with severe handicaps* (2nd ed.). Baltimore, MD: Paul H. Brookes.

Federal Regulations for Individuals with Disabilities Education Act (IDEA). Amendments of 1997 for Weds. October 22 (1997). Washington, DC: U.S. Government Printing Office.

Feuerstein, R. (1979). *The dynamic assessment of retarded performers: Learning potential assessment device.* Baltimore, MD: University Park Press.

Figueroa, R., Fradd, S. H., and Correa, V. I. (1989). Bilingual special education and this issue. *Exceptional Children, 56,* 174–178.

Figueroa, R. A. (1993). The reconstruction of bilingual special education. *Focus on Diversity, 3*(3), 2–3.

Figueroa, R. A., and Ruiz, N. T. (1994). The reconstruction of bilingual special education II. *Focus on Diversity, 4*(1), 2–3.

Flaugher, R. (1978). The many definitions of test bias. *American Psychologist, 33,* 671–679.

Franklin, M. E. (1992, October-November). Culturally sensitive instructional practices for African-American learners with disabilities. *Exceptional Children, 59*(2), 115–122.

Friend, M. P. and Bursuck, W. D. (2002). *Including students with special needs: a practical guide for classroom teachers.* Boston: Allyn & Bacon.

Friend, M., and Cook, L. (2000). *Interaction: Collaboration skills for school professionals* (3rd ed.). New York: Longman.

Frostig, M., Lefever, W., and Whittlessey, J. R. (1993). *Marianne Frostig Developmental Test of Visual Perception (DTVP).* Austin, TX: PRO-ED.

Fuchs, D., and Fuchs, L. (1989). Effects of examiner familiarity on Black, Caucasian, and Hispanic children: A meta-analysis. *Exceptional Children, 55,* 303–308.

Gardner, M. F. *Tests of Auditory Perceptual Skills-Revised (TAPS-R).* Hydesville, CA: Psychological and Educational Publications.

Gates, A. I., McKillop, A. S., and Horowitz, E. C. (1981). *Gates-McKillop-Horowitz Reading Diagnostic Tests.* New York: Teachers College Press.

Gearheart, C., and Gearheart, B. (1990). *Introduction to special education assessment. Principles and practices.* Denver, CO: Love Publishing.

Geary, D. (2002). *Mathematical disabilities: What we know and don't know.* [http://www.ldonline.org/ld_indepth/math_skills/geary_math_dis.html]

Gilmore, J. V., and Gilmore, E. C. (1968). *Gilmore Oral Reading Test.* San Antonio, TX: Psychological Corporation.

Ginsberg, H. P., and Baroody, A. J. (1990). *Test of Early Mathematics Ability-2nd ed.* Austin, TX: PRO-ED.

Goldman, R., and Fristoe, M. (1970). *Goldman-Fristoe Test of Articulation.* Circle Pines, MN: American Guidance Service.

Goodenough, F. L., and Harris, D. B. (1963). *Goodenough-Harris Drawing Test.* San Antonio, TX: Psychological Corporation.

Goodman, K. (1973). Analysis of oral reading miscues: Applied psycholinguistics. *Reading Research Quarterly, 5,* 9–30.

Goodman, Y., and Burke, C. (1972). *Reading miscue inventory manual: Procedure for diagnosis and evaluation.* New York: Macmillan.

Graden, J. L. (1989). Redefining "prereferral" intervention as intervention assistance: Collaboration between general and special education. *Exceptional Children, 56*(3), 227–231.

Graham, M., and Scott, K. (1988). The impact of definitions of high risk on services of infants and toddlers. *Topics in Early Childhood Special Education, 8*(3), 23–28.

Grandin, T. (2002). *Teaching tips for children and adults with autism.* Ft. Collins: Colorado State University, Center for the Study of Autism. [http://www.autism.org/temple/tips.html]

Greenspan, S. I. (2002). Early indicators of autistic spectrum disorders and related challenges. *Journal of Developmental and Learning Disorders, 6,* 1–7.

Grossman, H. J. (ed.). (1983). *Manual on terminology and classification in mental retardation* (3rd ed.; rev.). Washington, DC: American Association on Mental Deficiency.

Guerin, G. R., and Maier, A. S. (1983). *Informal assessment in education.* Palo Alto, CA: Mayfield.

Hager, R. (1999). *Funding of assistive technology: Assistive technology funding & systems change project.* [www.nls.org/spacedat.htm]

Halgren, D. W., and Clarizio, H. F. (1993). Categorical and programming changes in special education services. *Exceptional Children, 59,* 547–555.

Hammill, D. D. (1998). *Detroit Tests of Learning Aptitudes-4th ed. (DTLA-4).* Austin, TX: PRO-ED.

Hammill, D. D., Brown, L., and Bryant, B. R. (1992). *A consumer's guide to tests in print.* Austin, TX: PRO-ED.

Hammill, D. D., and Larsen, S. C. (1996). *Test of Written Language-3.* Austin, TX: PRO-ED.

Hammill, D. D., Pearson, N. A., and Wiederholt, L. (1996). *Comprehensive Test of Nonverbal Intelligence.* Austin, TX: PRO-ED.

Hanson, M., and Lynch, E. (1995). *Early intervention: Implementing child and family services for infants and toddlers who are at risk or disabled* (2nd ed.). Austin, TX: PRO-ED.

Haring, K. A., Lovett, D. L., Haney, K. F., Algozzine, B., Smith, D. D., and Clarke, J. (1992). Labeling preschoolers as learning disabled: A cautionary position. *Topics in Early Childhood Special Education, 12*(2), 151–173.

Harnisch, D. L., and Fisher, A. T. (eds.). (1989). *Transition literature review: Educational, employment, and independent living outcomes.* Champaign, IL: Secondary Transition Intervention Effectiveness Institute.

Harry, B. (1992). *Cultural diversity, families, and the special education system: Communication and empowerment.* New York: Teachers College Press.

Hart, D. (1994). *Authentic assessment: A handbook for educators.* Reading, MA: Addison-Wesley.

Hartman, R. C. (ed.). (1991). Transition in the United States: What's happening. *Information from HEATH, 10*(3), 1, 4–6.

Hayden, M. F., and Senese, D. (1994). *Self-advocacy groups: 1994–95 directory for North America.* Minneapolis: University of Minnesota, Institute on Community Integration, Publications Office.

Heiman, G. (1999). *Research methods in psychology* (2nd ed.). Boston: Houghton Mifflin.

Herman, J., Aschbacher, P., and Winters, L. (1992). *A practical guide to alternative assessment.* Alexandria, VA: Association for Supervision and Curriculum Development.

Heward, W. L., and Orlansky, M. D. (1992). *Exceptional children: An introductory survey of special education* (4th ed.). Columbus, OH: Merrill.

Hodgkinson, L. (1985). *All one system: Demographics of education.* Washington, DC: Institute for Educational Leadership.

Hoover, J., and Collier, C. (1994). *Classroom management and curriculum development* (3rd ed.). Boulder, CO: BUENO Center for Multicultural Education.

Hoy, C., and Gregg, N. (1994). *Assessment: The special educator's role.* Pacific Grove, CA: Brookes/Cole.

Hresko, W. P. (1988). *Test of Early Written Language-2.* Austin, TX: PRO-ED.

Iliesko, W. P., Reid, D. K., and Hammill, D. D. *Test of Early Language Development-2nd ed. (TELD-2).* Austin, TX: PRO-ED.

Jitendra, A. K., and Kameenui, E. J. (1993, September-October). Dynamic assessment as a compensatory assessment approach: A description and analysis. *Remedial and Special Education, 14*(5), 6–18.

John, J. L. (1985). *Basic reading inventory* (3rd ed.). Dubuque, IA: Kendall-Hunt.

Johnson, B. H., McGonigel, M. J., and Kauffmann, R. K. (1991). *Guidelines and recommended practices for the Individualized Family Service Plan* (2nd ed.). Bethesda, MD: Association for the Care of Children's Health.

Kamphaus, R. W. (1993). *Clinical assessment of children's intelligence.* Boston: Allyn & Bacon.

Kaufman Children's Center for Speech and Language Sensory Disorders. (2003). *Signs and symptoms: Central auditory processing disorders.* West Bloomfield, MI: Author. [http://www.kidspeech.com/signs_central.html]

Kaufman, A. S., and Kaufman, N. L. (1983). *Kaufman Assessment Battery for Children (K-ABC): Mental processing scales.* Circle Pines, MN: American Guidance Service.

Kaufman, A. S., and Kaufman, N. L. (1985). *Kaufman Tests of Educational Achievement.* Circle Pines, MN: American Guidance Service.

Kaufman, A. S., and Kaufman, N. L. (1990). *Kaufman Brief Intelligence Test.* Circle Pines, MN: American Guidance Service.

Kaufman, S. (1999). *Retarded isn't stupid, Mom!* (rev. ed.). Baltimore, MD: Paul H. Brookes.

Keith, T. Z. (1985). Questioning the K-ABC: What does it measure? *School Psychology Review, 14,* 9–20.

Keith, T. Z. (1997). What does the WISC-III measure? A reply to Carroll and Kranzler. *School Psychology Quarterly, 12*(2), 117–118.

Keogh, B., and Margolis, T. (1976). Learn to labor and wait: Attentional problems of children with learning disorders. *Journal of Learning Disabilities, 9,* 276–286.

King-Sears, M. E. (1994). *Curriculum-based assessment in special education.* San Diego: Singular Publishing Group.

Kirk, S. A., McCarthy, J. J., and Kirk, W. D. (1968). *Illinois Test of Psycholinguistic Abilities (ITPA).* Chicago: University of Illinois Press.

Kozloff, M. (1994). *Improving educational outcomes for children with disabilities: Principles for assessment, program planning, and evaluation.* Baltimore, MD: Paul H. Brookes.

Krebs, D. (1990, December). How to get a job and keep your benefits. *TASH Newsletter,* p. 9.

Lambert, W. E. (1977). The effects of bilingualism on the individual: Cognitive and sociocultural consequences (pp. 15–27). In P. Hornby (ed.), *Bilingualism: Psychological, social, and educational implications.* New York: Academic Press.

Langdon, H. W. (1992). Speech and language assessment of LEP/bilingual Hispanic students (pp. 201–265). In H. W. Langdon and L. L. Cheng (eds.), *Hispanic children and adults with communication disorders.* Gaithersburg, MD: Aspen.

Larsen, S. C., and Hammill, D. D. (1999). *Test of Written Spelling-4.* Austin, TX: PRO-ED.

Larson, S. L., and Vitali, G. (1988). *Kindergarten Readiness Test (KRT).* Aurora, NY: Slosson Educational Publications.

Leach, L. N., and Harmon, A. (1990). *Annotated bibliography on transition from school to work* (Vol. 5). Champaign, IL: Transition Research Institute.

Lerner, J. (1991). *Learning disabilities: Theories, diagnosis, and teaching strategies* (7th ed.). Boston: Houghton Mifflin.

Levine, M. (1994, October 3). *Educators: Some "don'ts" for those working with students.* Paper presented at the 13th National NEDO Conference. [http://www.angelfire.com]

Lezak, M. D. (1995). *Neuropsychological assessment* (4th ed.). New York: Oxford University Press.

Lieberman, L. M. (1985). Special education and regular education: A merger made in heaven? *Exceptional Children, 51*(6), 513–516.

Lipke, B., Dickey, S., Selmar, J., and Soder, A. (1999). *Photo Articulation Test-3rd ed. (PAT-3)*. Hydesville, CA: Psychological and Educational Publications.

Lovass, O. I. (1989). A comprehensive behavioral theory of autistic children: Paradigm for research and treatment. *Journal of Behavioral Therapy and Experimental Psychiatry, 20*, 17–29.

Luria, A. R. (1980). *The working brain.* New York: Basic Books.

Luttinger, H., and Gertner, M. (2003). Learning disorder: Written expression. *eMedicine Journal, 4*(7). [http://author.emedicine.com/PED/topic2801.htm]

MacGinitie, W., and MacGinitie, R. (1989). *Gates-MacGinitie Silent Reading Tests-3rd ed.* Itasca, IL: Riverside Publishing Company.

Madison, A. (2002). *Depression in school: A student's trial.* Bloomington: Indiana University, Center for Adolescent Studies. [http://education.indiana.edu/cas/]

Maldonado-Col¢n, E. (1983). *The communication disordered Hispanic child.* [Monograph] Boulder, CO: BUENO Center for Multicultural Education.

Markwardt, F. C. (1997). *Peabody Individual Achievement Test-Revised (PIAT-R).* Circle Pines, MN: American Guidance Service.

McCarney, S. B. (1989a). *Attention Deficit Disorders Evaluation Scale-Revised.* Columbia, MO: Hawthorne Educational Services.

McCarney, S. B. (1989b). *The Preschool Evaluation Scales (PES).* Columbia, MO: Hawthorne Educational Services.

McCarney, S. B. (1995). *The adaptive behavior evaluation scale-revised.* Columbia, MO: Hawthorne Educational Services.

McCarthy, D. (1972). *McCarthy Scales of Children's Abilities.* San Antonio, TX: Psychological Corporation.

McGloughlin, J., and Lewis, R. (1994). *Assessing special students* (4th ed.). Columbus, OH: Merrill.

McLean, M., Bailey, D. B., and Wolery, M. (1996). *Assessing infants and preschoolers with special needs* (2nd ed.). Upper Saddle River, NJ: Merrill/Prentice-Hall.

McLoughlin, J. A., and Lewis, R. B. (1990). *Assessing special students* (3rd ed.). Columbus, OH: Merrill.

McNair, J., and Rusch, F. R. (1991). Parent involvement in transition programs. *Mental Retardation, 29*(2), 93–101.

Mierow, S. A day in the life of a special educator: Self-contained regular school. *Who's teaching our children with disabilities? NICHCY News Digest, 27*, 1997.

Millette, A. Oppositional disorder and aggression. *The "Newsletter," 101*, October 1996. [Maine Foster Parent Association].

Ministry of Education of British Columbia. (1995). Adapting the Science Curriculum. [http://www.bced.gov.bc.ca]

Morris, G. (1999). *Psychology: An introduction.* Upper Saddle River, NJ: Prentice Hall.

Murray, H. A. (1943). *Thematic Apperception Test.* Cambridge, MA: Harvard University Press.

Myers, A., and Hanson, C. (1999). *Experimental psychology* (4th ed.). Belmont, CA: Brooks/Cole.

Naglieri, J. A., McNeish, T. J., and Bardos, A. N. (1991). *Draw-A-Person: Screening procedure for emotional disturbance.* Austin, TX: ProEd.

National Association of School Psychology. (1991). *Position statement on early childhood assessment.* Washington, DC: Author.

National Association of State Directors of Special Education (NASDSE). (1992). Alexandria, VA: Author. [http://www.nasdse.org]

National Council on Disability. (1995). *Improving the implementation of the Individuals with Disabilities Education Act: Making schools work for all of America's children.* Washington, DC: Author.

National Dissemination Center for Children with Disabilities (NDCCD). (2002). *Attention Deficit/Hyperactive Disorder* (Briefing Paper). Washington, DC: Author.

Newborg, J., Stock, J. R., and Wnek, J. (1984). *The Battelle Developmental Inventory (BDI).* Itasca, IL: Riverside Publishing.

Newcomer, P. L., and Hammill, D. D. (1997). *Test of Language Development-Primary: 3 (TOLD-P:3).* Austin, TX: ProEd.

NICHCY News Digest. (1990, December). Vocational assessment: A guide for parents and professionals. Washington, DC: National Dissemination Center for Children and Youth with Disabilities.

NICHCY News Digest. (1991). Questions and answers about IDEA. Washington, DC: National Dissemination Center for Children and Youth with Disabilities.

NICHCY News Digest. (1992, October). Sexuality education for children and youth with disabilities. Washington, DC: National Dissemination Center for Children and Youth with Disabilities.

NICHCY News Digest. (1993, March). Transition services in the IEP. Washington, DC: National Dissemination Center for Children and Youth with Disabilities.

NICHCY News Digest. (1994, September). Options after high school. Washington, DC: National Dissemination Center for Children and Youth with Disabilities.

NICHCY News Digest. (1996, March). Travel training for youth with disabilities. Washington, DC: National Dissemination Center for Children and Youth with Disabilities.

NICHCY News Digest. (1996, April). Assistive technology. Washington, DC: National Dissemination Center for Children and Youth with Disabilities.

NICHCY News Digest. (1996, June). Respite care. Washington, DC: National Dissemination Center for Children and Youth with Disabilities.

NICHCY News Digest. (1996, October). The education of children and youth with special needs: What do the laws say? Washington, DC: National Dissemination Center for Children and Youth with Disabilities.

NICHCY News Digest. (2003, January). Autism and pervasive developmental disorder. Washington, DC: National Dissemination Center for Children and Youth with Disabilities.

NICHCY News Digest. (2004). General information about disabilities which qualify children and youth for special education services under the IDEA act. Washington, DC: National Dissemination Center for Children and Youth with Disabilities.

Nihira, K., Leland, H., and Lambert, N. (1993). *AAMR Adaptive Behavior Scale-Residential and Community-2.* Austin, TX: PRO-ED.

Nisbet, J. (1992). *Natural supports in school, at work, and in the community for people with severe disabilities.* Baltimore, MD: Paul H. Brookes.

Norris, M. K., Juarez, M. J., and Perkins, M. N. (1989). Adaptation of a screening test for bilingual and bidialectal populations. *Language, Speech, and Hearing Specialists in Schools, 20,* 381–390.

Nurss, J. R., and McGauvran, M. E. (1986). *Metropolitan Readiness Tests-5th ed. (MRT-5).* San Antonio, TX: Psychological Corporation.

Office of Special Education and Rehabilitative Services. (2002). *Summary of existing legislation affecting persons with disabilities.* Washington, DC: Clearinghouse on Disability Information.

Ortiz, A. (1986). Characteristics of limited English proficient Hispanic students served in programs for the learning disabled. *Bilingual special education newsletter* (Vol. 4). Austin: University of Texas.

Ortiz, A. A., and Rivera, C. (1990). *AIM for the BEST: Assessment and intervention model for bilingual exceptional students* (Contract No. 300–87–0131). Washington, DC: Office of Bilingual Education and Minority Language Affairs.

Otis, A. S., and Lennon, R. T. (1996). *Otis-Lennon School Ability Test* (7th ed.). San Antonio, TX: Psychological Corporation.

Overton, T. (2000). *Assessment in special education: An applied approach* (3rd ed.). Upper Saddle River, NJ: Merrill.

Parker, L. (2002). *Tips on dealing with OCD in the classroom.* [http//www.tourettesyndrome.net]

Paulson, E. L., Paulson, P. R., and Meyer, C. A. (1991). What makes a portfolio a portfolio? *Educational Leadership, 48*(5), 60–63.

Pennsylvania Department of Education, Bureau of Special Education. (1993, March). *Instructional support.* East Petersburg: Pennsylvania Department of Education.

Pierangelo, R. (2003). *The special educator's book of lists* (2nd ed.). San Francisco: John Wiley & Sons.

Pierangelo, R., and Giuliani, G. (2000). *The special educator's guide to 109 diagnostic tests.* Paramus, NJ: Center for Applied Research in Education.

Pierangelo, R., and Giuliani, G. (2000). *Assessment in special education: A practical approach.* Boston: Allyn & Bacon.

Pierangelo, R., and Giuliani, G. (2003). *Transition services in special education: A practical approach.* Boston: Allyn & Bacon.

Repetto, J., White, W., and Snauwaert, D. (1990). Individual transition plans (ITP): A national perspective. *Career Education for Exceptional Individuals, 13*(2), 109–119.

Reschley, D. (1986). Functional psychoeducational assessment: Trends and issues. *Special services in the schools, 2*, 57–59.

Rueda, R. (1989). Defining mild disabilities with language-minority students. *Exceptional Children, 56*, 121–128.

Ruiz, N. T. (1989). An optimal learning environment for Rosemary. *Exceptional Children, 56*(2), 130–144.

Runyon, R., and Haber, A. (1991). *Fundamentals of behavioral statistics* (7th ed.). New York: McGraw-Hill.

Rusch, F. R., Hughes, C., and Kohler, P. D. (1991). *Descriptive analysis of secondary school education and transition services model programs.* Champaign, IL: Secondary Transition Intervention Effectiveness Institute.

Salvia, J., and Hughes, C. (1990). *Curriculum-based assessment: Testing what is taught.* New York: Macmillan.

Salvia, J., and Ysseldyke, J. (1998). *Assessment* (7th ed.). Boston: Houghton Mifflin.

Sattler, J. (1992). *Assessment of children* (3rd ed.). San Diego: Sattler Publishers.

Sewell, T. E. (1987). Dynamic assessment as a nondiscriminatory procedure (pp. 426–443). In C. S. Lidz (ed.), *Dynamic assessment: An interactional approach to evaluating learning potential.* New York: Guilford.

Shapiro, E. (1989a). *Behavioral assessment in school psychology.* Hillsdale, NJ: Erlbaum.

Shapiro, E. S. (1989b). *Academic skills problems: Direct assessment and intervention.* New York: Guilford.

Skrtic, T. M. (1988). The crisis in special education knowledge (pp. 415–447). In E. L. Meyen and T. M. Skrtic (eds.), *Exceptional children and youth* (3rd ed.). Denver, CO: Love Publishing.

Sleeter, C. E. (1986). Learning disabilities: The social construction of a special education category. *Exceptional Children, 53*(1), 46–54.

Slosson, R. L. (1990). *Slosson Oral Reading Test-Revised.* East Aurora, NY: Slosson Educational Publications.

Slosson, R. L. (1991). *Slosson Intelligence Test-Revised (SIT-R).* East Aurora, NY: Slosson Educational Publications.

Smith, D. (1998). *Introduction to special education: Teaching in an age of challenge* (3rd ed.). Boston: Allyn & Bacon.

Smith-Davis, J., and Littlejohn, W. R. (1991). Related services for school-aged children with disabilities. *NICHCY News Digest, 1*(2), 1–24.

Spache, G. D. (1981). *Spache Diagnostic Reading Scales.* Columbus, OH: CTB Macmillan/McGraw-Hill.

Sparrow, S., Balla, D., and Cicchetti, D. (1984). *Vineland Adaptive Behavior Scale.* Circle Pines, MN: American Guidance Service.

Sprinthall, R. (1994). *Basic statistical analysis* (4th ed.). Boston: Allyn & Bacon.

Stainback, W., and Stainback, S. (1984). A rationale for the merger of special and regular education. *Exceptional Children, 51*(2), 102–111.

Stanovich, K. (1982). Individual differences in the cognitive processes of reading. I: Word decoding. *Journal of Learning Disabilities, 15*, 485–493.

Swanson, H. C., and Watson, B. L. (1989). *Educational and psychological assessment of exceptional children* (2nd ed.). Columbus, OH: Merrill.

Sweetland, R. C., and Keyser, D. J. (eds.). (1991). *Tests: A comprehensive reference for assessments in psychology, education, and business* (3rd ed.). Austin, TX: PRO-ED.

Taylor, R. (1997). *Assessment of exceptional students: Educational and psychological procedures* (5th ed.). Boston: Allyn & Bacon.

Taylor, R. L. (1991). Bias in cognitive assessment: Issues, implications, and future directions. *Diagnostique, 17*(1), 3–5.

Terrell, S. L. (ed.). (1983, June). Nonbiased assessment of language differences [Special issue]. *Topics in Language Disorders, 3*(3).

Tharp, R. G. (1989). Psychocultural variables and constants: Effects on teaching and learning in schools. *American Psychologist, 44*(2), 349–359.

Tharp, R. G. (1994, June). *Cultural compatibility and the multicultural classroom: Oxymoron or opportunity.* Paper presented at the Training and Development Improvement Quarterly Meeting, Albuquerque, New Mexico.

The pocket guide to federal help: For individuals with disabilities. (1993). Washington, DC: U.S. Department of Education, Clearinghouse on Disability Information Office of Special Education and Rehabilitative Services.

Thorndike, R. L., Hagen, E. P., and Sattler, J. M. (1986). *The Stanford-Binet Intelligence Scale (4th ed.).* Chicago: Riverside.

Thorndike, R. L., and Lohman, D. F. (1990). *A century of ability testing.* Chicago: Riverside.

Trainer, M. (1991). *Differences in common: Straight talk on mental retardation, Down's syndrome, and life.* Bethesda, MD: Woodbine House.

Trohanis, P. L. (1995). Progress in providing services to young children with special needs and their families: An overview to and update on implementing the Individuals with Disabilities Education Act. *NEC*TAS Notes, 7,* 1–20.

Turnbull, A., Turnbull, H., Shank, M., and Leal, D. (1995). *Exceptional lives: Special education in today's schools.* Upper Saddle River, NJ: Merrill.

Turnbull, H. R. (1990). *Free and appropriate public education: The law and children with disabilities* (3rd ed.). Denver, CO: Love Publishing.

Ulrich, D. (1999). *Test of Gross Motor Development-2nd ed. (TGMD-2).* Austin, TX: PRO-ED.

U.S. Department of Education. (1995). *Seventeenth annual report to Congress on the implementation of the Individuals with Disabilities Education Act.* Washington, DC: Author.

U.S. Department of Education. (1997). *Nineteenth annual report to Congress on the implementation of the Individuals with Disabilities Education Act.* Washington, DC: Author.

Vacca, J., Vacca, R., and Grove, M. (1986). *Reading and learning to read.* Boston: Little, Brown.

Valles, E. C. (1998). The disproportionate representation of minority students in special education: Responding to the problem. *Journal of Special Education, 32,* 52–54.

Vellutino, F. R. (1979). *Dyslexia: Theory and research.* Cambridge, MA: MIT Press.

Venn, J. (2000). *Assessing students with special needs* (2nd ed.). Upper Saddle River, NJ: Merrill.

Wagner, M. (1989, March). *The transition experiences of youth with disabilities: A report from the National Longitudinal Transition Study.* Paper presented at the annual meeting of the Council for Exceptional Children, San Francisco.

Wallace, G., and Hammill, D. D. (1994). *Comprehensive Receptive and Expressive Vocabulary Test (CREVT).* Austin, TX: PRO-ED.

Wallace, G., Larsen, S. C., and Elksnin, L. K. (1992). *Educational assessment of learning problems: Testing for teaching* (2nd ed.). Boston: Allyn & Bacon.

Walsh, B., and Betz, N. (1985). *Test and assessment.* Englewood Cliffs, NJ: Prentice Hall.

Wandry, D., and Repetto, J. (1993). Transition services in the IEP. *NICHCY News Digest, 1,* 1–28.

Ward, M. J. (1992). Introduction to secondary special education and transition issues (pp. 387–389). In F. R. Rusch, L. DeStefano, J. Chadsey-Rusch, L. A. Phelps, and E. Szymanshi (eds.), *Transition from school to adult life: Models, linkages, and policy.* Sycamore, IL: Sycamore Publishing.

Watkins, C., and Brynes, G. (2001). *Separation anxiety in young children.* Baltimore, MD: Northern County Psychiatric Associates. [http://www.baltimorepsych.com/separation_anxiety.htm]

Wechsler, D. (1958). *The measurement and appraisal of adult intelligence* (4th ed.). Baltimore, MD: Williams & Wilkins.

Wechsler, D. (1991). *The Wechsler Scales of Intelligence.* San Antonio, TX: Psychological Corporation.

Wechsler, D. (1992). *Wechsler Individual Achievement Test-2.* San Antonio, TX: Psychological Corporation.

Wehman, P. (1992). *Life beyond the classroom: Transition strategies for young people with disabilities.* Baltimore, MD: Paul H. Brookes.

Wepman, J. M., and Reynolds, W. M. (1986). *Wepman Test of Auditory Discrimination-2nd ed. (ADT-2).* Los Angeles: Western Psychological Services.

White, E. A day in the life of an itinerant special educator. *Who's teaching our children with disabilities? NICHCY News Digest, 27,* 1997.

Wiederholt, J. L., and Byrant, B. R. (1992). *Gray Oral Reading Test-3.* Austin, TX: PRO-ED.

Wiggins, G. (1989). A true test: Toward more authentic and equitable assessment. *Phi Delta Kappan, 70*(9), 703–713.

Wilkinson, S. (1993). *Wide Range Achievement Test-3.* Wilmington, DE: Jastak Associates-Wide Range.

Williams, R., and Zimmerman, D. (1984). On the virtues and vices of standard error of measurement. *Journal of Experimental Education, 52,* 231–233.

Wilson, A. J., and Silverman, H. (1991). Teachers' assumptions and beliefs about the delivery of services to exceptional children. *Teacher Education and Special Education, 14*(3), 198–206.

Wilson, N. O. (1992). *Optimizing special education: How parents can make a difference.* New York: Insight Books.

Wood, J. W., Lazzari, A., Davis, E. H., Sugai, G., and Carter J. (1990). National status of the prereferral process: An issue for regular education. *Action in Teacher Education, 12*(3), 50–56.

Woodcock, R. (1997). *Woodcock Reading Mastery Tests-Revised.* Circle Pines, MN: American Guidance Service.

Woodcock, R. W., and Johnson, M. B. (1989). *Woodcock-Johnson Achievement Battery.* Itasca, IL: Riverside Publishing Company.

Woolfolk, E. C. (1999). *Test of Auditory Comprehension of Language-III (TACL-3).* Itasca, IL: Riverside Publishing Company.

Yell, M. L. (1995). *The law and special education.* Upper Saddle River, NJ: Prentice Hall.

Ysseldyke, J., and Algozzine, B. (1982). *Critical issues in special and remedial education.* Boston: Houghton Mifflin.

Ysseldyke, J., Algozzine, B., Regan, R., and Potter, M. (1980). Technical adequacy of tests used by professionals in simulated decision making. *Psychology in the Schools, 17,* 202–209.

Ysseldyke, J., and Regan, R. (1980). Nondiscriminatory assessment: A formative model. *Exceptional Children, 46,* 465–466.

Zappia, L. A day in the life of a special educator: Self-contained special school. *Who's teaching our children with disabilities? NICHCY News Digest, 27,* 1997.

Zimmerman, I. L., Steiner, V. G., and Evatt, R. L. (1992). *Preschool Language Scale-3 (PLS-3).* San Antonio, TX: Psychological Corporation.

You may also wish to find out more about the following laws, which can be accessed through the Internet:

Brown *v.* Board of Education (1954). 347 U.S. 483.

Carl D. Perkins Vocational Education Act, 20 U.S.C. Sections 2331–2342.

Covarrubias *v.* San Diego Unified School District (Southern California). *No. 70–394-T* (S.D., Cal. February, 1971).

Department of Agriculture's Food and Nutrition Service (NFS) Technology-Related Assistance for Individuals with Disabilities Act of 1988 (Public Law 100–407, August 19, 1988).

Developmental Disabilities Assistance and Bill of Rights Act, 42 U.S.C. Section 6012.

Diana *v.* California State Board of Education. *No. C-70 37 RFP,* District Court of Northern California (February, 1970).

Guadalupe Organization Inc. *v.* Tempe Elementary School District. *No. CIV 71–435,* Phoenix (D. Arizona, January 24, 1972).

Individuals with Disabilities Education Act (P.L. 101–476), *20 U.S.C. Chapter 33, Sections 1400–1485, 1990.*

PARC *v.* Commonwealth of Pennsylvania (1972). 343 F. Supp. 279, E.D. PA.

Pase *v.* Hannon (1980). *No. 74 C 3586,* N.D. Ill.

Pennsylvania Department of Education, Bureau of Special Education (1993, March). Instructional support. East Petersburg, PA: Pennsylvania Department of Education.

Public Law 94–142 Education of the Handicapped Act, 1975.

Public Law 99–372, Handicapped Children's Protection Act of 1986.

Public Law 100–407, Technology-Related Assistance for Individuals with Disabilities Act of 1988.

Public Law 101–127, Children with Disabilities Temporary Care Reauthorization Act of 1989.

Public Law 101–336, Americans with Disabilities Act of 1990.

Public Law 101–476, Individuals with Disabilities Education Act, 1990.

Rehabilitation Act of 1973, 29 U.S.C. Section 701–794.

Rehabilitation Act Amendments of 1992 (P.L. 102–569).

Wyatt *v.* Stickney (1972). 344 F. Supp. 387 M.D. Ala.

Other Books of Interest

The Special Educator's Book of Lists, 2nd Edition

Roger Pierangelo, Ph.D.

Paperback / 640 pages
ISBN: 0-7879-6593-6

Here's a unique time-saving resource for the special education teacher with 192 reproducible lists—all brimming with useful facts that cover essential assessment, diagnosis, remediation, legal, and procedural information. This new edition contains the latest information about Individualized Education Programs, early childhood intervention and remediation, inclusion, new medications, current research on dyslexia and autism, updated tests and measurements, and current special education terminology, materials, and readings.

Roger Pierangelo, Ph.D., has over 25 years of experience as a classroom teacher, school psychologist, administrator of special education programs, and professor in the graduate special education department at Long Island University.

Special Educator's Complete Guide to 109 Diagnostic Tests

Roger Pierangelo, Ph.D. and
George Giuliani, Psy.D.

Paperback / 352 pages
ISBN: 0-87628-893-X

Here is a comprehensive practical guide to the most frequently used and helpful tests for diagnosing suspected disabilities of all kinds—intellectual, perceptual, language, achievement, psychosocial and social maturity—from the early childhood years through adolescence. You'll find detailed information on the make-up and purpose of each of 109 different tests, including subtests, scoring diagnostic patterns if any, and specific strengths and weaknesses, all conveniently organized in four easy-to-use sections.

Dr. George Giuliani is a full-time Assistant Professor at Hofstra University's School of Education and Allied Human Services in the Department of Counseling, Research, Special Education, and Rehabilitation and earned his Psy.D. (Doctor of Psychology) from Rutgers University. Besides college teaching, Dr. Giuliani is involved in early intervention for children with special needs and is a consultant for school districts and early childhood agencies.

Other Books of Interest

The ADHD Book of Lists:

A Practical Guide for Helping Children and Teens with Attention Deficit Disorders

Sandra F. Rief, M.A.

Paperback / 496 pages
ISBN: 0-7879-6591-X

This book addresses the needs of teachers and parents working with ADD/ADHD students from preschool to teenage years. *The ADHD Book of Lists* contains information on recent changes in the law, definitions, new supports and interventions, new medication descriptions, new behavior strategies, and more academic strategies for both school and home.

- Assesses the needs of teachers and parents working with ADD/ADHD students from preschool to teenage years.
- Features almost 100 lists containing up-to-date information on the laws, definitions and characteristics of this disorder, and supports and interventions.
- Printed with a lay-flat binding for easy photocopying of any list.
- Written by an author who is active in the field and well recognized by special educators and parents.

How to Reach and Teach ADD/ADHD Children:

Practical Techniques, Strategies, and Interventions for Helping Children with Attention Problems and Hyperactivity

Sandra F. Rief, M.A.

Paperback / 256 pages
ISBN: 0-87628-413-6

Get practical guidance for addressing the "whole child," as well as the team approach to meeting the needs of students with attention deficit hyperactivity disorder. Includes management techniques that promote on-task behavior and language arts, whole language, and multisensory instruction strategies that maintain student attention and keep students involved. In addition you'll get sample contracts, charts, a student self-evaluation checklist, sample letters and documentation on communicating with physicians and agencies, observation sheets, and an outline for a social skills planning unit to help successfully manage children with ADD/ADHD.

Sandra F. Rief, M.A., is a leading speaker, author, and consultant on effective strategies and interventions for meeting the needs of children with learning, attention, and behavioral challenges. She is the author of the bestsellers *How to Reach and Teach ADD/ADHD Children* and *The ADD/ADHD Checklist*, as well as the video "ADHD & LD: Powerful Teaching Strategies and Accommodations," all available from Jossey-Bass.

Other Books of Interest

How to Reach and Teach Children and Teens with Dyslexia:

A Parent and Teacher Guide to Helping Students of All Ages Academically, Socially, and Emotionally

Cynthia M. Stowe, M.Ed.

Paperback / 368 pages
ISBN: 0-13-032018-8

This comprehensive, practical resource gives educators at all levels essential information, techniques, and tools for understanding dyslexia and adapting teaching methods in all subject areas to meet the learning styles and social and emotional needs of students who have dyslexia. Special features include over 50 full-page activity sheets that can be photocopied for immediate use and interviews with students and adults who have had personal experience with dyslexia. Organized into twenty sections, information covers everything from ten principles of instruction to teaching reading, handwriting, spelling, writing, math, everyday skills, and even covers the adult with dyslexia.

Cynthia M. Stowe, M.Ed., is a certified special education teacher and school psychologist who has worked with children of all ages and with adults. She is the author of *Let's Write* and *Spelling Smart!* from Jossey-Bass as well as children's novels, including *Home Sweet, Good-Bye; Dear Mom in Ohio for a Year;* and *Not-So-Normal Norman.*

ADD/ADHD Behavior-Change Resource Kit:

Ready-to-Use Strategies & Activities for Helping Children with Attention Deficit Disorder

Grad L. Flick, Ph.D.

Paperback / 416 pages
ISBN: 0-87628-144-7

Virtually all you need to help kids take charge of their own behavior and build effective life and social skills is here. One of the most practical resources available for diagnosing and remediating reading problems available, the *ADD/ADHD Behavior-Change Resource Kit* includes easy-to-follow explanations of the causes of disabilities, reproducible assessment devices, scores of activity sheets for improving ability in visual perception, and more.

Dr. Grad L. Flick, Adjunct Professor at the University of Southern Mississippi Regional Gulf Park Campus in Long Beach, has over 28 years' experience in both research and clinical practice and has numerous publication credits including *Power Parenting for Children with ADD/ADHD* (The Center for Applied Research in Education) and *How to Reach & Teach Teenagers with ADHD* (Jossey-Bass).

Other Books of Interest

Life Skills Activities for Special Children

Darlene Mannix

Paperback / 368 pages
ISBN: 0-87628-547-7

Help children acquire the basic skills necessary to achieve independence and success in everyday living with these 145 ready-to-use lessons and reproducible worksheets. Each lesson places a specific skill within the context of real-life situations. It gives special children the extra focus they need to understand how to fit into the real world and how to develop the skills needed to become more independent in their homes, at schools, and in the community.

Social Skills Activities for Secondary Students with Special Needs

Darlene Mannix

Paperback / 262 pages
ISBN: 0-13-042906-6

Darlene Mannix has taught and helped emotionally disturbed, learning disabled, mentally handicapped, at-risk, and language disordered children of all grades and ages. Currently she is teaching a public program for middle school students utilizing computers to teach thinking skills. Ms. Mannix holds a Bachelor of Science degree from Taylor University and a Master's degree in Learning Disabilities from Indiana University. She is also the author of *Life Skills Activities for Secondary Students With Special Needs* and *Social Skills Activities for Special Children*, both from Jossey-Bass.